VOICES FROM IRAQ

VOICES

FROM IRAQ

A PEOPLE'S HISTORY, 2003–2009

MARK KUKIS

COLUMBIA UNIVERSITY PRESS   NEW YORK

COLUMBIA UNIVERSITY PRESS
Publishers Since 1893
New York   Chichester, West Sussex

Library of Congress Cataloging-in-Publication Data

Voices from Iraq : a people's history, 2003-2009 / [compiled by] Mark Kukis.
p.   cm.
Includes bibliographical references.
ISBN 978-0-231-15692-9 (cloth : alk. paper) — ISBN 978-0-231-52756-9 (ebook)
1. Iraq War, 2003– Personal narratives, Iraqi. 2. Iraq—History—2003–
I. Kukis, Mark, 1973– II. Title.

DS79.766.A1V645   2011
956.7044'30922—DC22

2010045331

DESIGN BY VIN DANG

TO SARAH

CONTENTS

INTRODUCTION

WHEN I STARTED COVERING Iraq for *Time* magazine in the fall of 2006, going onto the streets of Baghdad to interview Iraqis was nearly impossible. Sectarian violence was at its height. Dozens of bodies littered the streets every morning, the bloody leavings of Shi'ite death squads who had roamed Sunni neighborhoods the night before. Each afternoon brought a steady drumbeat of car bombs across the city. I heard between two and five every day for months when I first started coming to Iraq. Some thumped ominously in the distance across the vast cityscape of Baghdad, barely audible from the confines of the private compound where the magazine's bureau sat outside the Green Zone. Others rocked our house, sending all of us inside crouching toward the floor as curls of smoke rose from a nearby street.

In those days, it was almost suicidal to consider venturing out to talk to Iraqis for any real length of time. Like most reporters working for big media outlets, I had a bodyguard detail to accompany me anywhere I might go. We traveled in two cars on the rare occasions when we did go into the city. I would ride in the front car with a driver and a gunman armed with pistols and Kalashnikovs. A chase car followed us with two more bodyguards similarly armed. Even this was not enough protection during Baghdad's bloodiest days, however. Some attacks on Westerners during that time involved dozens of armed men with heavy guns. There was even one instance in which a Western consultant was kidnapped from an Iraqi government agency in broad daylight, along with his entire team of bodyguards.[1]

There was danger to consider beyond my personal safety as well. My bodyguards and drivers were all Iraqis, not Western security men. They

---

1   British Broadcasting Corporation, "Five Britons Abducted in Baghdad," May 29, 2007. Accessed at http://news.bbc.co.uk/2/hi/middle_east/6700319.stm.

lived in homes across Baghdad and kept their work with me and *Time* secret to all but their closest confidants. Any time they appeared in public with me brought the risk that they might be seen by killers who would come for them or their families later. This threat was no abstraction or baseless fear. The magazine's initial Baghdad bureau manager, Omar Hashim Kamel, was shot to death on his way to work one morning in March of 2004. His killers were never found. My Iraqi colleagues were so fearful for their safety that they would never mention me by name outside of the bureau. Instead, they referred to me using two codenames, Farouq and Malik. They even entered those names into their cell phones instead of my own, in case they ever fell into the hands of militiamen, insurgents, or kidnappers.

Moreover, if I were to visit an Iraqi at his or her home or office with my drivers and bodyguards, I risked bringing danger to our host. Insurgents and militiamen had eyes all over the city, it seemed. Many of my colleagues who had covered Iraq in the years before I arrived told stories of how they went to interview an Iraqi, who soon afterward received threats. And unlike me, most Iraqis did not have the luxury of living under armed protection at all times.

I found myself in those early months of covering Iraq right in the middle of Baghdad but unable to see Iraq or Iraqi society in any real way. It was an impossible situation in many regards as a correspondent tasked with reporting on the country. So, I did what most journalists did—a lot of embedded reporting with the U.S. military. For roughly the next two years I spent much of my time in Iraq with U.S. troops in trouble spots around the country like Ramadi, Diyala province, Samarra, and Mosul. And of course I went along with U.S. troops in the many neighborhoods of Baghdad that became synonymous with sectarian violence, places like Ghazaliya, Dora, and Mansour. Such combat reporting had its dangers, but at least when embedded I did not impose the risk of death on anyone who wasn't facing it already.

Understanding the violence in Iraq was difficult sometimes for me as a journalist, because the phenomenon often appeared so intricate. The overthrow of Saddam Hussein unleashed a number of dangerous political currents that ran unchecked, gathering a terrifying force in the first two years of the war. A nationalistic guerilla movement had sprung up amid the presence of U.S. troops. Then just as quickly, that Iraqi resistance morphed into an insurgency dominated by Sunni radicals who drew inspiration from the ideology of Osama bin Laden. Shi'ite militias like the Mahdi Army formed at the same time, pitting themselves against occupation forces as well as the Sunni fighters, who were increasingly bent on sectarian violence and came to call themselves al-Qaeda in Iraq. Amid all this, meanwhile, violent criminality swept the country like an epidemic and became interwoven with the burgeoning militias and insurgency.

By 2006, on any given day in Iraq, people were killing each other for revenge, profit, ancient sectarian hatreds, or modern political gain. Often many reasons seemed to come together at once in the minds of those who had a hand in Iraq's violence, but usually only one was enough to set off carnage as lawlessness prevailed across the country. The result was not so much a civil war, as some believed. Rather, Iraq after the U.S. invasion simply fell into anarchic convulsions of mass violence, shaking the society to its core and nearly tearing the nation apart.

Iraqis often refer to the U.S. invasion and the period afterward as "the collapse." It's an apt description. The shattered remnants of the government only crumbled further rather than reforming into a new state. Disparate factions of Iraqi society who had once coexisted now drifted apart amid deepening mutual suspicions. The country itself was physically breaking down as well. You could see damage everywhere in the bullet scars and bomb craters. You could sense the depth in the decay of so many streets, buildings, farmlands, and oil fields all over the country. In many ways Iraq as a nation simply fell in on itself soon after invasion forces arrived—and then began to burn like a collapsed house ablaze with everyone inside.

When not out reporting around Iraq with the U.S. military, I wrote and recovered at the magazine's Baghdad bureau, a comfy little villa with sandbagged windows tucked into a compound surrounded by blast walls. There was a good Internet connection, generators for when the electricity failed, home cooking, and the warm friendship of the bureau's Iraqi staff, most of whom had worked with *Time* since 2003. Through them I began to hear my first in-depth stories about Iraqi life during the past years of war. They told me their own stories. They told me stories of their neighbors and relatives and stories they had heard second- or thirdhand.

Gradually, as the situation in Iraq improved in 2008, I began doing more interviews with Iraqis in Baghdad and less embedded reporting. Most often an interview subject would come to the bureau for a session. I found that was the best and safest way for me to conduct interviews with

Iraqis. It spared everyone the risks and difficulties of being seen in public with me, which remained a deep concern of mine throughout my time covering Iraq. And at the bureau we could make people feel comfortable and safe, and treat them as special guests. Several of the Iraqis who came to talk to me in 2008 at the bureau lingered and opened up about themselves. Only then for the first time did I feel I was getting to know Iraqis and what the war had meant to them. Hearing their stories was like a window onto a wholly different, parallel world, one barely glimpsed by me and all but invisible to followers of the war in America. I was fascinated and wanted to hear more.

Through 2008, I recorded a handful of long-form interviews in Baghdad with Iraqis who told me about their lives before the war and how the years following the 2003 invasion changed them. In January of 2009 I returned to Baghdad after a brief stint in Washington, D.C., with the idea of collecting enough interviews for an eventual oral history of the war as told by Iraqis. I brought with me then a book, *The Good War* by Studs Terkel. I called together the Iraqi staff and showed them Terkel's oral history tome on World War II, explaining that I wanted to tell the story of the Iraq war in much the same way, through Iraqi voices. I told them I needed to interview at least one hundred people, more if possible, for sessions as long as two hours or more each. And I asked for their help in finding me the people to tell the story. I could not do it without them. Apart from the bureau's staff, I could count the Iraqis I knew personally on one hand, despite the years I had spent covering the war. My ability to move around Baghdad remained limited, and I could not even make calls to find people because I do not speak Arabic. I needed them, my Iraqi colleagues and only friends in the country, to find the people to tell their stories, bring them to me, and translate what they said through long hours of conversation.

It was a lot to ask. Any one of them could have refused. Oral history research was not part of their roles as employees of *Time*. I stressed that any help they might give would be a personal favor to me, done in spare time around our work together reporting on Iraq for *Time*. The only thing in return I could give was a chance for them to play a role in the telling of the war as Iraqis saw it. I was moved by how quickly all said yes and threw themselves into the project. Like me, they felt the story of how Iraqis lived through the conflict had not been told enough.

In the days and weeks that followed, my colleagues in the Baghdad bureau brought me a stream of visitors. They invited dozens of friends, relatives, neighbors, acquaintances, friends of friends, and people known to them through tribal ties and shared hometowns. I rarely knew who would be coming to the bureau for an interview in the early days of our research together. People would simply appear, and after brief introductions conversations would begin as I recorded. Gradually their stories accumulated into a flow of memories that poured day after day through a haze of cigarette smoke and the steam from endless cups of sugary Iraqi tea and Turkish coffee we shared.

We became more selective with interviews as the months wore on, seeking out people with stories from specific times and places in order to ensure we gathered accounts of the war's important moments. We sought people with stories from all corners of Iraq apart from Kurdistan, a region that saw relatively little violence in the absence of a heavy American troop presence. We searched for people whose stories reflected widespread experiences among Iraqis over the years, and we sought those who had especially unique tales to tell. We took care to interview a wide variety of people in an effort to collect stories from as many cross sections of Iraqi society as we could.

The book offers a number of interviews expressing the dominant political views of the time. Shi'ite militia fighters, Sunni insurgents, secular activists, invasion advocates, and former regime supporters all give their perspectives throughout the pages. But political leanings and sectarian identities were very much a secondary concern to me during interviews. I simply sought Iraqis whose lives were unarguably changed by the war and invited them to explain to me what had happened to them. Many of the Iraqis I interviewed were indeed initially supportive of the U.S. invasion—even elated by it. Few remained so through the occupation, however. The sentiments expressed by Iraqis whose stories appear here are a function of their experiences, not interview selectivity on my part.

For many Iraqis, their interview with me was the first time they had a chance to speak at length to an American. Every Iraqi I interviewed was imminently gracious and said nothing to suggest they held me, as an American, personally responsible for the actions of my country. Yet many of the conversations held a palpable tension and sense of anger nonetheless. I felt again and again during interviews that many of the Iraqis were in a way speaking through me in the hope of being heard by those who supported the U.S. invasion and occupation, so that the war's advocates might understand what it had done to them. The fact that I was an American author—born and raised in Texas no less—shaped the interviews in a way that I feel made them more powerful, more meaningful than they otherwise might have been.

Whether it was just or not, the U.S. invasion of Iraq was the most ambitious undertaking by America on the world stage since the fall of the Berlin Wall. At the height of its power and influence, the United States plunged into the most ancient corner of civilization and tried to remake the region in its image by force. On some levels, the U.S. campaign might seem like a modern epic destined to fill history volumes for generations. The view on the ground was very different in Iraq, where the American presence and its many consequences became interwoven in the everyday lives of Iraqis. The war ultimately weighed most heavily on more than 6 million Iraqis caught up in the violence. About 2.3 million Iraqis fled the country. Another 2.7 million were internally displaced by 2008.[2] As many as a half-million civilians died, leaving behind grieving families. At the same time, millions of Iraqis were barely touched by the war. For them, the invasion and occupation passed like a distant storm. Many lives across Iraq have even improved in the wake of Saddam Hussein's downfall. The book captures some of this, but it is not the book's main purpose. The book at bottom is meant to be a collective portrait of those Iraqis who endured the most trying ordeals of America's war years in Iraq.

No one book could ever fully capture the immensity of the war's effects on Iraqi society. The human impact is simply too huge and complex for any single document to relate. Oral history, at least, offers a medium of storytelling that allows for many voices and perspectives. That's why I took this approach in trying to tell a fully Iraqi version of the time. Many more people sat for interviews than appear in the coming pages. The narratives here are ones I felt fit together as a whole to offer a sense of what it was like to live as one of the Iraqis who bore the brunt of the war. These stories are in the end a reflection of the saga lived by countless other Iraqis whose voices will likely never be heard.

2 Displacement estimates taken from the *Iraq Index*, the Brookings Institution, May 7, 2009. Accessed at www.brookings.edu/saban/iraq-index.aspx.

THERE IS NO FULLY RELIABLE count of civilian deaths in Iraq related to war violence for the period covered in this book at the time of writing. Estimates to date have ranged from more than a half-million on the high end to less than 100,000 as a low. One of the highest estimates comes from a widely disputed study published in the *Lancet* in October of 2006 that put the number of civilian casualties from 2003 to the summer of 2006 at 654,965. The findings flowed from a statistical survey and appeared as sectarian violence in Iraq was reaching a fever pitch, meaning thousands of other deaths were yet to be tallied.

The nongovernmental public database Iraq Body Count put the overall civilian death toll between 91,912 and 100,339 as of May 13, 2009. Most journalists, academics, and statisticians consider the IBC tally to be a credible minimum, because the database records only verifiable deaths. But the figure surely represents only a fraction of the civilian casualties in Iraq, where many, many killings have gone unreported.

Probably the best estimate at the time of this writing comes from another statistical survey done by the World Health Organization and the Iraqi government, which published their findings in the *New England Journal of Medicine* in January of 2008. Their study estimated that between 104,000 and 223,000 Iraqis died during the first three years of the war. Any estimate from the first three years must be doubled at least to arrive at a figure that approximates the civilian death count as of 2009, given that sectarian violence in Iraq was at its worst in 2006 and 2007.

All of the figures above represent a staggering war toll regardless of which you believe, especially when considering that Iraq is a society of about 30 million people. Take for example the number of just the missing in Iraq as a segment of the country's population. Iraqi government officials have told me that unpublished statistics of theirs show at least 140,000 Iraqis went missing from 2003 until mid-2008, with 82,000 documented cases in Baghdad alone. The real figure is likely much higher. Many Iraqis, particularly Sunnis, have been fearful of dealing with the predominately Shi'ite police because of their suspected ties to militia death squads, which were blamed for much of the kidnapping and murder during the height of the violence. Certainly many additional disappearances have gone unreported to authorities.

Still, even the known disappearances add up to a sizable portion of Iraq's population, which is roughly one-tenth the size of the U.S. populace. In proportional terms, the mass disappearances in Iraq since 2003 would be roughly equal to seeing more than 800 people vanish daily from an American city the size of Philadelphia, where George W. Bush accepted the 2000 Republican nomination for president, until it stood empty.

VOICES FROM IRAQ

The Sanctity of Guns and Shrines

✳

He has an easy smile with one dead tooth in the front. But he is an imposing figure nonetheless, with broad shoulders and a tall frame. He has jug ears and wears a longish flattop with gray spreading through the hair around his temples. Born in 1970, he joined the military at an early age and rose to the rank of major by 2003.

I WAS AN ARTILLERY OFFICER when the war started. I was second in command overseeing three batteries of long-range cannons, eighteen guns in all. Just before the bombardment started we were ordered to move our guns toward Nasiriyah in the south and hide everything so they would not be destroyed in the aerial attack. The idea was to keep the guns safe from the American planes and use them on any U.S. troops moving north into Iraq from Kuwait.

We had more than two hundred men in our unit and a lot of vehicles to move the cannons, which were meant mainly to support forward infantry elements. But I still didn't have enough men. Each gun needs six trained soldiers to operate it, and I was lucky if I had four for each any given day. Initially we put the guns at the edge of Nasiriyah, near a large airbase in the area. We spread the guns out, establishing three positions about a kilometer apart. I guess we were about 400 kilometers south of Baghdad just waiting for things to happen.

A few nights before the bombardment began the Americans started dropping leaflets in our area. On them were instructions detailing how to surrender, how to drive your car slowly so as not to seem like a threat, and how to approach on foot and all that. They even told us to lower the cannons so they would know we were not in the fight. We gathered up all the leaflets we could find—and burned them in a huge pile. Honestly, we were not expecting such a huge invasion. We thought maybe the Americans would attack for three or four days, and then it would be over. So no one was in the mood to surrender. Even the tribes in the area were talking of fighting the Americans if they came across the border. All of us had to fight, whether we wanted or not. Because if Saddam survived, he would probably execute anyone who didn't.

About eight o'clock on the night it started I was having tea with my commanding officer, Hamis, at our main camp. Suddenly we saw two red flashes toward our northernmost position. And then it started raining Hell on us. I think they were using B-52s. I don't know. But everything started exploding around us. We had ordered our soldiers to dig trenches for cover, and we dove into the ground. But the damn trenches were too shallow! They had not dug deep enough, because they did not take it seriously. We could barely cover up as we all hid together. Almost as soon as the bombing started we began getting word about casualties. So and so is wounded. So and so is dead. Names came with every bomb. Most of our soldiers were very young then and had not seen any fighting, much less a bombardment like this. Most started crying, so I took out a Koran and started reading from it to try to calm them down.

The area we were in was muddy, and that's what saved those of us who lived. Since the ground was soft, the bombs would go in deep and throw shrapnel straight back up. Hugging the ground left us buried in mud, but we escaped the flying metal.

We got word that the back position was destroyed in the initial attack, and we went to check the others once there was a lull in the bombing. We jumped in two trucks, but we didn't get far because one of the tires had been blown out with shrapnel. I got down from the truck to have a look, and then I heard another plane coming. We all ran like rabbits, thinking a cluster bomb was falling right on top of us. It was dark, and we could not find our way to the trenches, so we were just running in the open. I was racing across the mudflats when I heard my commanding officer scream, Ra'ad Down! I flung myself face first into the dirt, put my hands on the back of my neck, and started praying. A wave of explosions went over us like a rake. Then silence. We started running again, and the same scene unfolded. This time when I hit the ground, I saw a small hole. I stuck my head in it, because it was the only part of me I could shield. We ran again after that second bomb, and some of us managed to find a small trench. We all piled in, but there was not enough room for everyone. People were stacked on top of each other as the third bomb hit. I was at the bottom of the pile and was not hurt, but the people on top were shredded.

By two o'clock in the morning the bombing for that night seemed to be over, and we got an order to move our remaining guns into the city of Nasiriyah. We figured there would be a battle inside Nasiriyah if U.S. ground forces entered the area, and we had dug out some positions for the guns there previously and stashed a lot of ammunition. But when I relayed the order to my troops they started swearing at me. It was crazy, I have to admit. We were in total disarray. We were dealing with dead and wounded. Some of the soldiers had fled totally, especially the ones who came from that area. A bunch of our vehicles were badly damaged. And they wanted us to go pulling heavy guns over open road as bombers circled overhead. But what could we do? It was an order, so we had to go.

Only about fifty of us remained, and we were on the move toward Nasiriyah by dawn with sixteen guns. We had managed to salvage four from the destroyed position. Now we could see the planes overhead, but they were not bombing us. We figured paratroopers were coming to finish us off after bombing us out of our positions. But we thought we would be safe if we could reach the city, because the Americans would not attack heavily populated areas. The moment we entered the city with the artillery we had left, people started coming out asking what we were doing. We told them we were setting up firing positions, and suddenly everyone vanished. We spread the guns out over three positions some distance apart. We really only had enough men to work two batteries with six guns each, so we left a third position of four guns with just one officer who was like a vegetable because of the shock.

We pointed the guns south, toward our old main base, because we knew the Americans would move to seize it once they came into the area. By now everyone realized they were coming. This was no three-day attack. Soon news reached us that American troops were at our old base, just like we guessed. We still had pretty good intelligence at that time, and we knew that base so well. Now the war really started for us, because we could shoot back. For the next four days we hit at them, day and night, day and night. We must have fired more than three hundred shells. They never shot back because we were in the city. But then I guess they finally had had enough. We heard that an interpreter with the Americans on the base issued a message over a loudspeaker threatening to flatten the town unless our firing stopped. One of our infantry units toward the front heard this and sent word back to us. Shortly after that we got an order to stop firing, and we just waited there.

Some days after that a huge sandstorm blew in, and the skies were red all over. A lot of fedayeen were moving into Nasiriyah, and from what we could tell the Americans had bypassed the town on their way to Baghdad. It seemed to us that they had planned to go through Nasiriyah on the way to Baghdad. Instead they moved past and left us there, although gradually they surrounded the town. We sat wondering what would happen next.

Fifteen days into the war, our situation was getting really bad. We were not firing the guns at all, just watching over them and staying in the houses of people near the positions. People in the town were beginning to turn on us slowly. They started coming to us saying, Why don't you leave? You're going to cause us a lot of problems being here. But my commander would not leave the guns. He had abandoned his guns in the Persian Gulf War in 1991 and was badly punished for doing so. He told the people asking us to go, Look, we are here to defend you. But they clearly weren't on our side anymore. I thought we should go. I told him, Look, it's over. Forget it. He said no. He would not leave the guns unless he saw them destroyed with his own eyes. I decided to stay with him. Hamis and I had sworn an oath to each other as friends. If one of us would die, the other would take our body back to our family in Baghdad. How could I just walk away from him?

The Americans eventually started bombing the town, and we knew they were coming in. We could hear them nearer to the town, and we saw Chinooks in the air, meaning they were probably landing ground forces nearby. The gun position we left with just one soldier had been destroyed, and an Apache attack helicopter shot at our battery nestled among some houses and destroyed an empty home. From what we heard, people in Nasiriyah after that went to the Americans and said, Listen, please don't just shoot into the town trying to hit the guns. Let us show you where they are, and you can come and do away with them without blowing everything up.

What was left of my officers and me, seven of us altogether, were walking toward the position among the houses around then, and a woman burst out of her home suddenly screaming at us. What are you doing!? The Americans are here! They're here! Come inside! We hid with her and watched from a window where we could see our guns. Three American tanks rolled up. We had never seen such machines, and there were all kinds of rumors about how they were indestructible and could see everything in all directions. We didn't know what to make of them. After a moment some U.S. soldiers popped out and went over to our guns. They looked them over and then began stuffing the barrels with some kind of explosives. And one by one they blew the barrels of all six in that battery, flowering the muzzles.

I cried. I had lived with these guns for so long and worked so hard to take care of them. I had spent more time caring for these guns than I had my family. The army never gave us proper tarps for them, so we went to the markets and got our own. Some of my soldiers who were supposed to clean the guns would often do a poor job, so I would sometimes redo it myself with a special solution I mixed from propane and benzene. I loved them, and I cried and cried looking out that window. We all did.

Ra'ad Obaeid Hussein and his fellow artillerymen shed their uniforms and disbanded after their cannons were destroyed. Ra'ad made his way back to his family in Baghdad as the Saddam Hussein regime was in its final days. After the collapse, he began working with various foreign journalists as a driver and guide and eventually joined the Iraqi staff of Time *magazine.*

※

AHMED ABU ALI

He is a devout Shi'ite in his early thirties, poorly dressed and a little on the heavy side. His bare feet are covered with dust inside battered plastic slippers. He appears for the interview on a chilly evening in Baghdad, where he was a shopkeeper living a quiet life with a wife and two young daughters before the U.S. invasion.

A LOT OF PEOPLE were leaving Baghdad in the days before the bombing started, and I decided to take my family to Karbala in the south. I brought a blacksmith to my house in Baghdad before we left and had him weld all the doors and windows shut because we were expecting a lot of looting if the city fell. I myself was eager to see the Americans invade. Life was very hard for me under Saddam because I had avoided my military service. But I was afraid honestly the Americans would do again what they did in 1991, when Shi'ites rose up against that butcher Saddam with U.S. encouragement only to be abandoned.

We arrived in Karbala the night before the bombing began. We settled in with my wife's parents who have a house there. The city was quiet but afraid. Karbala and Najaf saw a lot of bloodshed after 1991, and everyone was scared that that would happen again.

One morning about ten days after we got there I decided to go to the Imam Hussein Shrine, and I was surprised to find a crowd of people out front. At that time Saddam's government was still standing. The Ba'ath party offices were open, and any gatherings, especially of Shi'ites in front of a holy place, was illegal. I started asking people what they were all doing there, and they said there was a rumor that the Americans were planning on entering the city. They had decided to make a human wall to prevent the Americans from entering the Imam Hussein Shrine if they tried. I don't know exactly how many people were there initially, but I would say about two thousand. Some were saying that American troops were only about seven or eight kilometers outside the city, so I decided to try to catch a glimpse of them. I wanted to see them with my own eyes. I walked with my brother-in-law about five kilometers to the edge of the city, but I did not see them. I only found some tracks from their armored vehicles, discarded wrappings from the food they eat, some empty shell casings, and the remains of a fire. From what I saw then and heard from others it seemed to me that the Americans had gone around Karbala initially, moving northward toward Baghdad and then swung back to surround Karbala. We started walking back, thinking maybe the Americans were already entering the city from the other side.

As we moved back into the city you could see that Saddam's government was crumbling. There were no Ba'ath party cars or army vehicles roaming the streets, for example. More importantly, you could sense it. Look, I am a Shi'ite. I know Saddam and his butchers. I had felt that tyranny and oppression touching me every day of my life, and at that moment I could feel it all just melting away.

Back at the shrine, more people were gathering. Posters of Saddam the party had pasted all around the shrine were being torn down. People from the houses in that area were passing out food and water for what was becoming a sit-in against the Americans entering the shrine. You have to understand that for us this shrine is sacred. We could never accept any foreigners setting foot in it. Never.

Still at this point no one had seen the Americans, but we kept hearing that they were nearer and nearer. At one point I was at the northern entrance of the shrine, and I finally saw them. From where I was standing I caught sight of an American tank facing the city. I spotted a cleric in the crowd and went up to him. I said we should try to talk to the Americans and explain about the shrine in case they did not understand. It was the least we could do for the sake of our conscience. After a moment he said, Okay let's go. He and I joined hands and began walking together toward the Americans. A third man fell in with us as well. I did not know who either of these men were at the time. I'm not from Karbala and don't know anyone there besides my family, and my brother-in-law at this point had gone home. I didn't even know the names of these two men as we walked together toward a column of American soldiers standing at the edge of the city.

As soon as we drew near the Americans, the closest armored vehicle pointed its gun at us. The third man with us froze. He was scared they would gun us down and considered turning back. The cleric said, Listen, we're already here. There's no point turning back. If we die, we will die for the sake of Imam Hussein and the shrine. Then the cleric grabbed my hand again and we continued with the third man following behind us. There were tanks, Humvees, armored vehicles, and all kinds of machines and weapons I had never seen before lining the road, and American soldiers were fanned out everywhere in fighting positions. Some were crouching on the ground, while others were poised on rooftops pointing their weapons toward the city. I don't know how many troops and vehicles were there, but I could not see the end of them from where we were. Each step we took toward them brought another gun aimed at us.

We saw a black man on top of a tank, and we approached him trying to talk. He didn't speak Arabic, and the cleric and I only knew a few words of English. But somehow we made it understood that we wanted to talk to someone in charge. He got down and motioned for us to follow him. We walked a bit more into the formation, and then an interpreter in a track suit appeared. I think he was Kuwaiti. He immediately began verbally abusing Saddam Hussein before we could even say anything. After he was done we told him what we wanted to say about the shrine and asked that he take the message to the commander. Our message was simple: Please do not enter the shrine because it is sacred to us.

The interpreter went off and we stood there waiting for some time. Suddenly there was an explosion in one of the buildings near the shrine as U.S. troops entered it. Then we started hearing gunfire from the armored vehicles toward that building. We didn't know what was going on. Then suddenly a very small soldier approached us with the interpreter. The soldier was tiny, a quarter of a bite. He was apparently the American commander, and we began explaining the situation at the shrine. We told this officer there was nothing of interest there for the army, that the shrine had only unarmed civilians around it. The officer told us that the soldiers thought there were some Arab fighters inside the shrine and that they had taken fire from that direction. The shrine had been closed for days, actually. No one had been allowed to enter. We tried to explain this to the officer, and we went back and forth with him for some time. This officer was insisting that he had to enter the shrine. He was a military man with orders, he said. Blah, blah, blah. I got the sense he was just playing us for time as they planned a raid on the shrine. So finally I told him, Look, if you enter, it will be over our dead bodies. We can never allow it. After talking a little more the commander promised us that American forces would not enter the shrine. We said we would go back and inform the others, and we expected him to keep his word. As we were walking back, I said to the cleric, I don't trust them.

Back at the shrine, we told the crowds what was said between us and the Americans. There were some young strong men in the crowd, and they volunteered to climb the fences of the shrine and go inside to see if indeed there were any fighters. We all decided this was a bad idea. It could raise suspicion among the Americans, and if there were fighters inside they might kill whoever entered.

It was getting late, almost dusk, and a lot of the people who had gathered around the shrine during the day were beginning to drift off. I was very tired myself and thinking of going home too. But then suddenly one of the tanks advanced toward the shrine and leveled its gun, and it appeared that the Americans had broken their promise and were moving to enter the shrine. For those of us still left, it was a matter of faith, and we knew what we had to do. About forty of us men joined hands and formed a human wall at the gate of the shrine facing the tank, and we began shouting insults at the Americans. We called them dogs and bastards and occupiers. You have to remember also the fear and hatred toward Americans implanted in most Iraqis during the Saddam years. None of us standing there I'm sure had ever really known Americans as anything other than ruthless foreign enemies who, as far we understood, were willing to kill us all right there in the street. Those of us who stood to face them had only our faith.

Events were moving so fast all of a sudden. Everything was a blur of noise and confusion in those moments. As the noise rose, people began returning and the crowd swelled again. More people joined us in front of the tank and began shouting as well. And then, after a moment, the tank notched its gun up a little and inched backward a bit. It moved a few meters back and then stopped. Apparently from what we could tell the Americans were essentially pouring into the city from every direction after sitting at the edge of it all day—but stopping short of the shrine because of our human wall. More tanks appeared but stood well off, and the first tank that approached backed farther away.

As darkness came, it looked as though the Americans were content to leave the shrine alone as they moved through the rest of the city. After some time I sat on a curb in sight of all these tanks and began to cry tears of exhaustion and frustration, wondering why the soldiers had done this to us. How could they have broken their promise by moving toward the shrine after they vowed they wouldn't? What kind of people would force a standoff with unarmed civilians? How could they insult our dignity by threatening such a holy place right in front of us? We are human beings, after all. Aren't we?

Ahmed Abu Ali later joined the Mahdi Army militia and came to consider himself a resistance fighter dedicated to ridding Iraq of the American occupation.

An Army in Defeat

✳

GASSAN ABDUL WAHED INED

He joined the army in September of 2001 and was serving as a young corporal in 2003. He was part of a light artillery unit based in Najaf, a city sacred to Shi'ites. Each year thousands of Shi'ite pilgrims pour into Najaf to visit the Imam Ali Shrine, where Ali ibn Abi Talib, a cousin and son-in-law to the Prophet Mohammed, rests in a gilded tomb beneath a huge golden dome.

I WAS AT HOME with my family in Baghdad the first night I heard bombs falling on the city. I was on leave, actually, even though the army was on alert. The very next morning I got a call from my commanding officer in Najaf, Lt. Col. Nabil al-Douri. He was my commander, but we were very close friends as well, closer than brothers. He asked me to rejoin our unit in Najaf. He sensed that this was going to be a real war even when a lot of people were still wondering if the Americans were serious about invading. A lot of people thought it would be a war like the one in 1991, but Nabil knew it was something much bigger. He wanted me there with him, and I wanted to be at his side too, as a friend.

I put on my uniform and headed down to the bus station to catch a ride to Najaf. I remember seeing American fighter planes in the sky. They were flying very low. We had never seen that before. And the bombing the night before had been so heavy and had lasted so long. It was not just a few strikes. I was beginning to realize too that this was something different. This was the real war. Everyone was realizing this after that first night of bombing, not just me. Passengers on the bus were talking about it. Several of them seeing me in uniform obviously heading to join my unit were like, Are you crazy? It was beginning to dawn on everybody that the Americans were coming and what that meant. Even my mother knew. She was crying as I went to leave the house, and my little sister was clinging to my leg and begging me not to go. But what was I supposed to do? I was in the military, and there was a war starting. I had to go, and I wanted to go because of

Nabil. Even if I didn't want to go, I probably would have been too scared to desert. The Ba'ath party was executing deserters then.

There were three or four checkpoints along the way from Baghdad to Najaf. At each one I had to get off and present my identification and explain who I was and where I was going. The guards on the road were suspicious of me. I think some must have taken me for a deserter. I'm sure it seemed strange to them to see a soldier on his way to a frontal unit in the south rather than fleeing in the other direction, but that's what I was doing. There was only one guard at a checkpoint in Hilla who treated me properly as a military man on duty. He looked over my identification and papers explaining my posting in Najaf. And then he gave me a salute and said, Go with God.

When I got to Najaf, I found our old base abandoned. The unit had broken up into several groups and based themselves in schools around the city to avoid being taken out all together in an airstrike. I went to the school that was serving as the new headquarters. There were about thirty men there, including Nabil. He looked really surprised to see me. He gave me a big hug. It was a very emotional moment. I'm sure he wouldn't suspect me of deserting, but I might not have made it for any number of reasons.

At the headquarters for arms we had Kalashnikovs, heavy machineguns, a few rocket-propelled grenade launchers, and several light and heavy mortar launchers. We were worried not just about defending the city from an American attack. We were worried about an uprising in the city as well. In 1991 the civilians in Najaf began attacking anyone in uniform. So, we had to be very careful about whom we trusted in the local population and our own ranks as well.

As the days passed, we began to run low on supplies. Our logistics support was collapsing. Our morale was fading, and we were scared, honestly. Most of us were young soldiers and had not been in a war before, and now we were expected to fight the U.S. army. We put a lot of hope in the Republican Guard. They were the experienced soldiers, and we thought if we had some of them among us we might have a chance. A unit of Republican Guard troops was supposed to join us from Baghdad, but they were all killed trying to reach us by the Americans. That was a shock to all of us, and we began to grow more afraid. People began deserting. Anyone who had family anywhere around Najaf disappeared. Eventually the only soldiers left in our unit were the ones who stayed for the sake of friendships, like Nabil and I. Men who could not just abandon each other.

Even after the Republican Guard troops failed to reach us we were getting messages from the Baghdad command saying the Americans had not entered Iraqi territory. We were left to believe that the campaign was just a bombing, not a ground invasion. There was a hotel in the city with a good rooftop view, the Zam Zam Hotel. We set up a lookout position on the roof. Very quickly we came to see U.S. troops maneuvering northward in the distance. We saw tanks and troop carriers and Humvees and all kinds of armored vehicles. We saw paratroopers dropping from the sky. That's when we basically just started ignoring messages from the Baghdad command. We knew we were on our own.

Did you think you had a chance after seeing all those forces?

To be honest, looking at them, I felt no urge to fight. Maybe you will think I was a bad soldier for feeling that way, but I didn't have the will to hurt any one of those Americans I saw. Saddam Hussein never personally harmed me or my family, but I knew how he hurt so many other Iraqis. And it was hard as a young person to see a future in the country. There were no jobs. There were no opportunities. What's the point in fighting for that? And even if we did fight, even if we won and drove out the Americans, none of us who did the fighting would ever see any benefit for it. Anything good in the country just went to Saddam.

One day I was at the lookout with Nabil watching the battlefield, and we decided to go together downstairs for a bite to eat. As soon as we were off the top floor, a missile flew in and destroyed the position. No one was hurt, but the roof was obliterated. It was like they were watching our lookout and waiting for a moment when no one was in it before striking. I'll never know for sure, but I always wonder whether they spared us on purpose. That's how it seemed.

Our situation started to get really bad after that. Our supplies dwindled further. We were running out of money. We had been spending whatever pocket money we had on chocolate bars and snacks, because we were so low on food. More men deserted. There used to be Ba'ath party officials who served as advisers to the unformed military officers. All those guys disappeared. The city's only defenses were the few of us still in uniform and some fedayeen units, who set up positions just outside the city. But the Americans weren't attacking. From what we could tell, there were two columns of American troops passing on either side of Najaf headed north. They seemed to be bypassing the city, but they closed off the main roads. We were effectively surrounded.

The city fell, as far as those left in my unit were concerned, on the fourth of April. By then almost anyone with any ties to the government or the Ba'ath party had vanished. Even the fedayeen were gone. I don't know where they went. We figured it was just a matter of time before our post at the school was bombed, so we were not even sleeping there at night. Nabil and I were staying with a family we knew in Najaf and going back and forth on foot to the post occasionally in civilian clothes.

On the day the Americans entered the city, Nabil was up a little before me and off to the post early. I followed after him a short while later. I went out the door and headed toward a roundabout near the house. I turned a corner, and there they were, the Americans. An infantry unit was moving through the city. There were thirty or forty of them on foot together right in front of me. I was actually sort of mesmerized seeing them so close up. I stared at their boots, their trousers, every bit of equipment on them up to their helmets I studied. I watched the way they moved and how they spoke to each other. Everything about them was so impressive to me as a soldier.

I followed them for a while, just watching. They were headed to the center of the city I think to rendezvous with other units that had entered from other points. There were a lot of people on the street watching them with me. Some were waving. Some were saluting. Some even came forward to shake their hands. I was close enough to hear the officer in charge talking with his interpreter as the unit came upon the Imam Ali Shrine. The officer seemed to ask, What's this? The interpreter did not fully explain the significance of the shrine. He just told the officer that it was the home of someone very important to the city. The officer looked at it for a moment and then shouted out loudly with an order. Suddenly all his men were at attention, and they all saluted the shrine before moving on again.

Eventually I broke away from the troops and found Nabil at our post. I told him what I had seen. He was silent for a long moment, and then he said, Okay, that's the end. The war was over for us, and we decided to go back to Baghdad together.

Gassan Abdul Wahed Ined made it safely back to Baghdad along with Nabil al-Douri. Gassan started a civilian life shortly afterward, first as help at a restaurant in western Baghdad called Blue Sky. He eventually got another job as a writer for a scholastic magazine called University Voice, *where he remained working as of May 2009.*

BAHA'A NOURI YASSEEN

Born in Basra in 1959, he looks like a drill sergeant with a buzz cut atop his sturdy, squat frame. His eyes are small, dark, close together, and dart as he speaks in English and Arabic, gesturing in choppy motions occasionally with small, toughened hands. A career military man, he was a senior officer in the Iraqi army's air defense wing in 2003 as the bombardment began.

I WAS A STAFF COLONEL at that time in command of a position in southern Baghdad that served as a headquarters for the air defenses. We had distributed a lot of anti-aircraft weapons throughout Baghdad. But right away the Americans destroyed our radar. We had no eyes. Then they started destroying all our anti-aircraft weapons. The more positions they destroyed, the more soldiers defected. Everything collapsed very quickly. We weren't surprised, honestly. There's no comparison between our air warfare technology and the American capability. It was a battle. We've seen enough battles to understand. Sometimes you win, sometimes you lose. We were definitely losing.

Morale collapsed when we lost contact with our superiors. All the communications were eventually cut during the bombing as well, even land lines, and soon we stopped getting orders. As a military man, I was ready to stay and follow orders, and so were many of my fellow officers even though things were going very badly. But suddenly there was no word from our commanders. Before U.S. troops reached Baghdad, we were cut from them. No communication. We stayed in our position on the idea that we could not leave unless we had an order, but we didn't even have food where we were.

After three days of this, we decided that it was useless to try and do anything more to fight with the air defenses, so we focused on just trying to minimize our losses. All I could do was protect my building and my men. More than two hundred soldiers at that time were under my command, and I had five or six other officers with me. But we had run out of fuel for our vehicles and were low on ammunition for the arms we had as the Americans neared Baghdad. Basically we just sat there and waited.

We heard that the Americans had reached a grain depot in the neighborhood of Dora, which was very near us. The city had no power at all, and bombs were dropping all around our position. There was some talk about trying to make our way to another air defense site and see if we could regroup with some other soldiers, but as the hours unfolded we began to realize that the entire city had fallen. From what we heard the Americans had entered Baghdad from all sides and had taken control of all the main routes. So we decided simply to go home and abandon our post before the Americans reached us.

I kept my uniform on and had some of my boys drive me to the edge of my neighborhood. I had to keep it on. I could no sooner shed my uniform than I could shed my honor. The real military men like me didn't care whether the army was under the control of Saddam or whoever. We were the army of Iraq, a professional army for the country. Many of us wanted to continue working for the country regardless of the political changes. We had the same mentality as most other good armies of the world. We served the state, not individual rulers.

I had kept a house in the Jihad neighborhood, right next to the airport. I knew there would be a lot of fighting in that area once the Americans arrived to seize the airfield, so I had moved my family to another house across town, near Kadhimiya. I figured they would be safer there, but I found heavy fighting there when I arrived at about ten in the morning. All I had to do was hop across some train tracks to reach my house, but I could not get there because of all the gunfire. The Americans were in the area but under attack by fedayeen and returning fire. I ducked into a house very close to mine and waited. Normally it would take me two minutes to walk from that house to mine. But it was at least four hours before the fighting slowed enough for me to move again.

Coming out I saw one of the saddest scenes of my life. Bodies were all over the streets. Smoke was flowing everywhere, blackening the sky.

Warplanes were roaring overhead, and I could hear tanks rolling in streets nearby. There was no water. No power. The streets were totally empty. It looked as though all life there had been crushed out in one afternoon.

My wife and my three children assumed I was dead. In those early days, amid all that destruction, any family with a man in the military figured they would never see him alive again. Honestly I was ready to die at any time. I was a military man in uniform on the streets of a city at war. I could have wound up killed or captured by the Americans at any moment. But I made it home, and I found everyone okay despite the scene outside. Only then did I take off my uniform.

Baha'a Nouri Yasseen eventually went back into uniform as a senior officer in the newly formed Iraqi National Police.

※

HUSSEIN AL-AWADIE

He is a wiry older man with a deeply lined, gaunt face. He chain-smokes slowly and smiles with a mouthful of gray teeth.

I JOINED THE IRAQI ARMY in 1970 and reached the rank of general in 1996. By 2003 I was semiretired. Like a lot of senior military commanders, I had an honorary post. I put on the uniform once a month or so to go down to an office and collect my salary, but that was about it.

My house was in Ghazaliya. It's a neighborhood on the western side of Baghdad where a lot of senior figures from the government lived. I remained in my house through the initial bombardment, staying there with my wife and four children. No bombs came into our neighborhood, but we could hear very well the bombing around the airport area. It's not so far from us. There's an open space between us and the airport, and we could see the flashes from the blasts as well as hear them.

By that time, I have to tell you, the Iraqi military was nothing. There were a lot of smart officers, even genius military commanders. But they were not in important posts. Those went to the high Ba'athist officials.

So the army really had no one capable of even attempting to lead a fight against the most powerful and technologically advanced army in the world. You could see a lot of tanks and missiles in the streets around Baghdad as the war started. But there was no real plan to defend the city, and the Iraqi military made poor use of what troops they had. Nobody seemed to make any plans for long-term fighting. The military mismanagement made it even easier for the Americans than it might have been.

In my neighborhood lived a bunch of other Iraqi military officers, who all knew like me how this battle would end. We used to gather during the bombing campaign to talk and share information and laugh, actually. Look, any military sometimes loses a battle, but you can lose with honor. There was no honor to be had in this.

Shortly after capturing the airport, American troops moved into our area. Overnight they suddenly appeared. They were everywhere with all kinds of vehicles all of a sudden one day. It was a real shock how quickly they just swarmed us. Things were tense at first. If you wanted to go out you had to wave a white cloth over your head. Close to my house there was a warehouse for the Republican Guard that had some munitions in it. The Americans quickly came to destroy all the weapons in a detonation, and the explosion broke all the windows of my house. They came around later to give us a little money for repairs. But the problem continued, because they turned that place into a demolition yard. Any time they found some explosives, they would bring it to that yard and detonate. The windows of my house were blown out four times.

Gradually things eased up, and there was a period of calm before American troops started facing a lot of attacks in our area and elsewhere. In the afternoons sometimes in those days the Americans would walk around the neighborhood and browse the shops and eat food from the street stands. They were very friendly toward everyone and seemed quite relaxed. They would play with the kids and sometimes have their medics look sick children over. Some in the neighborhood would try to talk to the soldiers, and they were all so very kind and polite. For me, watching the American soldiers there on the streets of my neighborhood brought such a strange feeling. Looking at them I would wonder what the future held. I could not see. And even though I knew the old army would fall from the very start, I still could not help but wonder, looking at these troops right there in front of me, how it all had come to this.

Hussein al-Awadie came out of retirement in 2004 and joined the Iraqi National Police, where he served as overall commander of the force.

※

MOHAMMED KHALIL HAMED

He has a thin, graying mustache and dark, heavy bags under his eyes. He speaks without any cheer at all, hardly showing any expression on his deeply lined face. He was born in 1961 in Baquba, coming of age in a time when Iraq arose as a power in the Middle East.

I JOINED THE IRAQI ARMY in 1982 and worked my way up to colonel in the Republican Guard. In 2003, as the war began, I was overseeing a military store north of Baghdad warehousing all kinds of equipment for use by the Republican Guard. That had been my job for three years. It made for a good life. My wife and I had a nice house in Baghdad. There was enough cash, even with four children. We never wanted for anything, really. But my suffering would come that April, in the downfall.

Of course we were on alert when the bombing started, and I was at the store while my family was at home. The facility where my store sat was not directly attacked, but bases all around us were destroyed. Those days were very difficult. Look, we knew as military men things would go badly for us. We knew the Americans would not be stopped on their march to Baghdad. All of them didn't come thousands of miles just to lose some stupid battle in the southern deserts. They were coming, and we knew what that would mean for us after. A whole picture of misery was drawn for us from the start.

I stayed at my post until the ninth of April, when a column of American vehicles passed our area. They didn't attack or even stop. They were on their way to someplace else. But a mob following them forced their way in and began looting. It was chaos. There were hundreds of them, running like crazy everywhere to grab something. Boys of no more than five were alongside 80-year-olds. I tried to argue with some of them, saying, Listen, this belongs to the state. This does not belong to Saddam or you or me. It belongs to Iraq. This is against the law. This is against religion! They told me to shut up unless I wanted to get killed right there. What could I do?

They went into my office, and one reached for an inventory file I had. I was very organized, and the file was put together nicely. But what good is an inventory file to anyone for a store that's being looted right in front of you? What are you going to do with that, I asked the guy? Nothing, he said. I just like the colors. And he took it. They took the spare military clothes I had hanging on the wall and the boots that went with them. They took everything, everything they could carry, and torched the heavy equipment they could not move.

That night we had no idea what was going on in Baghdad. Since I was a military man and somewhat known, I decided to leave my family there and head to Baquba to stay with relatives. I stayed there for about a week. We were hearing so many rumors about how the Americans were going to capture and kill all the officers of the former regime. But things started cooling down, and I decided to go back to Dora to see my family.

Man, my neighborhood was a disaster scene when I got there. The wreckage of destroyed tanks and artillery pieces was strewn everywhere. Bombed-out buildings were still on fire. Bodies were rotting in the road. The only signs of life to be seen were the warplanes in the skies and the U.S. soldiers roaming the streets. I felt so helpless when I looked at them, these occupiers. The Kuwaitis looked at us the same way when we invaded there, and they had the right. Now I knew how they felt.

I finally made it home, and thank goodness everybody was alright. But the whole family was in sorrow, because we all understood that our lives as we knew them were over. It was the moment when we all began counting backwards, and we would go down, down, down until we had less than zero.

Mohammed Khali Hamed tried repeatedly to join the new Iraqi army but was rejected for reasons never made clear to him. In 2007, his oldest son, Ali, was murdered by Shi'ite militants as sectarian violence raged in his neighborhood. The family was forced to flee their home after that and eventually settled into a two-room flat in another neighborhood in Baghdad, living mainly off a meager military pension as Hamed remained without work.

The Roads of Falling Cities

✳

RAHMA ABDUL KAREEM ABBAS

She is in her early forties, but her face appears much younger beneath a silky head scarf patterned with leopard print and flecked with sequins. She comes to the interview in dress clothes, wearing a pressed black pantsuit with heavy gold buttons. She stands very tall, much higher than most Iraqi men. And she motions with long, elegant hands as she remembers hearing the war come to her family's home in a poor area of southeastern Baghdad called Zafaraniya.

IT WAS JUST ME in the house with my mother and father. All my brothers and sisters had married and moved out. We decided to stay at the house as the bombing was beginning, because many of my brothers were in the military. We wanted to be home if they came. My father and mother are very old, and it is difficult to manage alone. Those days unfolded like a dream. Our house sits very near an Iraqi airbase. How would we survive when the Americans attacked it? I didn't know.

The bombardment was savage when it started, really strong. All the windows shattered as the bombs hit the base, and a rain of debris showered our house. You could hear it landing on the roof and in the yard, nuts and bolts and I don't what else. My mother was shaky. But my father had been in the military and seen wars. You know, as an Iraqi from the time you open your eyes coming into the world until you die, you see wars. So he stayed calm, and I tried to be like him. The good thing about the bombardment was that the Americans only attacked at night, not in the daytime. In the daylight I would go out in the street and talk to the kids and collect bits of shrapnel for souvenirs.

When we heard that American troops were nearing Baghdad, we decided to leave the area. My sister and her family were living nearby with a lot of young girls, and we were afraid the soldiers might do bad things to them. We have a family farm in Diyala province east of Baghdad, and we all left Zafaraniya as the Americans were entering the area. This was around the fifth of April. We stayed at the farm for four or five days, and everything was fine. Then I started hearing the American helicopters landing at night near the farm. You could hear the soldiers talking to each other as they walked the ground nearby. They were so close! That really scared us. Most of us were women, and my father is so old. We decided to move again, this time going north to stay with another relative who lives near Kirkuk. He offered one room for all of us, but our problem wasn't solved.

The Peshmerga, the Kurdish fighters, were in that area, and they were trying to stop Arab families from settling there. They would search houses and go through the streets whooping war cries, like Indians of the Wild West or something. We were lucky, because we were staying with a Kurdish family. They kept us inside and did not let anyone search the house.

Of course we were listening to the radio. We heard on a lot of stations that Baghdad had fallen and the era of Saddam Hussein was over. I cried bitter tears, because I knew worse days were coming. Living in the time of Saddam Hussein was like trying to breathe underwater. He destroyed my dreams. I had good marks in high school and wanted to go on for a degree in engineering. But the sons of the martyrs for Saddam's wars were always first in line for the programs, and in the end I got nothing. Even with all the bad things Saddam did to Iraqis, though, I have to admit he was very effective as a leader. And I knew what was coming would be worse.

After about fifteen days in the north we decided to go back to our house in Baghdad. No one really knew what was happening. When we reached the main road into the city, we saw a huge number of people walking in both directions. I saw boxes of ammunition everywhere on the road, and people were digging through them taking bullets. At the edge of the city we came upon a weird scene. People in dishdashas were wearing stethoscopes, carrying medical instruments, and dragging around heavy hospital equipment. It had all been looted. Looters were everywhere. I kept crying the more we saw.

We finally reached the house. The place was a mess from all the bombing destruction around it, but it was standing. We started cleaning up. A lot of the things in the house were so damaged we needed professional help to fix them, but of course there was no one around to hire or help.

In the days that followed we lived in agony. No word had come from three of my brothers who were in the military. I tried to comfort my father, telling him I could feel that his sons would return. We'll see them, I would say. We'll see them. I have a very active sixth sense. I always have. I learned later that my brothers hid with other family during the invasion and were safe. By the end of it, we were all back together again.

Rahma Abdul Kareem Abbas eventually found work as an administrative assistant for a sponge factory in her area. And in her spare time she established a small nongovernmental agency focusing on prisoners' rights.

※

MOHAMMED ABBAS ABDUL AL-HUR

He had served in the Iraqi army for nearly twelve years until 1991, when he settled in central Baghdad and opened a supermarket. A Shi'ite born in Baghdad, he was living near the store with his wife and four children when the war started in 2003.

IN THE EARLY DAYS of the bombardment, we used to go to the roof of our house to watch the explosions. I had a small satellite dish too, so I could watch the news on television. I would see images of military planes taking off from airbases far away and then see the explosions from the bombs across the horizon. Bear in mind that the sky was often black. The army had dug trenches all around Baghdad, filled them with oil, and set them alight to create smoke that could obscure visibility from the air. It really hurt to see all these scenes. It was really painful, I think for all of us.

At first the airstrikes around Baghdad were far away from us. But day by day the explosions drew closer. And groups of Iraqi soldiers began appearing in our neighborhood. They had been bombed out of different military installations throughout the city and were just adrift or hiding out in our area.

Before it all started I went to my store and grabbed as much as I could off the shelves so we could have a food supply at home. Then I closed the place up. My family and I stayed in the house throughout the bombardment and lived off what I had taken from the store. We thought we would just wait things out. When we heard that American soldiers were entering Baghdad, however, we decided to leave the city in case there was some kind of big fighting on the ground. We had relatives in Hilla in the south, and we thought we would try to make it to their house for a stay. So we packed up the car one day and went.

On our way out of the city we were surprised to see an Iraqi army unit digging defensive fighting positions along the road, as if they were expecting to see the Americans appear coming at them on the same road we were going down. Meanwhile, from what we had heard, the Americans were already inside parts of Baghdad. There were reports saying they had entered the western portion of the city, which meant the government was probably finished. So, why these soldiers would be setting up positions there was a mystery to us at the moment. In any case, we stopped to ask them if the road going south was safe, and they waved us through like everything was normal. We drove on heading south for a short distance, and then suddenly we saw American forces, right there. Soldiers were taking up positions on the road, fighting positions, with their weapons pointed at us as we approached. I was afraid they would start shooting, so I slowed way down, put the hazard lights on, and hung a white cloth out the window. As we got nearer the soldiers stopped us and ordered us all out of the car. They separated me from my wife and children and asked where I was going. I was truthful. I explained that we were leaving the city because we were afraid there would be fighting there. They told me to turn around and go back, because the roads farther south were too unsafe. The Americans told us to go home for our own safety, put us back in the car, and turned us around.

We definitely did not want to go back to Baghdad, so as soon as we were out of sight of the Americans I hopped on a country road I know going south along a riverbank. We took back roads to Hilla and never saw either Iraqi military or Americans the rest of the way.

Hilla seemed untouched by anything, and it was safe enough at our relatives' house. But we did not stay long. The day after we got there I watched on television the statue of Saddam falling in Baghdad and knew it was really over. Then the images of the looting came. I got really scared for my house and my store. That was everything we had. Everything, all sitting there unguarded as the city went crazy. Our relatives urged us to stay, but we headed back to Baghdad after just a week in Hilla.

We took another country road back into the city. As we neared Baghdad I was astonished at what I saw. Such destruction. Our route into the city took us past several military installations, which had of course been bombed. People were crawling over the ruins like ants, looting things. Missile batteries that had been abandoned by their soldiers were just sitting in the open. Children were playing on some of them I passed.

When I got back into Baghdad, it was not the city I had left just a week before. It was like some other place. And it was a depressing sight. You saw people walking everywhere carrying looted goods. All kinds of things. When I got into my neighborhood, I found the streets littered with weapons and Iraqi military uniforms. All those soldiers had just vanished and left their things. Nowhere could you see any sign of law and order. No police. No military. No government. Nothing. Everything had collapsed.

Mohammed Abbas Abdul al-Hur found his home and his supermarket thankfully untouched by looters. He eventually reopened his store later in 2003. Sectarian violence in the years that followed forced him to relocate his family several times around Baghdad, but they all remained safe. He hoped to leave Iraq nonetheless. As of April 2009 he was looking for ways to emigrate, because he felt the future of the country looked too bleak.

⁂

FARID HADI ABDUL ZAHRA

He wears a thin beard on his young, handsome face and offers a pleasant smile often while speaking. For five years before the war he had been working as an apprentice to an upholsterer in Baghdad and living a life he considered fortunate.

WE NEVER EVEN DARED to dream that someone would remove Saddam Hussein. When I used to talk against Saddam even to my family they would tell me to shut up, because you never know which walls have ears. So, yes, I was happy to see the Americans invade, but I did not expect it to cost me a hand.

Shortly after the Americans entered Baghdad there was basically a media blackout. We did not even know they were in the city until we saw them with our own eyes, and we had no idea what was happening elsewhere in the country. Around this time a very close friend of mine from my neighborhood, Razeq, came to me and asked me to go with him to Mosul. His brother, Nakeep, was with the Iraqi army up there, and he wanted to try to find him since it appeared the army was disbanding. So, one morning we set out together heading north hitching rides.

We made it all the way to the southern edge of Tikrit, where there was a huge number of people on the road heading south in the direction we had come. Many were on foot, and we began asking them what was happening farther north. The situation was very confused. No one seemed to know exactly what was happening. Some people told us that American paratroopers had captured Tikrit the night before without a fight. Many we talked to on the road said the military was in fact in collapse. They said that officers in the northern areas had abandoned their posts and ordered their troops to go home since the country had fallen and it was no use to fight anymore. The Iraqi army had left Mosul from what we gathered. Most of the people we saw on the road were actually from Mosul heading toward Baghdad, and we figured that Nakeep was probably somewhere in the mass of people moving south. Maybe we had already passed him on the road. In any case it seemed impossible to find him even if we made it all the way to Mosul, so we decided to turn back. The road for the most part seemed safe, and we thought he would likely be okay returning to Baghdad like the rest of the people on the road.

We walked for a while in the crowd moving south and then came across a white pickup truck with four men in it. Two of them looked like typical tribesmen wearing robes and head scarves. But the other two looked like military men who had ditched their uniforms for civilian clothes. Anyway, we didn't ask a lot of questions. They said they were heading toward Baghdad and let us jump in the back. Most of the cars on the road had some kind of white cloth waving from them in order to show the Americans they were peaceful. The guys in the truck had done the same, but the cloth had blown off and was in the bed of the truck where we sat.

We saw no American tanks or troops or armored vehicles anywhere around as we neared the northern edge of Baghdad. Everything looked normal. About four or five cars ahead of us on the road was a minibus moving along. Behind us the road was empty for some distance except for one car trailing. All of a sudden without warning the minibus exploded. It had clearly been bombed, but we never heard or saw a plane or the shot of a cannon or anything. It just blew up and sent black smoke curling everywhere, totally destroyed. A second later the car behind us exploded too. We had no idea where the firing was coming from or why we were being attacked. But it seemed as though they bombed the vehicles at the head and rear of our line in order to trap the rest of the cars and destroy them one by one. That was my guess. The driver of the truck must have thought the same, because suddenly he slammed the accelerator and began speeding around the cars in front of us to try and get away. I reached into the bed of the truck and found the fallen white cloth and held it up as we raced ahead.

Just as we moved past the burning minibus I heard a sound in the distance, a single thump. Boomp. And then it felt like someone kicked me hard in the hand. I drew down my arm and saw my hand just above the wrist hanging only by a bit of skin. To this day I have no idea what did that. A bullet? A grenade? A cannon shot? A laser beam? I never saw anything.

The driver kept going toward Baghdad, and nothing else hit us. I bandaged myself up the best I could and asked the men in the truck if they could take me to the hospital near my neighborhood in northern Baghdad. Initially they refused, if you can believe it. The driver stopped the truck just outside my neighborhood and said, Sorry, I can't take you any further. He was afraid of getting arrested or something if he took me to the hospital. Razeq had to beg him, with me standing there bleeding and screaming. A group of women walked up on us and saw the scene, and they started screaming at the driver to take me as well. Finally he relented and drove me to the hospital.

By the time I got there my arm felt like it was in an oven, and I was so, so thirsty. I was getting delirious because of the blood loss, but I was still conscious. There were only two doctors in the hospital, which had been virtually abandoned like most others after the Americans entered Baghdad. One of them looked me over and said my case was serious and that the hand had to be cut. I asked if he had morphine, because I had heard someone in the emergency room saying they were out. The doctor assured me there was morphine, so I told him to go ahead and cut it. It was already cut anyway. I knew I had lost the hand. I was really only concerned about bleeding to death. I was lying for a while in the operating room, and two nurses, a man and a woman, were standing next to me talking. My mouth was so dry. I managed to ask the man for a drink of water. He ignored me and continued talking to the woman, and the two of them started laughing about something. So I kicked him with my foot. Seconds after that I fainted.

When I woke up, I found my right hand gone. The end of my arm was just a mass of bloody bandages. The doctor came in soon after I opened my eyes, and so did the male nurse I kicked. He apologized for not getting me water, explaining that he could not give me anything to drink right before surgery because I might throw it up after taking morphine. He and the doctor both came over to me and bent over my bed and kissed me on the cheek.

Farid Hadi Abdul Zahra could no longer continue working as an upholsterer because of his injury, and his financial situation worsened drastically in the years following the incident. As of February 2009 he was unmarried and eking out a living by selling scratch cards for mobile phones from a makeshift street stand.

※

ALI AL-SHAHEEN

He speaks perfect English with a slight Scottish accent from his years as a student in the United Kingdom. Born in 1956, he normally wears a cross expression on his haggard face, but he has a sharp wit and is quick to laugh.

I WAS A CHICKEN FARMER. I had been running a chicken farm on a plot of land just south of Baghdad for about three years before the war with a couple of business partners. The money was good. We were all doing well. Everybody needs eggs, you know.

Twice a week, Mondays and Thursdays, I would be in Baghdad for a gathering of old men. I was the youngest member of the group. Most of them were in their sixties, retired judges and professors and other educated people. It was a salon for elder intellectuals, basically, and we would talk about all that was happening, over drinks of course. There were a lot of arguments about what would happen once it became clear the Americans would invade. Some said it would be a turn for the better. Others said the country would break up. I had mixed feelings about it. Sometimes I was happy about the idea of the Americans coming and bringing down Saddam. Sometimes I would worry a lot about the future.

When the war started I was on the farm with my wife, three kids, and my mother, who was very old and frail at that point. The bombing of Baghdad started very late one night, I remember. From the roof of the chicken farm I could see the flashes of light over the city, but I did not hear anything. It went like this night after night. The city would flash with explosions in the distance through the darkness, but by day most everything seemed more or less normal in our area. Finally we started hearing bombs as the Americans began targeting spots around us. And we began to see army deserters moving through the fields, coming from the south heading toward Baghdad. We saw high-ranking officers hiding in ditches to avoid execution squads sent out by the Ba'ath party to kill deserters.

When we heard that the Americans had made it to Nasiriyah and were headed our way, we decided to leave the farm and join family at our house in Baghdad. We put everything in a truck and headed for the city, where the Americans had not reached at that time. Nobody was on the road. The only things to be seen were ditches here and there full of burning oil. The army or someone had lit them to send up heavy smoke in the hopes of obscuring bombing targets. Inside Baghdad the feeling was sad. Nobody was in the streets. Believe me, nobody.

Since I was back in Baghdad, I decided to see if the oldies were still meeting. They were, on a daily basis now. They were running low on booze. And I said, This is not good. We are about to pass through a lot of shit, and we are going to need some drinks. Two of us went all over the city looking for someplace we might buy alcohol. Almost nothing was open. Finally we found one tiny shop tucked away in a back alley. The place was packed. Everybody was there buying up any booze they could. We bought several bottles of really bad liquor, which is all they had left, and paid six times the price. We got four blocks of ice too and put everything in the back of my car and headed for my neighborhood. The streets were still virtually empty. Any shop that was open was in chaos as people rushed to buy up everything.

Some days later we started hearing rumors that the Americans were in the city. We heard that the Americans had tried to take the airport but failed. We heard they were destroying tanks at the edge of the city. We heard a lot of things, but it was impossible to really tell what was happening. Each night I would sit with these old men. They had always debated with each other. But now they were really fighting. Not physically but verbally, in a mean way. They would shout at each other, tell each other to fuck off, and storm out. Of course there were nightly bombings throughout the city, though our area was not directly targeted. We heard the war in the city every evening as we sat together through the bombs. For days all we heard were the airstrikes. But eventually we began hearing the sound of tanks, and not Iraqi tanks. The planes that had flown so high before were suddenly swooping very low over the city, and the gunfire that had been in the distance began sounding in the streets around our house.

We had a satellite dish, and all the news channels began reporting that Baghdad had fallen. We still had not seen any American troops. Then on the television we saw the images of mobs pulling down the statue of Saddam. I cried. My wife cried. Not for him, mind you. I cried for Iraq. To me the fall of that statue was a symbol for the fall of the country, not just one dictator.

In the days after that we never left our area. The mobs were everywhere looting, and a bunch of us from the neighborhood began organizing watches to try and keep our houses safe. We knew the mobs would come, because our area was wealthy and home to several prominent figures from Saddam's regime. The looters came like ants. They started ransacking houses near us, in sight of the Americans. There was a tank at either end of the main road in our neighborhood, and six or seven shot-up cars sat on the street with several dead people in them who had apparently been killed by the Americans for whatever reason, getting too close to the tanks I guess. There were bodies on the street as well. The Americans were just sitting in the tanks overlooking this for days but not coming out. I went with some neighbors of mine who also speak English to try and talk to them. They shooed us away without speaking. So, we were left on our own to protect our houses. We set up roadblocks, and we would stand guard on the rooftops. If anyone saw anything, he would fire and we would all grab our guns. I always had with me in those days a Kalashnikov and a revolver.

We managed to keep ourselves safe even as the mobs tore through the houses around our block for four days. Eventually the mobs took what they could carry from the houses around us and disappeared, and all was quiet. Some of my neighbors suggested we try to talk to the Americans in the tanks again. I said no. They had refused to talk to us last time, and some attacks against them had already started. We could be killed if we tried to approach them again if they thought we were suicide bombers or something. Well, some of my neighbors went without me and tried to talk to them anyway. This time the Americans were willing to talk, but my neighbors could not communicate with them well. So they sent for me. I speak English, but I had never heard it like the way they talked with their southern accents. One said, Whaaat's the prablam? I said, With all respect, all we need from you is some help clearing the bodies from the street. The flies were unbelievable. Huge balls of them were rolling over the street with the bodies there. They gave us body bags and said we could bury all the corpses except the ones in the cars nearest to the tanks. They did not want us near the tanks.

We buried about seven bodies in shallow graves just in the partition of the road. I had to cover my mouth with a cloth, because the stench was horrid. The weather was warm, and these bodies had been out for days. They weren't even bodies, just rotting remains.

Two days later the smell from the corpses in the cars near the tanks was so unbearable that the Americans shoved them off some distance with one of their vehicles but still left them sitting in the street. Six or seven days after that someone came running to me saying the Americans wanted to see me. I went to them, and they told me that if we wanted to bury the bodies now, we could. At this point, they were just piles of bloated, rotting flesh. You could see worms crawling out of them. Many had no heads. And the cars were so damaged that you could not just open the door and get them out. You needed tools. I told them we simply couldn't do it. They said they would help by getting tools to wrench the cars open. They could not stand the smell any longer and were eager to do something. They got started, but I could not stand it and had to turn away. Somehow they got all these bodies out. I went through some of their identification cards. One of them was a pilot, a civilian pilot. I remember that. We buried him and the others from the cars there in the road along with the rest.

Ali al-Shaheen eventually shuttered the chicken farm and became the manager of Time *magazine's bureau in Baghdad.*

✻

TAHSEEN AL-SHAIKHLI

Born in 1956, he is fluent in English and has a taste for expensive suits and good cigars. He was a computer science professor at a college in Baghdad before the war began, living a relatively privileged life.

WELL, I HAD TO LEAVE MY HOUSE because Saddam Hussein put a huge missile in front of it. The military was putting mobile missiles all over the city just before the war, and they parked one right in front of my house. A giant missile on the back of a truck mounted on what looked like a launcher was just sitting there one morning on my street. I honestly don't know what kind of weapon it was, whether it was meant to shoot down airplanes or be launched at ground targets. I'm not a military man. In any case it would be clearly seen from the air when the Americans attacked. And if they bombed it, our house would definitely be destroyed.

There were two officers and about eight soldiers manning it. No one was looking after these poor guys. We gave them some food and tea. They had no idea what they were supposed to do, actually. They were just following orders by setting the missile there. You could see the weakness in their spirit when talking to them. They didn't have the courage to fight. The believed they had already lost everything even before the war had begun. They knew the end was coming. We all did.

I have a wife and five children, three boys and two girls. All of us went to my brother's house, where many other family members of mine gathered to wait out the war. It's in the same neighborhood as my house, but far enough away. We were fortunate because we had a satellite dish, so we could see all the television news. We watched CNN and al-Jazeera, mainly al-Jazeera. Watching the television through those days we all understood that this was the end of the regime. The government of course was still broadcasting propaganda saying most of the operations were outside Baghdad and so on. But we could see otherwise. Finally, when it became clear that the Americans had taken the city and the government was destroyed, we went back to our house.

The missile was still there. The soldiers manning it of course had fled, but we were still worried. It was a huge missile sitting right in front of the house. We didn't know whether it would explode or if the Americans would bomb it or what.

Apart from the missile, getting food was our main concern. Food grew a bit scarce in the days just after the fall of Baghdad. I went to a bakery around the corner, and that's when I saw American troops with my own eyes for the first time in my life. I saw a group of them moving on foot from street to street, and they were coming my way. I stood there with some others on the street as they approached. The came toward us, looking around as soldiers on patrol do. They didn't talk to us. They just walked right through us and moved on.

Tahseen al-Shaikhli went on to become a spokesman for the government of Iraqi Prime Minister Nouri al-Maliki and was a good friend to many journalists in Iraq.

A Guest for Mr. Axe

茶

ALI ABDUL MAJID

He is in his late twenties, recently married, and wears thick sideburns and hair spiked with heavy gel. Both his pinky nails are grown long. Altogether he would look at home in one of the new Iraqi nightclubs beginning to open in 2009.

I WAS LIVING with my mother, father, and my two younger brothers in Malaysia at the time of the invasion. My father was working in the Iraqi embassy there. He was a career intelligence man under Saddam Hussein. He had held a number of senior posts over the years in the Department of General Intelligence, the Mukhabarat. He was well known to Saddam and around Baghdad in general, partly because of his posts and also because of his nickname, Abdul Majid Axe. He had picked up the nickname in high school. The story as I heard it many times was that there was fight at his school one day among some of the students. My father grabbed an axe that was supposed to be used as a prop in a school play and went at some of the other kids. No one was hurt, so I was told. Later when the headmaster was gathering up all the kids involved, he called for my father but did not know his name. He just asked for the Axe, and everybody knew who that was. The name stuck with him his whole life.

Of course he was fired from his embassy post as the regime collapsed. We stayed in Malaysia until August of 2003 so I could finish up high school, and then we returned to Baghdad. Iraq was not the country we knew when we came home. Our house was badly damaged during the bombing, so we had to settle in a rental in another part of town. Our situation was not good. We were running out of money. There was no work. The city was lawless. Violence was rising, and my father had a lot of enemies. We were always hearing rumors about various people looking for him. We were very afraid to go out, all of us. My father grew his beard long as a kind of disguise and only occasionally left the house. On top of all this one of my younger brothers looks a lot like one of Saddam's sons, Uday. That caused him and us a lot of trouble after the collapse. It became a habit for us to murmur a prayer before walking out the door.

One afternoon my father went out. When he came back he told us he had made contact with Saddam Hussein, who was still at large then. Apparently the meeting was by chance. Saddam was of course then sleeping in a different place every night to avoid capture by the Americans. My father said Saddam told him he might come to our house for a stay soon.

We immediately began making preparations. We got a room ready. We chose an unused room in the back of the house, where the window faced the yard, not the street. We put a television in the room and hooked it up to a satellite dish. We knew he probably had not had a chance to follow the news because he was traveling a lot. We installed an air conditioner for him in the room. We had not bothered to put one in that room before. We bought him a change of clothes in case he might need them. My father knew his measurements. We called some of our cousins whom we could trust and asked them to be ready to come over and serve as lookouts and guards. We even drew up a shift schedule so that we could keep guards posted all day and all night. In case he needed to escape, we stacked a few bricks as steps at the foot of the wall separating our yard from the neighbor's. We did all of this very secretly to avoid being noticed by anyone.

Was there any discussion among the family about how this might be a bad idea?

No. We were excited that he might pick our house for a visit. He was our president. And to our family he was much more than that. To tell you the truth, most of my family used to work in the intelligence or the Ba'ath party. As far as we were concerned, all those accusations about him torturing people were all fake. And even if they were true, that happens all over the world. Why should Saddam take so much blame for it?

Saddam had given us our whole life. In the old Iraq there was a saying: Life was about money and power. We always had plenty of both. We had cars, we had drivers, bodyguards. We traveled to Egypt, to Malaysia, to Jordan. Sure, there were some who were richer than us, but we never wanted for anything.

Of course it was risky to bring Saddam into our home. We could have all been killed or captured if the Americans found him and raided the house. We didn't care. We wanted to help him. As long as he was alive, we still held hope for getting our old lives back. Look, overnight the Americans were in Baghdad when many thought they would never come that far. Maybe if Saddam were still free, things could change back just as fast. That's how we thought then. My father even planned to join him if possible. He pulled me aside one day as we were making preparations and said that if Saddam was willing, he would join the group traveling with him. He only told me this because I was the oldest son and would be responsible for taking care of the family if he wound up leaving.

For about a week we stayed ready, thinking he might arrive at any moment. Then after that we started to doubt whether he would come. The weeks turned into months, and he did not show. We figured he had found some safer places than ours. He had a lot of places to hide. We left everything in place nonetheless but began to assume he would not visit and went about our daily lives. We were sad, actually, that he never came.

Ali Abdul Majid and his family fled to Damascus, Syria, in October of 2004. As of May 2009, Ali was in Baghdad looking for work without luck. The rest of his family remained in Damascus with no plans to return. U.S. forces captured Saddam Hussein in December of 2003.

Home No More

※

ABDUL HADI ISMA'IL

He is tall and thin with a thatch of gray hair atop his head. He has a warm smile and an easy confidence. He looks the part of a principal, the job he held at a middle school in a poor area of northern Baghdad during the time of the U.S. invasion.

THE MINISTRY OF EDUCATION ordered us to dismiss classes the day the war started. I did but stayed at the school in order to watch over the campus. I was alone in my house, which was very near the school. I had sent my wife and five children to stay in Khalis, northeast of Baghdad, before things started. But I had many students still with me at the school each day. A lot had volunteered to remain with me to keep an eye on the place. About 850 students normally attended the school, ranging in age from 12 to 15. After we dismissed classes, there were probably about 150 various people, students and others, who came to the school each day during the bombardment.

One morning very early two fuel tankers were passing through our neighborhood, probably going to Kirkuk. The Americans I think targeted them, suspecting they were full of chemical weapons or something. But they were not. They just had fuel for cars in them. The trucks were moving down a road about 500 meters away from the school when they exploded, sending fire everywhere. I was inside the school with some others when the blast went off. We all went running at the sound, maybe thirty of us. The scene was unforgettable. Fire covered the whole of the street. The heat was unbelievable. The two tankers with two people in them each were totally destroyed. A number of other cars on the street were ablaze as well, two pickups and a minibus. I saw people inside alive trying to get out but unable to because the blast had crunched their doors shut. At least two people who had been standing on the street were dead as well. The fire was so intense that the ambulances and the fire trucks couldn't even approach the street for some time. There must have been fifteen, twenty people dead. This is what liberators do? The Republican Guard came to my school some time after that, and I left the place to them and joined my family in Khalis and waited out the fall of Baghdad there like a lot of other families.

I'll never forget coming back to the city a few weeks later. I was born in Baghdad and lived my whole life there. To me, the city had always been like a beautiful bride. What I saw of the city after the invasion made it look like an old widow. The destruction was everywhere. Charred military vehicles were all over the streets. Everybody was at home behind locked doors. My school had been looted, of course. I had been in charge of that facility for six years. I had even brought some of my own furniture there to try and make it a little homier for the students. Everything was gone. The looters even took the doors off their hinges. The only things left were the bricks in the walls and some of the files. At least the looters had not burned the place like they did several other schools in the area.

My house was very old and did not do well amid all the bombing. A water pipe had broken and flooded the whole place. We lived in water up to our ankles as we tried to settle back in. It stayed like this until I got my first threat only a few weeks after returning to Baghdad.

The first threat I got was not a letter. Someone simply tossed a grenade into my yard. Fortunately it did not explode. It was a dud. I did not see anyone throw it. My son found it in the yard one morning when I sent him out for bread. It was just sitting there with the pin out. I have no idea who threw it. The most likely suspects are the students I failed in years past. Or it could have been someone from the neighborhood who was jealous of me and my position. My neighborhood was a semislum. I was a rich person by the standards of many of my neighbors. Most were laborers. I was one of the only professionals from the area. And I was a Ba'ath party member. I had to be because I also coached the women's national handball team in addition to working as a principal. Only party members could get visas for traveling as we needed to for competitions. I was poor, to be sure. But I had some privileges, and some saw me I guess as one of Saddam's men.

Many of my neighbors tried to put me at ease over the incident, telling me it was probably just some sick joke by kids in the neighborhood. But I didn't believe that. I was afraid. Assassins seemed to be everywhere in the city then. There was no government. I believed someone was after me. I hardly left the house after that. I didn't even go to the market. If we needed anything, my wife or my children went.

About a month after the grenade appeared I got a threat letter. Of course I was out of work then with the schools still closed. So my wife and I made a little shop in our house, selling cigarettes and candy and other small things out a window. It was just a little something to make money day to day so we could get by. We hardly even opened it, actually. Mostly neighbors would come by and knock on the window if they needed something, and we would sell it to them. One day I was napping in the afternoon. My daughter woke me up and said she had found a piece of paper in the shop. Atop the note was a drawing of a sword and some Islamic quotations. The letter itself accused me and my family of being unbelievers and said we would die.

I immediately called some of my former students, young men I remained friends with who were now college age. I showed the letter to them, and they did a little investigation. They found out that some children in the neighborhood had been told to put the letter through the window, but the children could not say who ordered them to do so. Again, people told me it was child's play, a bullshit prank, and not to worry. But I felt it was serious, and I decided to leave.

I had coached handball in Yemen for a year back in 1997 and had an invitation to return. It seemed like a good time to go. I didn't have enough money to relocate my whole family, however, so I would have to go alone. I didn't even have enough money to get myself there actually. I had to sell my car, a 1986 white Volkswagen Passat, which I had bought with the money I earned coaching in Yemen, ironically. I had always been poor. The house I was living in was not mine. I inherited it from my mother. I had never owned a car before. Finally I was able to afford one after going to Yemen, and I took very good care of it. I loved that car, and I hated to sell it. Even then I still didn't have enough money. I had to sell all my wife's jewelry too before I could raise enough to get out of the country. I was gone by the end of May 2003.

Abdul Hadi Isma'il was in Yemen for only three months. He had a falling out with his employers and was forced to return to Baghdad, where he settled on the western side of the city away from his family home to remain safe. He eventually found work as an educator again.

Hitting Back

※

OMAR YOUSEF HUSSEIN

A Sunni born in Baghdad, he is thin and bookish-looking in his late thirties. He had served roughly eight years in prison for political dissidence but was released toward the end of 2002, when he began pursuing a career as an academic and historian in Baghdad. As the U.S. invasion grew imminent, however, he began mingling with some of the earliest figures of a nascent resistance movement that was taking shape in Baghdad even before U.S. forces reached the city.

I KNEW FROM MY READING of history what was coming—an occupation. None of us figured Saddam's regime would survive the American invasion. The only question on our minds was what to do after the collapse. My first connection to the insurgency was through writers and intellectuals who, like me, had spoken out through published articles before the collapse about what was to come and what should be done. We shared an ideological view about the coming occupation, and we began thinking about how we might act.

The first serious discussion about forming a resistance I took part in came about three weeks before the fall of Baghdad. There were about 64 of us. We met at a farmhouse south of Baghdad. We were all different ages. We all had different backgrounds, different levels of education. But all of us had two things in common: we had all been imprisoned under Saddam, and we were all Sunnis. The purpose of the meeting was to come up with a plan, basically, on how to organize a resistance. There were four senior figures who led the meeting. I cannot reveal the names, however, because several of them are still prominent figures in politics and religious affairs today.

The first thing we decided to do was to reach out to all the Sunni officers in the regime and urge them not to fight the Americans. It was no use to see them die for Saddam Hussein. We would need them for our cause. They had military experience, and they knew where to find all the weapons.

Why just Sunnis? There were a lot of Shi'ite officers, nationalist men, who might have been interested in your cause.

We did not want to complicate things. A lot of us, myself included, were very conservative religiously. But that was not the point. We did not want to waste time on arguments over religion. Doing so would have been a distraction. That's why we excluded Shi'ites. We knew there would be conflicts about that. Our base of support then was basically conservative rural Sunnis who in general took a dim view of Shi'ites. If we were working closely with Shi'ites, we might have lost some support in Sunni areas like where we held the meeting. So we just decided to avoid this whole problem mostly for organization purposes, not sectarian or ideological reasons. Look, reaching out to former Ba'athist officers in Saddam's army was already complicated enough. Most of us hated them and their socialist ideological view and their years serving the old regime. But we knew we needed them. They had military experience, and they knew where to find weapons. When the meeting broke up, we had all vowed to go out and recruit as many Sunni officers as we could to the cause and gather as much money as we might find from sympathizers. We agreed to meet again on the first of May. We all figured Saddam would be out of power by then at the latest, and that would be our time to begin.

The area where I was living at the time was home to many Iraqi army officers, and I personally recruited about eleven high-ranking officers and about fifty in lower ranks. I convinced them to keep whatever weapons they could find in a safe place and be ready to start the real war, the one that was coming. By the time Baghdad fell, altogether we gathered enough weapons to fight for three years, we estimated. We gathered a lot of money also in the days of the looting. A lot of the looting was organized by gangs. We went to the heads of these gangs after the fall and demanded half of what they had taken, for the cause. They knew we were serious. They knew that we had been gathering men and weapons, and they did not argue with us. In return for half the money, we promised to leave them alone from then on.

We met again as planned at the same place. There were a lot of arguments, of course. We had a lot of money and weapons, and some in the group were getting greedy. They wanted shares of money to support their families and so on. Some in the group were putting forward ideas about forming an Islamic state led by an emir. Others in the group like me were more concerned about coming up with attack strategies and getting started right away with strikes. That meeting broke up without any firm decisions or directives, but it didn't matter. We had set things in motion with all the work we had done. We had opened the field for anyone who wanted to fight.

I decided along with a few close friends of mine to ignore all these political arguments and simply get started with what we meant to do, fight the occupation. We had among ourselves enough money, vehicles, and weapons to form our own little guerrilla group. Five of us began planning our first operation, a roadside bomb on Canal Street in Baghdad near a newly built American base.

To begin, none of us had experience in explosives. So we had to be taught how to make the device. There was an Egyptian from al-Qaeda who showed us how.

You mean from Osama bin Laden's followers in Pakistan and Afghanistan?

Yes. He had come from Afghanistan, through Pakistan and Iran to Iraq. From our group we dedicated an engineer who took lessons from this Egyptian. He was a typical Egyptian al-Qaeda guy. He had felt oppressed by the Egyptian government and had gone to join the fighters in Afghanistan during the Soviet invasion there. He had worked in Iraq in the oil fields in the 1970s, however, so he knew the place pretty well. He knew the roads. He knew the accent. And he had come to Iraq for jihad after the Americans invaded.

After a few lessons from this Egyptian, our engineer came back, and we went about making the device. We made it in a mosque one evening near the base, just after evening prayers. We took an old artillery shell and bored into the casing with a hand drill to reach the explosive material. You have to drill very slowly. You don't want the friction to set it off. Then after you have a proper hole you put in a little C-4 explosive. On top of that you put a blasting cap or primer. We put several blasting caps, actually, because they were from old Iraqi stores and might be busted. When we were done making the bomb we carried it out of the mosque, all five of us. A lot of people saw us. Everyone knew what we were doing. No one said anything to us. We had made the thing in front of many people in the mosque. Even children were running around us playing as we worked.

We made our way to the road. There were some shepherds there with sheep. They saw us planting the bomb but said nothing. It all seemed like a game, honestly. A game you might play as a child. We ran a wire from the bomb through the fields off the road and found a hiding place where the leaves and grass kept us from view. From there we watched. We did not have to wait long. It was a busy road. The Americans used it a lot. After about an hour we saw a Humvee. This was in the early days, when Humvees were often seen alone, not always in armored convoys like later. The Humvee approached, and at the right moment we detonated. The explosion flipped the Humvee onto its side, and after a moment a crowd gathered. We eased out of our hiding spot and joined the group on the street. I don't know if the Americans in the Humvee were dead or not. I just saw them being carried away on stretchers. No one walked away as far as I could tell.

I can't say how the others felt at that moment, but I was in tears. I didn't know whether I was crying out of sadness or fear or happiness. Maybe all those reasons. For me, that first operation was like breaking free from a whole life of oppression. I had grown up under Saddam Hussein. I had spent nearly a decade of my youth in his jails. I had seen my country invaded by a foreign army. All my life I felt beaten down by one hand or another. And now, finally, for the first time I was hitting back.

Omar Yousef Hussein, who requested an alias for fear of arrest by either U.S. or Iraqi authorities, said he and his fellow insurgents planted eleven more roadside bombs in the same area where they did for their first operation. Over the next several years he participated in or helped organize roughly thirty attacks on American forces, he said. He eventually drifted away from the insurgency, however, and ceased participating in attacks in July of 2007. He felt the chaos in Iraq then was benefiting the designs of Iran, a notion he despised even more than the American occupation. He resumed an academic life but kept up his relationships with militants.

An End to Exile

✳

AYAD ALLAWI

*Born in 1945, he is soft-spoken and serious when talking, carrying the air of an
aged professor. A former Ba'ath party official, he had since the 1970s been heavily
involved in Iraqi dissident politics. For decades he plotted against Saddam Hussein while living in various corners of the Middle East and London. One night
in 1978 he narrowly survived an attack by assassins likely sent by the Saddam
Hussein regime who tried to murder him and his wife in bed with an axe. He
rushed back to Iraq in 2003 as the Americans moved to strike down his longtime
tormentor, returning to the country for the first time in more than thirty years.*

A FEW MONTHS before the war I got to Jordan, and during the war I
started moving across the western desert of Iraq with tribal leaders of that
area, through Ramadi and toward Baghdad. With their help I was reaching out to various Iraqi military officers, urging them not to defend the
regime as the Americans advanced from the south. That's why in Ramadi,
for example, U.S. forces faced no resistance initially. There were scores of
tribal leaders and army officers all over western and northern Iraq eager
to see the regime fall at the time, people who believed a new dawn was
breaking over Iraq.

I was in Baghdad by the ninth of April when the regime fell. Arriving
was incredible. I came with about eighty people, friends and colleagues
and supporters of our party, the National Iraqi Accord. We drove of
course, coming through Fallujah and into the capital. We were in a convoy
of mostly four-wheel-drive vehicles we had purchased in Lebanon. As we
were moving into the city, lots of emotional memories came rushing into
my mind. When I last saw Baghdad, it was a beautiful city, very nice, very
clean, very authentic. I had always known the people to be extremely nice
and friendly. When I came in again, I saw the reverse. I saw a broken city.
It was destroyed, collapsed. What really was very painful was the level of
poverty I saw. I wondered to myself how such a wealthy nation could suf-

fer such poverty. By then the average salary of a working Iraqi was in the range of a dollar or two a month. So you can imagine somebody with a family who earns one or two dollars a month trying to provide. It was very sad to see all the effects of this.

At the same time we were euphoric. We thought we were going to make a civilized country out of all we saw around us. We were going to have real democracy with rule of law, a country worthy of its citizens. We were in a way daydreaming as we looked at the city, imagining how we would remake Iraq. Even as we looked we saw some very distressing signs, however. The looting was heartbreaking. This was all because of the sanctions placed on Iraq that caused so much misery and poverty and never really affected Saddam's regime.

Inside Baghdad there was no electricity as we all settled at friends' houses. A lot of people inside Baghdad were expecting our arrival. We had been communicating with them through satellite telephone calls. Over the days that followed, hundreds and hundreds of visitors came to see us, mostly members of the armed forces, members of the police, and members of the Ba'ath party. We spent most of the first two weeks just meeting with these guys. I had always advocated for change to take place in Iraq from within, not through war. And I had always advocated for Iraqi institutions like the army to remain intact. Only the upper crust should be removed. But of course the Americans ignored this advice.

I got my first shock about how badly the occupation would go after being back in Iraq for just a few weeks. Jay Garner and other senior American officials had been holding a series of meetings with various opposition figures like us. Finally it was our turn, and I went with five or six of my associates to the Republican Palace. Garner was there with many U.S. and British officials, and he opened the meeting by saying he had called us in to get our views on how to set up a new government in Iraq. Frankly, I was shocked. I said, Are you serious? He said, Yes, we are very serious. They had no plan. None. Here was the United States of America, the only superpower in the world. And their leading decision makers on Iraq had no idea what to do? You know, the opposition had discussed with the U.S. State Department and the foreign ministries of some Arab countries for at least a year and a half what should be done once Saddam was gone. Everything had been discussed. How to create a judiciary, how to run the agricultural sector, what to do with the army. Experts from the Iraqi opposition and experts from the United States and Britain had sat down and discussed virtually all aspects of a transition. Piles and piles of reports were written, all to be tucked away and forgotten in cellars around Washington when the Pentagon was given the authority to run the country as they saw fit. And they clearly did not have a clue what to do.

Ayad Allawi went on to serve as interim prime minister of Iraq from 2004 to 2005 and remained a prominent voice in Iraqi politics after leaving office.

☀

MITHAL AL-ALUSI

He has deep, watery eyes and offers an intense gaze when speaking. He is an independent Sunni secularist politician who returned to Iraq in 2003 after nearly thirty years in exile spent mostly in Germany. In the early days of the occupation he earned a reputation for his outspokenness against sectarianism, among other issues. His views made him a number of enemies in Baghdad among Shi'ite and Sunni partisans alike as the city grew increasingly violent through 2004 and 2005.

COMING BACK, how can I describe the feeling? I had not been in Iraq since 1976. I felt delirious. I felt nervous. Being in Baghdad again was a chance to begin realizing our dreams, wishes, and goals. But we were still so far from our dreams even being back in Baghdad. I began to understand this in the weeks after returning. Even with Saddam gone there were many big dangers. Iran is not a joke. Saudi Arabia is not a joke. Syria is not a joke. The remnants of the old system are not a joke. The damage done to the society by the years of oppression is not a joke. You begin to feel very small against such big, dangerous waves.

I was politically active from the first moment I returned. I spent most of my early days back just connecting with old friends. Iraq had changed more than I could have imagined. Saddam once said that if he had to leave Iraq he would leave it as a house on fire. That's what he did. The country was like a house gutted by fire. I used to think that whatever damage

Saddam did to Iraq we could fix in a few years. We could fix the economy. We could fix the infrastructure. What I did not understand was how much damage had been done to the minds of Iraqi people. I was naive.

The first assassination attempt against me came in the fall of 2004. I was living in a small house in western Baghdad. It was at night. I heard a small sound, a thump. I had a dog at that time, and I thought it was him bumping something outside. I went to check and found a bomb had been tossed into my garden but had not gone off for some reason. I told my wife and my two sons to go to the second floor of the house. I armed myself with a Kalashnikov and went looking around the outside. I saw two armed men. They clearly had thrown the bomb and were waiting around to make sure it killed me after going off. I jumped out at them from a dark corner and opened fire. They had the advantage in numbers, but I had surprised them. I must have shot fifty or sixty rounds at them, and they shot back at least as much. I know I managed to injure one of them before they fled. The police came about an hour later and examined the bomb. When they threw the explosive into my yard, one of the wires dangling from it snagged on the fence and disconnected. That's why it did not go off. We were so lucky that night.

Some time after that they tried again, but I was lucky that night too. I was in the upstairs bedroom. I had gathered up some things to take downstairs and just walked out the door into the hall. I left the light on, so I reached around backward to flip the switch. That's when they tossed another bomb through the window. This one went off. Only being on the other side of the wall saved me. If the bomb had come a few seconds earlier, I would be dead. There were other assassination attempts in those days, maybe fifteen or sixteen in all. Most were people shooting from a distance and not much of a concern. But those two and the one roughly a year later were the most serious.

I had an appointment in the Green Zone the day of the third big attempt on me. It was supposed to be at eleven in the morning. I got a call asking if we could make it at one-thirty. I said sure, and as the time approached we prepared to leave. I didn't travel with a proper armored convoy or anything. I just had two regular cars. My two sons and my bodyguard jumped in the first car, and I got in the second. The lead vehicle moved onto the street and rounded the corner, getting maybe sixty meters. That's when they opened fire. We learned later that at least a dozen of them had come to set an ambush for me, and they unloaded into the first car because they thought I was in it. I knew what was happening as soon as I heard the gunfire, and I ran with my Kalashnikov to try to help. But I was too late. The whole thing was over by the time I reached the car. The shooting had stopped, and I saw my sons and my bodyguard dead where they sat.

My oldest son, Ayman, was born in 1975. Jamal was born in 1982. They were my only children. I never saw who shot them. The attackers had run away by the time I got there. Maybe some of them hid their guns and joined the crowd on the street that quickly gathered around the scene. Maybe I saw their faces among those people. Maybe. I don't know.

Mithal al-Alusi successfully ran for a seat in the Iraqi parliament in December of 2005.

The Coming of a War Within

✳

ABU MUSTAPHA

In his mid-thirties, he has a calm, simple face with a deep dimple on his chin. He is missing the pinky finger of his left hand, which he lost to a piece of farm equipment in his youth. He made a career out of farm work nonetheless and eventually joined the Iraqi Department of Agriculture, where he was working as a procurement bureaucrat at the time of the U.S. invasion.

MY JOB AT THE MINISTRY came with a pickup truck. Just before the bombing, as you know, a lot of people were leaving Baghdad. But I had to stay, because I could not leave this truck. It would have been wrong for me to drive it out of the city, since I was only supposed to use it for official tasks and coming and going from work. And I could not just abandon it. It might be destroyed or stolen. So I parked it at my house, where I remained with my wife through the bombing. We were living in a neighborhood called Jamia, in western Baghdad, not far from the airport.

Those were hard days. Bombs blew out all our windows. Some bombs even fell close enough to our house to crack the walls. All the shops were closed, so getting necessities was difficult. There was no electricity and no gas for cooking. On top of all this we had no idea what would happen to us.

I was still going to the ministry sometimes during those days even though most government offices were closed. Some of us who worked there came periodically to check on the place. I remember on one of the days I visited the ministry a huge sandstorm rose. I had never seen one like this, not in all my years in Iraq. I watched the storm for a while from one of the upper levels of the ministry. The city was largely deserted below, where the wind was strong enough to pull up small trees. And the sky had turned completely red. This was not long before the American troops entered the city. I think that was the day the Americans bombed the Republican Palace. I can't exactly remember, but it was toward the end. Standing there in that storm you could feel the end was coming. All of us in the ministry there that day knew it, and we all decided to go home to our families and not come back until things were clearer.

A short time after that, American troops entered Baghdad and moved into our area. I had never seen such soldiers before and did not know what to make of them, honestly. They had all this equipment and strange eyewear and were always pointing weapons around. I felt scared whenever I saw them. And embarrassed, especially if my wife was with me. We didn't know what they might do. I felt really sad in those days. I had read in history about the armies that had captured Baghdad, like the Mongols. I never thought I would be forced to watch an army enter Baghdad in my lifetime. It's not easy to witness such a thing, you know. I cried many times during those days. Many times. Gradually the American troops withdrew from our area for the most part. And things started to seem somewhat normal again as the weeks passed.

I started going back to the ministry, where I found I still had a job. Things were strange, however. All of the senior officials had simply vanished, and no one really was in charge initially. But soon we began to see a new sectarian order. Posters of Shi'ite religious icons started appearing in the halls. And all these Shi'ite clerics were suddenly around the ministry all the time. I never had any idea what they would be doing there, but they walked around like they owned the place. Gradually people claiming to be doing the bidding of Shi'ite religious authorities began to fill the posts left open by the vanished Ba'athists. People known to be thieves or incompetents, even illiterates, were suddenly running important offices, and they began verbally abusing and firing Sunnis or anyone they distrusted. More than two dozen senior officials who had been important to the ministry's work were kicked out by these new bosses. These were the ministry's technocrats, scientific men who didn't have any sectarian leanings to speak of. Their dismissals were a huge loss to the ministry and its work.

As things grew more tense, people began changing offices. The remaining Sunnis all put their offices in certain halls, and Shi'ites did the same in others. No one would ever have thought of doing this at the ministry in the old regime. We were all just colleagues at the Ministry of Agriculture. None of us cared who was Sunni or Shi'ite before. We would never think of such a thing. Later some senior officials began coming to work with bodyguards, as if they might be attacked in the building.

Life at home in the early period was good, even though things at work were weird. My wife and I had our first child, a boy. I managed to buy a car of my own. We had cell phones and the Internet. Our neighborhood was in general safe and doing well. That began to change in 2005 and 2006. Policemen in my neighborhood started getting killed. A senior official working with the new government who lived in my neighborhood was assassinated as well. They were targeted killings in the beginning. The insurgency was after police and prominent government officials then, so you really only had to worry if you were on that list. Not like later, when everyone had to worry because of the sectarian violence.

Abu Mustapha kept his job at the Ministry of Agriculture and remained living in Jamia, which became the scene of serious sectarian violence in later years. He and his family managed to remain safe through the height of the killing despite several close calls, including an assassination attempt by unknown gunmen against Abu Mustapha as he waited for the bus one morning.

※

AZHAR ABDUL-KARIM ABDUL-WAHAB

Born in 1957, she holds a PhD in constitutional law from Baghdad University, where she was a lecturer in the political science department in 2003.

BAGHDAD FELL ON A TUESDAY I THINK. I went driving around our neighborhood, Karada, with my husband a day or two after that just to have a look around. The looters were everywhere. I saw women and children pushing trolleys full of things out of an old intelligence office. At the national theater, they were loading a garbage truck with the seats from inside, and streams of people were coming out carrying all kinds of props. I saw plastic models of the planets bopping down the streets in the arms of thieves. They took everything you can imagine taking from a theater. Everything.

I used to talk a lot with my colleagues in the days before the war about what would happen if the Americans invaded. Most of us wanted a change from Saddam Hussein, even if it meant having foreign troops destroy the republic. It's not easy, you know, to swallow the idea of a foreign army coming to your country. Not even for us under Saddam Hussein who wanted to see him go. But a lot of us felt that change needed to come, no matter how. What we did not know was whether that change would be for better or for worse.

The Baghdad University campus was not really harmed, thank goodness, during bombardment and invasion or even the looting that followed. Not many classes were held in the weeks after the fall of Baghdad, but many people were gathering at the campus to meet each other and share information. Not all of my colleagues were happy about what they were seeing then. Like I said, many of us wanted change. But others did not. Some felt that Saddam was better than an American invasion and were vocal about it, and the first lines of division on the campus began to be drawn. There began to be a lot of quarrels among the staff, with those of us who believed the change was a good thing on one side and others against the invasion on the other.

I'm a Sunni and my husband, who was also a professor at the university, is a Shi'ite. A lot of the Sunni staff members simply could not accept what was clearly happening—that is, the rise in power of the Shi'ites. They could never accept the idea of an Iraq dominated by Shi'ites. Even though I am Sunni I took another view. The Shi'ites and the Kurds had suffered a lot in the previous regime. Why should they not have a chance to run the country? That view caused me a lot of problems with my colleagues at work and even my close family.

In September of 2003 we started the fall session. There was a big problem. There were a lot of groups saying we should not hold classes because we were under occupation. In the minds of insurgents, we should be boycotting the college as part of a resistance to the occupation. In class, I found that many of the students who came that fall despite the threats were totally unwilling to accept the idea that this change was for the better. I would say most of them viewed the Americans simply as occupiers, not liberators. And clearly some of them felt that armed resistance was in order. Of course we discussed all that was happening in class. I often tried to tell them this situation was simply a fact of life, something we all must deal with the best we can in our everyday lives. Basically I said to my students, Look, I know many of you didn't want to see change come to Iraq this way. But it has. So now we have to make the best of it. I stressed to my students that the birth of the Iraqi republic also started with an occupation, the British at that time. Of course you cannot discuss Iraqi history without mentioning Saddam, whom I viewed as a kind of occupier. I tried to put it in those terms to my students. Saddam stole freedoms from Iraq. He stole money from Iraq. He brought wars on Iraq. All the bad things an occupier might do Saddam actually did. I told them this. For the most part their reply to me was the same. At least he was an Iraqi, they would say. At least he was an Iraqi.

Azhar Abdul-Karim Abdul-Wahab went on to serve as minister of women's affairs in Iraq in 2005 and 2006. After leaving government she devoted herself to women's rights activism.

✳

AHMED IBRAHIM ABDUL WAHAB

Born in 1981, he was an engineering student at a technical college in Baghdad when the war began. He lived a basic student life, coming and going to class from his home in the western Baghdad neighborhood of Ameriya. His area began to change shortly after the invasion. It would emerge as one of the birthplaces of a Sunni insurgent movement that would come to call itself al-Qaeda in Iraq.

AMERIYA WAS BUILT UP in the 1970s as a new, rich residential neighborhood. It's a big area sectioned off into several quarters. There was a quarter for economists, a quarter for the intellectuals, a quarter for the members of the intelligence agencies. Our quarter you could say was the best in Ameriya. All the houses were very nice. The streets were shady and green, and the place was well attended. The people who lived there had money, in other words. A number of foreigners working for international companies lived on our street in particular. There were some Bulgarians, some Indians, some Turks.

In the chaos after the invasion, we were surprised to see some of our Iraqi neighbors taking part in the looting. Our area was not looted. But some people we knew from Ameriya went to other areas to join the looting and brought things back to the neighborhood. That gave me a bad feeling. That gave a lot of us a bad feeling. Because you know, they did not need to do that. Anyone living in our area had enough money so that they did not need to go looting. Until then we would never have thought someone from our neighborhood would run with mobs.

These same people who went out and looted, and it was clear to everyone who they were, greeted the Americans so nicely when they first began patrolling our neighborhood. That really annoyed me, and a lot of others. The old government made a lot of mistakes but in the end ruled the country better than anyone else. And invaders should not be welcomed in any case.

I'll never forget a scene I saw one day shortly after the invasion. There was a woman who used to be a teacher of mine back in grade school. She was on the street with her daughter and her dog when she saw an American patrol. She approached them and offered a flower. And she told them,

I named my dog Saddam. The interpreter who was with the Americans, I think he was a Kuwaiti, was even shocked by the insult. He told her, You don't have to say such things to them. There was no need for her to say that, to disrespect Iraq like that.

As 2003 wore on, you could say our neighborhood became divided. There were those of us like me and my family who rejected the invasion and the occupation and did not participate in the looting. There were others in our neighborhood who supported the invasion and some who did participate in the looting. My family and others who shared our thinking began avoiding the neighbors who disappointed us. We even began to fear them. We placed barriers at the ends of our streets, in case they got ideas about looting our houses. And we watched carefully for strangers coming and going from our blocks.

In 2004, gangs started forming in Ameriya. You know, the city was largely lawless, and these gangs, just criminals, moved in and started robbing shops and kidnapping people for ransom. Some in these gangs were from Ameriya, and we knew them. Others in these gangs were from elsewhere, strangers to us, people who had moved in for one reason or another after the invasion. This was the beginning of al-Qaeda in our area, these gangs. At first they were interested mainly in just thieving. Gradually they grew more violent.

By June of 2004, many residents from our area of Ameriya were leaving because the neighborhood was going bad. It was not a sectarian thing at this time. The crime was just too much for many. My family and I decided to stay for a lot of reasons. In our family house at that time was me, my widowed mother, an older brother of mine, and the children of another brother who had died some years back. I didn't want to leave my studies. The children of my brother were also in school. And the only place to go for us, really, was abroad, which would have cost a lot of money in order to keep up our studies. We simply didn't have that kind of money. Also, we wanted to stay for emotional reasons. It made us sad to see people go, and we felt like we had to stay, sort of, for the sake of the neighborhood we had known and loved. If everybody left, what would become of it?

In 2005, we began to see how insurgents, al-Qaeda, were taking root in the gangs roaming Ameriya. The first sign that al-Qaeda was moving into our area was the graffiti. They started writing their slogans on the walls. They wrote simple things like "jihad" and "Islam" and "fight the occupier."

One of the mosques in the area known for its sectarian leanings became a gathering point for those of the al-Qaeda mindset. That was when this new ideology began emerging in the neighborhood. People started saying that Shi'ites were infidels. Many of my Shi'ite neighbors fled then. Strange edicts started coming from the al-Qaeda circles as well. They didn't formally announce any rules, but they had laws and made them known all the same just by whispering them on the street. Barbering, for example, was considered illegal by al-Qaeda, since it sometimes involved trimming beards, which many militants believe should be grown long. In the beginning it was just talk on the street, you know. People sharing rumors about what al-Qaeda was thinking and doing and saying among themselves. But some scary realities would follow such talk. A barbershop would be bombed. Someone rumored to have broken some other al-Qaeda law would be shot. That's how they made their laws known to those of us living there in the neighborhood with them. That's how they made their presence felt.

In December of 2006, unknown gunmen fired on Ahmed Ibrahim Abdul Wahab in Ameriya as he left an area mosque one evening, shooting him seven times. He believes the attackers were al-Qaeda operatives who targeted him because he had been looking after the homes of Shi'ite neighbors who had fled Ameriya under threat from Sunni militants. He remained living in Ameriya after that nonetheless and was still a resident there as of February 2009.

❋

KA'AB ZUHIR AHMED

Born in 1978, he was unmarried and living at the family house in Ghazaliya at the time of the invasion. He had a comfortable government job overseeing a warehouse for military computer hardware and other electronics. He likes to lift weights in his spare time and has the heavy build of a guy who spends a lot of time in the gym.

THEY WERE ROUGH DAYS immediately after the invasion. Everyone in my family was out of work. What's more, I had left most of my savings in my office at the warehouse, which was looted. I found the place completely cleaned out when I returned to it after staying at home through the bombardment. So, I was jobless and broke. I needed money fast, and there were basically two ways to make quick cash in those days. You could get involved in the buying and selling of looted government vehicles, or you could deal guns. I was too afraid of getting caught with stolen vehicles. Guns are easier to hide.

Why not sell cooking oil, sugar, or propane—something else people needed badly immediately after the collapse? Why guns?

None of those things make money like guns. And all of those things were in short supply on the street. Guns could be found everywhere right after the invasion. There was a huge number of Kalashnikovs available. Iraqi soldiers who died fighting the Americans entering Baghdad would have the guns and ammunition taken off their bodies by people who stashed the weapons in their houses. A lot of the Iraqi soldiers in the final days of the regime fled their posts in uniform. Out in the streets many of them traded their guns for civilian clothes so they would not be killed by either the Americans or the Ba'athist execution squads looking for deserters. Houses near military bases wound up with six or seven Kalashnikovs, because so many fleeing soldiers passed. People with a lot of guns in their houses started to get worried about being caught by the Americans with so many weapons, so they wanted to get rid of them quickly. Also, there was a huge arms depot in my neighborhood. Looters emptied it, and many of the weapons wound up in houses around the area. All of this made it easy to collect inventory for sale.

I had two partners who helped me get started. They were guys from my neighborhood I had known since boyhood. We would hear by word of mouth about people in need of money wanting to sell their guns. At the same time we were hearing about people looking for guns. We developed a network of friends, friends of friends, and acquaintances from other neighborhoods who pointed us to buyers and sellers. Making money was just a matter of going between the two. It was so easy.

I didn't have any experience with weapons when I started, but I got to know guns gradually. Mostly for show I used to wear two pistols, one on each hip like a cowboy. I would wear the pistols when driving around making deals. It was good for business to have the look. I wore my hair long then and was built up from having been in the gym. That plus the guns made the image. I thought I looked like Che Guevara, and I carried a picture of him on my cell phone.

One of my regular customers was from Ramadi. He would come to Baghdad driving a government truck that had clearly been looted. We used to call him simply Haji. No one in this business liked to give names or answer too many questions about themselves, so I can't say I knew who he was. But he would hang around Ghazaliya practically going door-to-door looking for guns in this looted truck. He was buying in bulk. He bought almost everything I could find for him. There were others like him too from Ramadi and Fallujah. They were some of my best customers. They were quantity purchasers. They sometimes even bought broken guns saying they had someone who could do repairs. And they never argued over the price. They just paid what you asked.

You were dealing in guns when violence was beginning to rise. You had to know the guns you bought and sold were destined to be involved in killings. Did that ever bother you?

We thought about it the other way. We knew sectarian violence was coming, and families needed guns to protect themselves. We were providing a service in that sense. At the end of the day, to be honest, I didn't care where the guns went or how they were used. My family was out of money. I had to do something to earn, so we could eat. There were twelve of us in the house, and I was the only one able to bring in money. I never thought at the time, however, that the sectarian killings would get as bad as it did.

I was an amateur, and I only stuck with it for about a year. The Americans started getting more aggressive about confiscating weapons, and those fighting the Americans had bought up a lot of the guns on the streets too. So, weapons were growing more scarce. It wasn't as easy to do business as it had been in those first days after the invasion. I remember there were boxes of hand grenades and mortars just sitting around in places then. People would take the boxes and use them but leave the grenades and mortars, piles of them sitting in the open untouched. Gradually those piles of grenades and mortars began to shrink and disappear. You could tell people were getting ready for a big fight.

Ka'ab Zuhir Ahmed worked as a day laborer for a time after getting out of the gun trade. Eventually he got a job with the new Iraqi government again, overseeing a warehouse for computer hardware and electronics.

SAMAN DLAWER HUSSEIN

Born in 1978, he wears a faint beard on his smooth, youthful face. He was a junior in high school when the United States invaded, the son of a judge who did well by the old government. Just before the invasion his family had settled in a new rented house in what was then one of the nicer neighborhoods of Baghdad, Mansour. But Mansour and its adjacent neighborhood, Washash, became two of the bloodiest killing grounds in Baghdad early in the sectarian violence.

SHORTLY AFTER THE INVASION, we were living in what was like a golden age for us. I was back in school. My father was back at work, and our family was largely untouched by the chaos that happened after the government fell. But everything started to change for the worse I would say around the beginning of 2005.

There is a main road that separates Washash from Mansour. Our house overlooked that road. It was like living in the backyard of Washash. The troubles started with three suicide car bombs in Washash. Around that time we started to hear about a new Shi'ite militia forming, the Mahdi Army. And then we started to hear stories about how the Mahdi Army was forcing Sunni families to leave Washash. There was no killing during this time that we knew of, no murdering of Sunni families. Sunnis were being made to leave Washash under threat, but widespread murders were not happening yet. There were only leaflets scattered around Washash warning Sunnis to leave. Some of the wealthier Sunnis forced to leave Washash settled in Mansour. Others left the area entirely. All of this was happening literally right across the street from our house in Mansour. The Mahdi Army could have easily crossed the main road dividing the neighborhoods and done the same thing to houses around us. But they didn't initially for some reason. They seemed content to stay in Washash, at least at first.

Around this time I had enrolled in a private college in Mansour studying criminal justice. As things got bad, fewer and fewer students came to
class. The students were from all over Baghdad, not just our area. And as
the neighborhoods around Baghdad split along sectarian lines, it became
difficult to move around the city because of the checkpoints set up by insurgents and militias. I don't know exactly how many students stopped
coming as the violence rose, but you could see and feel a huge absence on
campus.

Thankfully no one was killed on our campus. But a lot of my classmates
began dying in their neighborhoods. We always knew when a fellow student had been killed, because the dean would put their names in white
on a black banner and hang it on a special wall on campus. Five banners
went up, two of them with names of close friends of mine. But these were
just the students who the dean knew had been killed. There were a lot of
other students who had vanished or been kidnapped and not released.
They were probably dead too, but the dean would only put up a banner if a
student was confirmed dead somehow.

Things in the neighborhood got even worse after the bombing of the
shrine in Samarra in February of 2006. Not all Sunnis had been forced
out of Washash by then. There were some prominent Sunni families who
had lived there for a long time and been able to resist the pressure put on
them to leave by the Mahdi Army. The night of the bombing, the head of a
prominent Sunni family was murdered in Washash and left in the street.
It was a statement by the Mahdi Army saying no Sunni was safe there anymore, no matter who they were. Everyone understood what that one killing meant for our area, and we were afraid. And after that the real killing
started. For a while the murders of Sunnis were only in Washash. Just a
block away, where we were, things were fine, just like with displacements.
But after a while the Mahdi Army started coming into Mansour looking
for Sunni families who had fled Washash to kill them. That's how the violence finally came directly to us.

Murders, usually shootings, began happening all over our neighborhood almost daily. I remember once not far from my house I personally
saw gunmen pull a man from his car and shoot him to death. In front of
my house, probably twenty people were killed. Another thirty people
were killed on or around our block. All shot. And these were just the bod-

ies I saw with my own eyes coming and going around the neighborhood. Who knows how many more there were.

Saman Dlawer Hussein and his family fled Mansour in August of 2007 and moved to a safer neighborhood very near the Green Zone, where they remained living as of January 2009.

Old Foes

※

MOHAMMED RA'AD AHMED

Sometime shortly after the U.S. invasion, neighboring Iran began to offer training, arms, and funds to Iraqis out to fight American forces in Iraq. Hundreds, perhaps thousands, of Iraqis journeyed from Iraq to Iran for training in guerrilla tactics.[1] The Iraqi fighters who returned to Iraq formed cells American forces came to call "Special Groups." Ahmed was a career military officer in the Saddam Hussein years and fought against Iranian forces in the Iran-Iraq war. But anger at the U.S. occupation drove him to get involved with the Iranian Qods Force, a paramilitary arm of the Tehran's Revolutionary Guards that organized and backed Iraqi guerrillas fighting U.S. troops in Iraq.

IN 2004 I WAS TRAVELING by bus from Baghdad to my home province of Maysan. On the way we came across a bloody scene on the road. The Americans had just shot a whole load of people in a minibus. I couldn't tell whether the shooting was an accident or not, but that didn't matter in my mind in any case. Everyone inside was dead from what I could see. At that moment I realized how heavily we are suffering under the occupation. The

---

1   Joseph Felter and Brian Fishman, *Iranian Strategy in Iraq: Politics and "Other Means."* Combating Terrorism Center at West Point, Oct. 13, 2008. Accessed at http://ctc.usma.edu/Iran_Iraq.asp.

occupation was like a weight on all of our chests. We were without our will. I talked to the man next to me for the rest of ride discussing the situation in Iraq. Let's call him Mr. X.

When we reached Amarah, Mr. X suggested we meet again. We did at a teahouse in Amarah shortly after our first talk. At that next meeting, we discussed the situation in Iraq more thoroughly, and he suggested that we form an armed group to resist the Americans and the British. I thought, That sounds like a good idea. Of course I had kept in touch with many friends of mine from my army days, and together Mr. X and I reached out to a group of nine people we knew felt like we did. One of the people I recruited was actually a former commander of mine in the Iraqi army. We all agreed that Mr. X would be in charge of the group once we got together, and he began suggesting we go to Iran and train before doing any operations.

Mr. X made all the arrangements through contacts of his, and by early 2005 we were on our way into Iran. We traveled from Maysan province to Basra. We crossed through Shalamcheh and then into Iran at Khorram-shahr. From there, we went to Ahwaz. When we got into Iran, a person named Ali Braheem received us. That guy spoke perfect Arabic with a Lebanese accent. I suspected he was from Hezbollah, but I later I found out he was an officer in the Iranian intelligence. Then we moved to Qom. And then we moved again northward toward the Caspian Sea to the site of our training camp.

There were several other groups like ours already at the training camp when we arrived. The total number of people there was about sixty. None of us Iraqis could bear the cold, actually. It's freezing so far north in Iran that time of year. So they had to take us to another area nearer to Qom where a lot of Iraqis had settled after the Shi'ite uprising following the first Gulf War in 1990. Once there the training started for real finally.

Initially there were just two weeks of lectures. They gave us a short break back in Iraq, and then we returned to Iran for forty more days of intensive training at a site near Kafajia. Instructors gave us lessons in detonating charges, magnetic circuits, and laser circuits, which were being used in Iraq for these new explosives against occupation forces. Basically they taught us the newest bomb technologies, which had changed a lot since my days in the army dealing with explosives. All the instructors spoke Arabic with a heavy Lebanese accent. You'd think they were Lebanese hearing them, but we found out by talking to them that they were either Qods Force or Iranian intelligence.

After that, they moved us yet again, to a camp called Hamidi. If you ask me what I saw on the way, believe me I didn't see anything. It was totally dark as we traveled, always using a convoy of regular cars.

After Hamidi, we went back to Maysan province in Iraq through Kafajia. We were given a cache of light weapons, medium weapons, and very sophisticated explosives. They gave us money too, of course. I needed money badly then, believe me. We all did. I used my share to move my family to Syria since the situation in Iraq was getting very bad then. All of us who went for training settled back in Amarah afterward, and we were told to wait for orders.

In the following months our group organized two bombing operations, one near Nasiriyah against an Australian convoy and one near Basra against the British. In the attack on the Australians we destroyed one vehicle and caused some casualties, though I don't know how many. We destroyed two British vehicles with our attack near Basra. Mr. X paid us for each of these operations with money I understood to be from Iran.

We began to rethink things as time went on, however. How long were we supposed to keep this up? How long would it take to drive out the occupation with such tactics? If we attacked the occupation without an end in sight, what benefits would we get out of it? More chaos in the country? And we were being paid by Iranian money. What did that make us, mercenaries? None of this seemed to us a benefit to Iraq, so we broke up our group and went our separate ways again.

Mohammed Ra'ad Ahmed, who requested an alias for fear of arrest, said he remained uninvolved in militant activity as of October 2007, when he sat for a videotaped interview with Time *at a location south of Baghdad.*

The Edge of Battles

※

H A Y D E R   H A M I D   J A W A D

Married and a father of five, he moved to Kirkuk from Baghdad in 1988, trans-
ferred as an officer with the police. Around this time Saddam Hussein was un-
dertaking a campaign to increase the Arab population in the city in an apparent
effort to edge out the Kurdish population. The Hussein government built apart-
ments and encouraged Arabs to settle there with financial incentives. Kirkuk has
long been home to Kurds, Arabs, and Turkmen and sits atop significant oil re-
serves. A simmering dispute chiefly between Kurds and Arabs over control of the
city began to boil over shortly after the U.S. invasion, and Kirkuk quickly became
one of the most volatile flashpoints in Iraq as the country slid toward civil war.
Jawad had lost his job as a police officer in 1994, because a cousin of his ran afoul
of the Hussein regime. He had been making a living as a day laborer from then
until the time of the invasion.

THERE WAS AN ANNOUNCEMENT shortly after the collapse. The central
government announced on television that policemen dismissed by the
former regime could get their jobs back now that Saddam was finished. To
re-apply, you had to go to the police with two serving officers who could
vouch for you and submit papers. I went right away and tried to get my
job back, but it was like some kind of joke. They weren't hiring Arabs in
Kirkuk, only Kurds. The city was slowly being taken over by Kurds.

One of the first things I noticed as the change took hold were the street
signs. All the signs for government offices, schools, hospitals, and official
buildings had been all in Arabic before. But slowly they began to change.
The Kurds were remaking them in Kurdish, so outsiders began to have a
hard time navigating the city. This started happening at the end of 2004.
And of course anything named after Saddam Hussein was renamed. As
this happened, groups of Kurdish men began to appear in Kirkuk. They
seemed to come from Irbil and Sulaymania. They would go into the markets and approach men wearing dishdashas or Arab dress and harass

them, create an altercation, and then beat them badly. They would say the people they were beating were servants of the former regime, but really they were out to intimidate any Arab.

I saw two brutal beatings take place right in front of me around this time. I was in the market one day when suddenly there was a commotion. A group of about fifteen Kurds were beating an Arab man right there. Everyone was standing around too afraid to interfere. They bloodied him badly and then dragged him to a nearby bridge and hurled him off. It wasn't a far enough drop to kill him, and he lived. He was probably glad to be away from them. When people asked the attackers why they had done this, they of course said the man was a servant of the former regime. I didn't know the man personally, but others did and said it was not true. But none of us dared to say a word to the Kurds, because then we might be labeled as Ba'athists too. A short time after that I saw a similar incident in a street not far away. This time a group of Kurds were beating a local doctor, right there in public.

It was all very strange to me, actually, this change. I had never known Kirkuk to be a violent place. For me it had always been a peaceful, dignified city where Arabs, Kurds, and Turkmen all mingled together. I had never experienced any problems like this in my time in Kirkuk, and I had friends of all kinds in the city.

I kept checking about my police application, but nothing ever came of it. Gradually I realized I would never be hired again because I was Arab. The police force was growing. You could see the new faces in the ranks on the streets, but they were all Kurds. Many were new recruits with no experience—Kurds. Arabs like me were passed over. Getting odd jobs became harder too as an Arab as time went on. In years past when I was doing odd jobs I was able to find work. It was not such a great life, but we had a place, and I was working most of the time doing fix-it jobs, plumbing repairs, and the like. But as the Kurds began to move on the city, I struggled to earn. Some weeks I would only work two or three days. Life became very hard financially.

I had found some temporary work loading rice onto trucks in June of 2004. I was at the site hefting bags with the other workers one morning when we began to hear shouts, then gunshots. There had been another beating, but this time a mob of Arabs formed and went after the Kurds responsible. A riot was breaking out right around us. I joined the people fleeing the area. I didn't want anything to do with it. I went home for a while but ventured back later in the day to see what had happened. The riot had lasted almost two hours before the police could break it up. On the streets where it happened I saw two or three cars that had been flipped and set on fire. There were several bodies in the street under sheets. Most of the storefronts had broken windows and bullet marks. I had never seen anything like this in all my life. Looking over the scene, I began to cry. I struggled to understand what was happening, honestly. It was so strange to see Kirkuk like that. How could a heaven turn into such hell?

Hayder Hamid Jawad and his family fled Kirkuk in late 2005 after watching many other Arab families go ahead of them. Jawad was struggling to make a living with a small tea stand in central Baghdad as of May 2009. Unresolved disputes over claims on Kirkuk remained a major cause of tension in Iraq even as U.S. forces began withdrawing from Iraqi cities in the summer of 2009.

LUAY ALI HUSSEIN

In his mid-thirties, he has hazel eyes, grimy hands, and a hoarse voice. In the late 1980s he moved from Baghdad to Fallujah, where U.S. forces launched a counter-insurgency offensive in 2004 following the public slaying of four Blackwater security contractors in the spring of that year. Mobs dragged the bodies of the contractors through the streets after gunmen attacked their convoy, and later charred remains swung from a bridge over the Euphrates River. The Blackwater episode and the U.S. assault that followed marked one of the early turning points in the war, a moment when Iraq's accelerating slide into violence became an undeniable reality even to those in Washington still insisting the country was on the mend from the invasion. A Shi'ite, Hussein was working as a blacksmith in Fallujah's industrial sector as insurgents began to gather in the city following the invasion. He saw the beginnings of the sectarian war from inside the mounting insurgency.

AT FIRST THE AMERICANS WERE WELCOME in Fallujah. They came saying they were liberators, and we felt they were. They freed us from a terrible regime. But people's feelings toward them began to change as the occupation wore on. I began to hear sermons coming from the mosques about how the Americans were occupiers, not liberators, and should be fought. I began to think so too, even though I supported the invasion. Why does one fight? Usually for money or honor. Having the Americans in our city was painful for many people, including me.

As you know, there was a huge amount of weapons left behind by the collapse of the former regime, and as a blacksmith I began helping to mount heavy machineguns on trucks for fighters. I helped make about thirteen gun trucks, but I wasn't the only one doing this. A lot of others were helping to make more trucks. Some other people I knew helped make roadside bombs. We were becoming a kind of armory for the resistance, you could say.

Foreign fighters began to drift into the city as things got tenser, Yemenis, Saudis, Moroccans, Palestinians, Syrians, Lebanese. An uncountable number came. Thousands of them. They took over the whole city. Eventually it seemed like the foreigners outnumbered us, at least in the industrial sector where I lived and worked. They began to run the place, ordering us around as though we were slaves to them.

The foreigners were uneducated and had weird ideas about religion, like they had been brainwashed by fanatics. They forbid smoking, for example. Anyone caught with a cigarette would have his fingers chopped off. They would not allow vegetable sellers to display cucumbers and tomatoes next to each other, because they considered that too erotic. The cucumbers looked to them like male parts and the tomatoes were somehow female in their mind. And believe it or not, they would put underwear on sheep. They apparently thought it was against Islam to allow a female animal to expose her genitals.

The foreign fighters went around putting underwear on sheep?

Yes, I'm serious, believe it or not. They were really weird. It was these foreign fighters who began to start with the sectarianism. I never had any troubles being a Shi'ite in Fallujah during all my years there. Neither did other Shi'ites. And in the early days of the resistance Iraqi Shi'ites and Sunnis were working together just fine. But as the foreigners began to take over, Shi'ites like me were pushed to the side. We began to feel ignored and eventually threatened by these outsiders. Even before the Blackwater incident, bodies were appearing in the street, Iraqis who'd been shot in the head or the chest. Often a note was attached to the corpses saying the person was a traitor or a spy for the Americans. There were American spies and collaborators in the city of course. Those of us involved in the resistance had spies among the Americans, and we assumed they had spies among us. So, at first many of us did not question these killings, but it began to seem like people were getting killed for reasons other than working with the Americans.

For a long time I had known these three very poor Shi'ite men who made money by rummaging for scrap metal they might sell. They actually lived in Sadr City in Baghdad but would come to Fallujah once a week or so to scavenge for scraps in the industrial sector. I didn't know their names, but I considered them friends nonetheless. I gave them some things from my shop. I sometimes offered them food, knowing how poor they were. I felt for them, because they were strangers in the city, and I knew what that was like from my early days in Fallujah. They had nothing to do with the Americans or the insurgency or anything else besides trying to get a little money day to day so they could survive.

One morning about a month after the Blackwater incident I was in my shop early, and someone came in saying there were three bodies in a dumpsite nearby. Come and see the dirty American spies, everyone was saying. So I went with the crowd to see the bodies. The men had been shot to death and were in a trash heap with newspapers over their faces. I'm too curious, so I went and lifted the paper of one of the faces to have a look. I was shocked to see it was one of those three guys who used to come up from Sadr City. He had been shot in the head twice and six or seven times in the body. I lifted the newspapers off the faces of the other two. It was them, all killed the same way. I didn't say anything as I realized this. You have to be very careful in such moments with so many people around. If I said something that revealed I knew them, I could be dead. I kept my composure and went back to my shop, and when I was finally alone I cried.

That's when I began to realize that the insurgency was turning against Shi'ites even while it was fighting with the Americans. There was no way those men had anything to do with the Americans. They had been killed because they were Shi'ites—and right next to where I lived. Shortly after finding those bodies I was telling my suspicions to a Shi'ite friend of mine in Fallujah, Abu Hayder. He had lived in the city for more than two decades. I told him I thought the resistance fighters were going to start killing Shi'ites. He told me not to worry, that holy warriors would never do such a thing. He was murdered the day after we had this conversation. There was another Shi'ite man I knew, a generator installer and repairman originally from Basra named Abu Hassan. He wound up murdered around this time too. I had known him for about seven years, and there was no way he was working with the Americans. One by one the Shi'ites in Fallujah were being killed off, even those who were supportive of the insurgency. I knew I had to go before someone came for me.

Luay Ali Hussein fled Fallujah for Baghdad two days after his Shi'ite acquaintance from Basra was killed, abandoning his shop entirely. He settled into a Shi'ite enclave in the capital and joined the Mahdi Army in early 2006. He said he spent about a year and a half participating in fighting against both Sunni militants and U.S. forces as a member of the militia. He never returned to Fallujah.

ADEL RASHEED MAJEED

In August of 2004, just a few months after heavy fighting erupted in Fallujah, another major battle broke out in the southern Shi'ite holy city of Najaf. This time U.S. forces faced off with fighters loyal to Shi'ite cleric Moqtada al-Sadr, leader of the Mahdi Army militia. The battle lasted for roughly three weeks, with much of the fighting in the city's vast necropolis. Majeed, a carpenter and lifelong Baghdad resident, was among those who answered Sadr's call for foot soldiers to fight back the Americans. Born in 1963, he is skinny with a mouth full of crooked teeth and a heavy mustache streaked with gray.

I REMEMBER THE FIRST TIME I saw American soldiers. We were in a car on our way back to Baghdad from Kut shortly after the invasion. We had left Baghdad to stay with my wife's relatives in the south during the bombardment. We were there for about a month before deciding to return to Baghdad. As we neared Baghdad I first caught sight of American troops manning a checkpoint overlooking a bridge going into the city. They were just checking cars and standing watch as soldiers do. I grew very angry seeing them there. It's not easy to see a foreign army in your country, you know. I remember I was smoking a cigarette, and I crushed out the lit end with my fingertips as I watched those troops. I could hardly feel the pain because I was so angry looking on these occupiers.

When we got back in the city, the situation in our neighborhood, Kadhimiya, was terrible. There was no power. The streets were still smoky from the fighting. Bomb damage was everywhere. In the weeks and months that followed, I got a lot of work repairing doors and windows blown out during the bombardment. At night some neighbors of mine and I would patrol our area, since there was no army or police to watch over things at that time and looters were everywhere. Seventeen of us worked together to keep watch over the neighborhood, and eventually we all became members of the Army.

Joining the Army is not like joining a regular army. There was no recruitment office, no paperwork or training or ceremonies. You simply made it known to the right people at the right mosques that you are willing to fight if needed. If the need arose, they would send the word to you through trusted people. Then you get your gun, and you go. That's how it worked. The Army in the early days was a cause, a belief and a movement more than it was an organization. It changed later, of course, as the ranks grew. Gradually commanders and bureaucracy emerged. But in the beginning this is how it was.

In the summer of 2004, a call came. Al-Sadr put the word out that fighters loyal to him should arm themselves and go to Najaf, where the Americans were attacking the city. Al-Sadr needed men to reinforce the fighters already in Najaf, and many of us from Baghdad decided to go. Roughly twenty of us from my neighborhood went to our homes, got our weapons, said goodbye to our families and all together boarded a minibus bound for Najaf. There were a lot of cars on the road to Najaf even though by this time the battle was already happening. We only came across one Iraqi police checkpoint as we approached Najaf. They stopped us and realized who we were. We had all our weapons with us in the vehicle, and we were not making a secret of what we planned. They tried to block us from going, but we refused their orders. What could they do? We were nearly twenty armed men, and there were only three or four of them. They let us go without a fight.

We didn't go to Najaf directly after passing the checkpoint. We went to Kufa, which is a short distance away. A lot of fighters were gathering there since the battle was already happening in Najaf. In Kufa, we got off the bus and took a short rest. Then we walked all together carrying our weapons toward Najaf. It was about an hour by foot. Once inside the city you could hear the fighting all around. The Americans were offering heavy fire from the ground and with helicopters, and the Army fighters were hitting back as best they could with machine guns and rocket-propelled grenades at the American Humvees and infantrymen on the ground. The battle was on all day and all night by then.

It was nearly sundown by the time we entered the city, and a group of us made our way to the main shrine in the city to pay our respects and pray. Then we had a simple dinner of rice, beans, and tea. We ate on the street near the shrine with the sounds of the fighting all around us. By then it was dark, and we headed for the cemetery with our weapons.

Most of us had been in the military, so we know how to move in battle. We didn't need orders or a commander. We broke up into twos and threes and crouched behind gravestones. Those of us who were coming late to the fighting found positions wherever we could. From what I could see where I was, there were three Humvees and a tank grouped together in fighting positions at the edge of the cemetery. It was completely dark, but we could tell what was sitting out there because of the muzzle flashes. A number of infantrymen were firing from positions around the vehicles from what I could tell as well. Spread out in front of me were the Mahdi Army fighters firing toward the American line, all of them crouching behind gravestones. I was far back with two others, well out of the range of hitting anyone, especially with my junky gun. Most of the guys had Kalashnikovs, but I only had an old Egyptian rifle that barely worked. I would have gone closer, but there seemed to be a fighter behind every gravestone in the cemetery.

I just watched the flashes in the darkness across the cemetery for a long time, hours, without shooting. I was too far back to hit anything or be of any use. But after watching the gun battle for so long I could not resist the urge to fire. I took aim in the darkness toward the American positions as best I could and pulled the trigger. I knew I probably wouldn't hit anyone. But at least they would know I was there. I just wanted to let them know that yet another person ready to fight them was there.

Adel Rasheed Majeed managed to squeeze off just a few shots at the American line before his gun jammed. After that he fell back, ditched his weapon, and returned to Baghdad. He gradually drifted away from the Mahdi Army but said he remained ready to fight for al-Sadr if another such call came.

A Saying About Luck

＊

ABDUL WAHAB FUAD ABDUL WAHAB

He cannot sit or stand without help and only moves with the aid of a walker. Much of the right side of his face and neck is a mass of burn scars. Born in 1975, he worked for most of his adult life alongside his father in an electronics repair shop off Sadoun Street, the main road in a commercial district of central Baghdad just outside the Green Zone. Militants began targeting the area regularly with bombs as violence rose in the period after the invasion, shattering building after building until the neighborhood was virtually abandoned.

I HEARD A NUMBER OF BOMBS near my shop and my house, which is not far from where I work. There were a lot of bombs. But only three were near enough to kill me. The first close call came one day when I was at work. I have a favorite falafel stand very near my shop, and I would go there almost every day for a snack just before lunch. The place is steps away from my shop. I walked in one day, and the guy behind the counter, who knows me well, told me to wait just a second because he had some hot, fresh bread coming out of the oven that he wanted to give me along with my falafel. A moment later he brought me a to-go package. I ate a little of it there. It was so good. I thought about staying to eat a little more, but I decided to head back to my shop instead. My mother would not like me eating so much early in the day.

I went back into the shop. My father was there. I put the bag down. Just outside the door to our shop was a tea stand. From the doorway I called to the guy and asked him to make two teas. I lit a cigarette as I waited for the tea in the doorway. I was just taking the first puff when a huge explosion hit the street. The first few seconds we were just in shock. Then I stepped outside to see what had happened, trying to peer through a cloud of dust and smoke. The tea guy I had just spoken to was alive but on the ground burning. Both of his legs were on fire. A little ways down the falafel stand was completely destroyed. We learned later that someone had placed a bomb just inside the door of the place and walked away. I was probably standing right next to it as I waited for my food.

Only luck saved me a second time shortly after that. I left for work one morning early as I usually do and went walking to the stand where I catch a minibus. I paused before crossing a street, and another man came and stood next to me as we watched the avenue. We saw an American convoy of Humvees coming toward us. We were about to cross ahead of them, but they flashed their lights, which we understood was a signal to stay put as they passed. They didn't like anyone moving near them because of all the suicide bombers. So we stood there watching and waiting for them to go by. On one of the side streets there was a maroon sedan edging toward the main road where the convoy was about to pass. I turned to the guy next to me and said, That guy is crazy. The Americans will kill him if he keeps coming like that. The maroon sedan stopped as the convoy passed. One, two, three Humvees went by, and nothing happened. The last Humvee in the line seemed to notice this car all of a sudden, and then everything happened in seconds. The sedan suddenly bolted toward the last Humvee. The driver of the Humvee saw it coming and jerked the wheel hard trying to veer out of the way. The sedan was almost touching the Humvee when it exploded. It was a huge explosion! A massive fireball went through the street sending things everywhere. I was surprised to see myself still standing in one piece a second later. Then the guy next to me suddenly yelled, I'm hit! I looked over at him, and he was split up the middle, just like a gutted sheep. I started running like crazy. As I'm running, things from the explosion are still falling all around me. I ran all the way to my shop, where a guy who keeps another shop nearby saw me. He could tell I was in shock and asked what happened. I told him everything. After hearing, he said a common saying in Arabic: You survived two, may God save you from the third.

It was the third one that got me, only a few days later. I've thought about that day so much since then that I can remember every detail almost perfectly. Usually when I go to work in the morning, I leave very early, half past seven. My routine is the same. I kiss my little girl goodbye and wave to her from the street as she watches me from the window. One of my neighbors is an old Christian woman. She's always up and about early and talks to me as I pass. Usually I see a few other neighbors on our street as well before getting to the main road. That morning I was running about forty-five minutes late. As I walked down my street I did not see anyone. Even the newsstand by the bus stop was closed for some reason.

Minibuses were a target for bombings during the bad period, and we were always reminding each other to stay off the crowded ones. The idea was that a bomber would probably not waste explosives on a minibus carrying few people. He would rather wait for a packed one. So, if your bus pulls up and it's packed, better to wait for the next one in the hope that it is less crowded. This was a common practice during the bad period, and I was usually careful about it. But that day I got on a crowded bus without thinking about it for some reason. I don't know why. I even took a seat in the back of the bus. Normally I try to sit by the door in case I need to rush out.

We were rounding a corner not far from the bus stop when it happened. I don't remember hearing the explosion initially. All I knew was that all of a sudden I felt like I was being electrocuted. I even screamed, Cut the Power! Cut the Power! Then, the next thing I know, I look to see the side of the minibus where I am sitting is gone, stripped away, and I am on fire. I tried to leap out but just fell into the street and could not move. I looked up and saw a few people running toward me with water. It felt so, so good when they poured the water on me. So good. I was surprised as I lay there not to be feeling any pain after they doused the flames. I lifted up my right leg, and it seemed okay. I lifted up my left leg and saw my foot dangling with what looked like a very bad break. It took a long time for them to get me to the hospital. Shortly after I got there I blacked out.

I fell into a coma for about two months. When I woke up I was covered in bandages, and both my legs were missing. Infection set into the wounds on my legs while I was comatose, and they had to amputate them.

I have to tell you, I was thinking it would be a good thing if the Americans came before the invasion. We saw the countries following American policies, like the Persian Gulf states, and they all were living a good, prosperous life. Even countries like Jordan. We expected to see the same thing happen to us, a better life. What can I say? I thought it would be something different.

Abdul Wahab Fuad Abdul Wahab remained largely housebound as of January 2009, struggling with complications related to his injuries.

PART
THREE

A New Order

❊

ALI JAWAD KADHEM

A married father of four, he was serving as a guard at a largely abandoned Iraqi airbase near the border with Saudi Arabia as the war began, a job he had held for four years.

THERE WERE ONLY FIFTY OF US garrisoned at the base, and half the men were on leave when American helicopters flew in from the desert and came low overhead. An interpreter's voice sounded from a loudspeaker on one of the helicopters. He said anyone who wanted to live should change into civilian clothes and leave the base. Anyone who stayed on the base in uniform would be killed by soldiers on the way. Then the helicopters disappeared. We all took the advice and ditched our uniforms and abandoned the base. Some of the officers had their own personal cars and drove away in them. The rest of us took a minibus from the base and began heading toward our homes.

I eventually made it back to Baghdad. My family had lived on the western edge of the city for a long time, and I went home to them. There were fourteen of us in one house. We had always been very poor. Everyone worked either as a farm laborer or in fishing. It was the kind of life where you were lucky to eat meat once a month. Things went on much as they had after the invasion for us until 2006, when the violence started.

The area where we lived was mostly Sunni, but there were several Shi'ite families. After the Samarra bombings, all the Shi'ite families got threat letters from al-Qaeda in Iraq. The notes were delivered to every Shi'ite house. The letters said we were dirty collaborators working with the Americans, the Iranians, and the Jews and said we had 72 hours to leave. We didn't bother to take anything from the house, just some blankets for the children because it was cold weather then.

At first we lived for a few months in Sadr City, all together in one room of a house belonging to a brother-in-law of mine. Eventually, though, I was able to find a cheap house built on land around an abandoned cement plant in Kadhimiya. Shortly after we settled in, one of the longtime residents of the neighborhood came to my door. He said the neighborhood was organizing some volunteer guards and wanted me to join. I did. There was a lot of thievery and murder in the area at the time and no police of course.

Twelve men from my neighborhood including me agreed to form a volunteer guard force. All of the volunteers were just neighborhood guys. Some were out of work. Some were students. Some were men from rich families in the area. All different backgrounds. We were split into two groups and worked twelve-hour shifts. During the day we would check cars coming into the area. If we knew the car, we would let them pass. If not we would stop them, looking for car bombs or strange guys who may be coming to the area. At night we would patrol the streets just keeping watch. We carried weapons all the time, unless we saw American troops. We'd hide our guns when U.S. patrols were around and take them back out when they were gone.

We weren't part of the Mahdi Army then in those first days, but the militia was in our area and would talk to us. There was a guy, a commander for the Mahdi Army. His name was Abu Isra'a. He would hold meetings with us, usually calling us together in a mosque to avoid attention. He was a tall guy, a bit fat, with a big mustache. He preached a bit about the importance of looking after our neighbors and being good Muslims. He warned us not to get involved with anything Moqtada al-Sadr would not like. And sometimes he asked us to help with some chores or missions the Mahdi Army was doing in our area and in nearby neighborhoods.

Some of the missions were to watch people, to see if they were doing anything wrong. Some of the missions were raids on houses where people were doing bad things, like making pornography or cavorting with prostitutes. If we found anyone in those houses we were sent to, the people inside were dragged out and beaten in the street. Not killed, just beaten and told to leave the neighborhood. Some people had to be killed, though. The Mahdi Army found out that some people were selling the names of Shi'ites to al-Qaeda. Shi'ites from the area were doing this for money. They would sell names of Sunnis to Shi'ite killers too. Those people had to be killed.

I didn't go on very many missions, and I never had a big role. I was only ever asked to stand watch on the street as the others went into the houses we were told to raid. We never went to attack Sunnis. I would not have done that. We were just working with the Mahdi Army to police our area, keeping out bad elements and making the place safe. But for the Mahdi Army, it didn't stop there. Sometimes they would attack checkpoints manned by Iraqi security forces and ask some of us volunteers to help them. Some of the men who first volunteered as guards for our area joined them. When I heard about this, I had words with these men. I did not think this was right. The men at the checkpoints were there to protect us. There was no reason to attack them. Those who were joining the attacks called me a coward when I argued with them, but I didn't care. I said how I felt.

I was at home one night when there was a knock at the door. It was one of my fellow guards. He said they needed me for a mission assigned by the Mahdi Army. Get your gun, he said, and come along. I asked what the mission was, and he said we would be attacking a nearby government checkpoint. I went and got my gun and handed it to him. I said, Take this and give it to Sadr himself and call me a coward to him for all I care. I won't attack a checkpoint with you. Taking my gun, he said, Okay. But he said it in a way that was meant to be a threat. Like he was saying, Okay, we know what do to with you . . .

Ali Jawad Kadhem said he never had any further dealings with the Mahdi Army or the volunteer guard force in Kudhimiya. He worried for a time that someone would come after him because of his refusal to get deeper involved in militia activities, but nothing ever happened. He was living in the same area and struggling to make ends meet as a house painter as of May 2009.

SADDAM HATIF HATIM AL-JABOURI

Born in 1979, he was a college student at a local university in Diwaniyah, a town in southern Iraq. He remembers celebrating with friends and family in 2003 as the U.S. attacks began, knowing as the news spread across the airwaves that Saddam Hussein was finished. In the lawlessness afterward, however, Diwaniyah and other towns around the area felt the tightening grip of the Mahdi Army as the militia sought to spread its influence from Baghdad into southern Iraq.

THERE WAS A GROUP OF STUDENTS on campus who were involved with the Mahdi Army. We called them the militia students, and they went around trying to spread the Mahdi Army's religious ideology. The biggest issue was females on campus. People involved with the Mahdi Army tended to believe that having females in school was against Islam. It was very hard for female students, believe me. A lot of the women who insisted on going to class came under threat. There were beatings and kidnappings targeting women just because they wanted to go to school. I didn't believe in this kind of thinking, and neither did many of my friends.

It wasn't just on campus where militia members and zealots pressed their ideas on people. In Diwaniyah generally, both the Mahdi Army and the Badr Brigade tried to intimidate people into conforming to their religious beliefs. People affiliated with one religious party or the other would go around in the streets as enforcers. If they thought the way you were dressed was against Islam, they might push you around or beat you up. Sometimes these enforcers would check people's cell phones for pictures. If you were a guy and you had a picture of a woman on your phone, for example, they might rough you up or take your phone. This kind of crap. Initially it was an annoyance to have such people in the streets, but gradually it became so widespread that everyone began to fear. It got to a point that you could not as a man even walk alongside a woman anywhere in public who was not your wife or your sister. If you did, someone from these enforcers would stop you, rough you up, and haul you off to one of the party offices, where you would be questioned and lectured about religion and society from these goons. It was not just beatings and lectures they doled out, however. Some people who defied these zealots wound up dead. Look, it was the same religious bullshit that al-Qaeda in Iraq and its followers imposed on Sunni areas. The exact same thing, only one group did it in the name of Shi'ites and the other in the name of Sunnis. I didn't see firsthand what happened in Sunni areas, but I've heard enough to know how similar the situations were to ours in places like Mosul and Anbar province in 2005 and 2006 as parties, gangs, and religious groups took over where the police and military were absent.

One day in the summer of 2006 I was on campus talking to a female friend of mine in one of the gardens. As we were sitting there talking, three of the campus guards came up along with five of the militia students and tried to break up our conversation, saying it was against the rules.

It was bullshit. We weren't doing anything wrong. These guards, like the militia students, were known members of the Mahdi Army. They were just harassing us, because they thought it was against Islam for a male and female student to be talking together on campus. I argued with them, and they ordered my friend and me to come to the campus security office.

All eight of them marched the girl and me away. I continued arguing inside the guards' office, telling them they had no right to interfere in our personal lives on campus. They were lecturing me about rules and Islam. One of the guards, I don't know his name, got up in my face, yelling things about how I should be ashamed of myself for such behavior and that I had no honor. He's a tall guy, slim, dark-skinned with an ugly face. As he was berating me I heard one of the militia students standing around us say, Beat him. The guard suddenly gave me a hard shove. That's when I lost my cool. I punched the screamer in the face. I boxed as a youth, so I know how to hit. I got him good in the nose, and blood began to pour over his mouth. I can't tell you very well what happened in the moments after that, because it got very confusing. But a fight broke out. I was punching at the guards whom I could reach with my fists. They were punching me and tearing at my shirt. There were weapons in the room but so far no one was reaching for them.

This ruckus erupted toward the end of the day, so a lot of people were leaving the campus. The guards' office is near the main campus gate, so some passing students saw what was happening through the window. Word spread quickly, and suddenly a group of my friends burst in and joined the fight. There were a lot of us who really hated the militia students, and they knew what was going on instantly. Then some more militia students came running. And more guards jumped into the fray. Soon my altercation with the guards had turned into a massive brawl. On the one side were the militia students and their friends among the guards. On the other side were the students like me who had been growing angrier and angrier at their intimidation and religious bullshit. All this tension on campus between the two sides was finally boiling over, and I was right there in the middle of it.

The fight got rougher and rougher until finally guns were drawn. The guards pulled out their pistols and began chambering rounds. The students fighting them backed up and began arming themselves with whatever they could—chairs, a bit of wood, whatever was within reach. I don't know what would have happened next if the dean had not jumped in the middle and broken things up along with some of the other faculty.

I avoided school for a few days after that to let things cool off. After a bit I got word through a friend of mine that the militia students and the guards who had started all this were willing to let things go if I apologized. I can imagine why they would want to smooth things over. My brother is a local police officer. And my family is part of the al-Jabouri tribe, which is powerful and well respected in our area. My brother dropped me off in his police vehicle on my first day back and told me to keep in touch with him through the day on my mobile. I went straight away to the security guard I punched, to apologize. I found him in his office. I had broken his nose, it turned out. His eyes were still blackened from the blow. He said to me, My dear, the devil is inside you. What's wrong with you? Why can't you control yourself? All we were trying to do was guide you to the right path in life. I didn't argue with him because I was trying to make nice. I just stood there listening to him and thinking, What an imbecile.

Saddam Hatif Hatim al-Jabouri went on to earn a master's degree in archaeology from Baghdad University. He was working as a part-time lecturer at Baghdad University in the archaeology department as of May 2009, when the interview was conducted. He said the money was not enough, however, and that he was considering leaving Iraq to find better work outside the country.

SAMI HILALI

Born in 1956, he worked with Time *as a driver, bodyguard, and cook from the magazine's early days covering the war in Iraq. From the beginning Hilali was one of the most beloved personalities in the Baghdad bureau. When not at work he lived in a rented house in Huriya, an area of northwestern Baghdad that fell under the sway of the Mahdi Army. The Mahdi Army's civilian wing was widely known as simply the Sadr Organization, which opened offices around Baghdad in Shi'ite areas that offered public services and aid. The Mahdi Army and the Sadr Organization were always deeply intertwined, however, and the Sadr Or-*

ganization's offices stood as a transparent front for the militia in neighborhoods
where its presence was meant to be felt.

I WENT HOME ONE NIGHT and parked my car across the street from
my place as usual. All of a sudden this guy walked up and said, You cannot leave your car there. He was not wearing a uniform, but I guessed he
was from the Mahdi Army or the Sadr Office. They liked to make a show
of being bosses in the street. I said, No, you're wrong, this is my place,
and this is where I always park. I don't know what his problem was or
why he wanted me to move my car. He wasn't clear with me. I argued with
him, and then he got mad. He said, If you don't move your car, I'll have
you chopped to pieces and dragged through the streets. I decided to ignore
him. We have a saying in Arabic: *Ruha, baba, ruha.* It's sort of like fuck off,
but more dismissive. It means roughly go away, little one. Something you
might even say to a dog. I said this to him. The guy replied, Okay, you have
a lesson coming. And then he walked off.

About half an hour later I was outside, and someone grabbed my shoulder. I turned and saw this same guy, and he had a hand under his jacket
like he was gripping a gun or a knife. I thought it was a knife, actually,
since he was talking about chopping me up earlier. In any case I told him I
didn't want to fight and crossed the street. As I was walking away he called
after me, saying I was a coward and all this. I should have kept ignoring
him, but I lost my temper. I turned around, drew my gun, and put a bullet
in the chamber. The guy ran into a nearby shop as soon as I did this and
hid. A group of people appeared and got between the two of us. Some of
them were telling me to calm down and forget about it, that he was just a
punk. But I was angry, and before going away I shouted some insults toward him, cursing his mother and things like this.

About a half hour after that, this guy appeared again and found me
on the street. This time he had with him a known member of the Mahdi
Army, who came up to me and asked my name politely after the other guy
pointed me out. I told him who I was. He wanted to know if I had a gun.
I told him yes. Then he asked me to come to the Sadr Office in a very nice
way. I said okay, and the three of us went.

The office the Sadrists were using previously belonged to the Ba'ath
party. After the fall of Baghdad it stood empty for a while until the Sadrists reopened it. Initially they billed it as a learning center for Shi'ite

religious studies, but gradually they started doing community services, things the government should have been doing but wasn't. They organized trash pickups when no one else would. That was a big thing everyone in the neighborhood was happy about. They did traffic control, and posted night guards around the streets since police almost never entered. They would try to solve people's problems, too. For example, a neighbor of mine was accidentally wounded by the Americans, and the Sadr Office paid his rent for seven months while he recovered. They would find homes for Shi'ites who'd been forced out of other areas of Baghdad and fled to Huriya. They distributed gasoline and kerosene when both were scarce. These were the kinds of things they did to give themselves a good reputation in the neighborhood. I have to admit they kept order on our streets, and we were grateful, especially in the early days of the looting. No shops were broken into and no vehicles were stolen from our area.

The Sadr Office itself was a tiny place with almost nothing in it. When we entered, there was nothing in the main room except a desk in the middle and a couch along the wall where a few old people sat waiting for I don't know what. Two brothers ran the office, Adel and Raheem. They had a bad reputation for being involved in sectarian killings and displacement. Both were clean shaven and well dressed, not with heavy beards or looking ragged or anything.

Once inside Adel said to me, Why did you threaten to shoot him? Why, if you were having a dispute, did you not come to us? I said, You are not the police. Why should I come to you? Adel said, No, we are the police now. Then they drew up a letter, a contract, spelling out a kind of truce between me and this guy to settle our fight. It said we promised not to attack each other and to come to the Sadr Office if there were any further problems. And it said some stuff about how the Sadr Office represented the law and all this. They told each of us to sign the document, and we did.

Sami Hilali remained working for Time *until the magazine shuttered its Baghdad bureau in the summer of 2009. After that, he found part-time work as a driver with National Public Radio's Baghdad bureau. He continued to live in Huriya.*

✳

HAYFA KAREEM SABI'A

She and her husband, Mohammed, were living a fairly comfortable life raising three young children in Baghdad's Jihad neighborhood at the time of the invasion. He had been working as an accountant for a poultry business, but the outfit folded when the occupation began.

MOHAMMED USED HIS CAR as a taxi for a time to make a little money after his accountant job ended, but then a roadside bomb went off near him one day and he was badly hurt. Shrapnel from the explosion went into his neck and back, and he's never been able to get around the same since then. So, I had to go to work to support the family. I did domestic work, cleaning and cooking for people. We managed. But we could tell even before the Samarra bombing that sectarian violence was getting bad in Baghdad. We felt we needed to get out of the city. We thought any place would be safer than Baghdad, sensing what was coming.

Mohammed had a little savings, and we decided to buy a house in a small town about halfway between Baghdad and Fallujah. We didn't know much about the place, honestly. Mostly we bought the house because we could afford it, and the area was close enough to Baghdad, where both of our families live. The town is called al-Haswa. It's a small place. To tell you the truth I never saw much of it. We moved there but only stayed for a month. This was in late 2005, and the sectarian violence was spreading to that area. We're a Shi'ite family, and soon after we arrived in al-Haswa we started hearing about violence against Shi'ites. Several Shi'ite homes were burned, and some older Shi'ite residents were found murdered. We decided to go back to Baghdad rather than wait for something to happen to us, even though we had no place to stay. We had almost no money and no income at this point. We spent most of what we had on the house, which we abandoned completely along with everything in it in our rush to go.

Without a home in Baghdad anymore, we had to split up the family among relatives who could take us in. I went to stay with my sister and her husband back in Jihad. I had a newborn baby girl then, and the two of us were allowed to stay there. But there was not enough room for my husband and three other children. They went to stay with relatives of his in a house not too far from where I was living in Jihad. As we settled in with family, the sectarian violence got really bad. I was able to visit my husband and my children only about every three days or so. It was hard to move around with a baby, especially then. The streets in Jihad were chaos. There were bodies in the road every day, Shi'ites and Sunnis. Snipers would attack the markets. I was out one day and saw a man walking on the street. Suddenly a car pulled up, and several men jumped out. They started beating this man very badly right in front of me, and eventually they threw him in the trunk and drove away. These were the kinds of scenes you saw almost every day in the neighborhood. At night you could hear gunshots and explosions. We spent most of the days just sitting in the house, totally terrified.

The Mahdi Army was active in Jihad, and a number of members lived in houses right around my sister's place. One of the Mahdi Army men came over one day and asked to speak to me. He was a neighbor who noticed my situation and wanted to help. He said the Mahdi Army would give us a house in the area where we could live together. I cannot mention the man's name, even now. It could cause problems. He was just someone who took pity on us and offered to help. I was told the house belonged to a Shi'ite family who had left the country. So long as we took good care of the house, he said, we could stay there until the family returned. They were very organized about this. They had a list of contents for the house they said would be double-checked when we moved out. Of course we said yes.

Did you have any problems accepting such help from the Mahdi Army, knowing as you must have that they were involved in a lot of the violence you were seeing?

I knew what the Mahdi Army was doing, and I didn't like it. I don't think there is ever a reason for a Muslim to kill another Muslim. Just because I accepted help from them doesn't mean I supported them. You have to understand. We were desperate. They were offering my family a home. How could I refuse? For the sake of my children, for the sake of my marriage, I had to accept. I could not say no. It isn't even such a nice house in any case. It's small and very old. The walls had mildew, and the place was almost empty when we arrived. The only furniture was a broken locker for clothes, a wooden wardrobe, a couch with burned cushions, a couple of broken chairs, and an empty oil drum.

We were lucky to have the house, but our situation was still difficult. I began doing domestic work again, getting jobs wherever I could. It's the only way we survived. On the days I worked, there was food in the house. If I missed a day of work, there was no food. That's how we lived through the violence, and it's the same now. I've even had to take my oldest daughter, Teba, out of school so she can manage the house while I work. She's twelve. Someone has to look after the baby and my husband. She cries so much begging me to let her return to school so she can see her friends and continue with her education. I try to explain why she cannot.

The family who owned the house in which Hayfa Kareem Sabi'a lived had given her and her family notice to vacate as of April 2009. They apparently wanted the place back either for themselves or to sell. She was unsure where the family would go next at the time of the interview.

RASIM HASSAN HAIKEL

A Shi'ite and former Ba'athist, he had served as a distributor of government food rations in his northern Baghdad neighborhood since 1997. The Saddam Hussein government, under international sanctions, licensed a number of neighborhood merchants like him to distribute government-subsidized staples such as flour, rice, cooking oil, sugar, and tea on a monthly basis. The program continued after the U.S. invasion.

THE OLD REGIME always gave complete shares of rations. After 2003, you never saw complete shares. Things went missing from the ration packages. Three or four items were always gone from each. Part of it was corruption. Part of it was just incompetence of the new government in power. They were not used to running such a program.

My distribution shop is right next to my house. In 2006, I was in charge of monthly rations for about 450 families. I knew all the families well. Twenty-three of them were Sunni families who lived in the area. But as the sectarian violence grew, the Sunni families left our neighborhood.

They moved to Sunni neighborhoods mostly on the western side of the city, like a lot of other Sunnis.

Normally, if a family moved, I would take them off my list, and the central distribution office would stop sending me their rations. The family was supposed to re-register wherever they moved. But I left the Sunni families who'd moved on my list. They had not left because they wanted to. They left because they felt threatened. So, I collected their rations, stayed in touch with them, and tried to deliver them whenever I could. It was dangerous for me to go to Sunni areas where they lived and difficult for them to come to me. Often I would meet them somewhere in the center of the city and hand off the rations in the middle of the road.

The Mahdi Army had basically taken over our neighborhood by the middle of 2006. They were very open about it. They established checkpoints on the main roads to search cars coming and going. At the end of my street was a big house that belonged to a family that had been forced to emigrate by the old government to Iran during the Iran-Iraq War. The only person in that house for years had been a guard and caretaker hired by the family to watch over the place. When the Mahdi Army moved into our area, they told the guard to leave and made the place a safe house of theirs.

There were always rumors that they were torturing people inside. Neighbors said they heard screams coming from there at night. I heard a scream myself once. I was walking down the street, coming home after doing some shopping. I passed that house and saw what must have been twenty cars parked all around it. There was some kind of gathering. As I was looking toward the place wondering what was going on, I heard someone inside scream. No one dared to ask any questions about what was happening inside. Everyone feared the Mahdi Army. You had to. At that time, in our area, they controlled everything and were involved in everything.

One day in the middle of 2006 they summoned me and a bunch of other ration distributors in the area to that house at the end of my block. They made it seem like an official meeting. They said the government had given them authority to collect any rations dedicated to Sunni families and redistribute them to families of Shi'ite martyrs. Most of the distributors were so scared that they agreed to cooperate without asking questions, even though it was not clear whether there had been such an order from the government.

How could they have me do that to people who have lived for centuries alongside my family? I was not satisfied with the ideology of these Mahdi Army people and decided not to go along with them. They were losers. They were thugs. They were ruining our neighborhood. It used to be a good place, a place where people of both sects wanted to live. Now it had a reputation as a militia haven.

That night I called all of the Sunni families I'd been giving rations to. I told them I was going to go to the central records department and alter the books to make it look like the government had stopped handing out their rations some months before. I could not give them their rations anymore because of the Mahdi Army. They were sure to come and check my records as they collected food from the distributors. But at least I could keep them from stealing food that was not theirs. A lot of the Sunni families told me I should just cooperate with the Mahdi Army, especially if trying to trick them would put me at risk. It was risky, but I knew how to do it so they would not know.

I went to the central records department. Two friends of mine worked there, a Sunni woman and a Shi'ite man. They didn't like the Mahdi Army. Few did. I explained the situation to them, and they helped me doctor the records to make it look like the rations for the Sunni families on my list stopped months before. After that, anyone looking at my records would see no signs of rations for Sunnis they might take. It was easy to do so no one would know. And the Mahdi Army does not have a reputation for smarts after all. They are quite stupid in general. If they really wanted to get a hold of the food, they would have gone to the central records department first and presented the distributors like me with lists they had gotten there.

I got married around this time, too. Her name is E'nas. She is Sunni, but neither of our families cared about this sectarian thing. We weren't like that. She was a friend of my sister. I saw her just a couple of times with my sister that year before we got married but felt something in my heart toward her. From the time I first saw her to the time we were married was less than a month. I would have done it in two weeks if I could. It's not much of a love story. It was not a time for romance. Love has no taste in war. When you see the misery of others, how can you love? When you go out and see all these black banners, and burned houses, homes belonging to people you know standing empty because they have been forced to leave, how can you have feelings of love?

Rasim Hassan Haikel was still serving as a rations distributor as of January 2009, when the interview was conducted in Baghdad. He said the Mahdi Army's safe house at the end of his block had been closed down after several raids by American forces starting in 2008. But the Mahdi Army, he said, still maintained an underground presence in the neighborhood.

Moving Days

❋

KHAIL IBRAHIM AL-NASIR

He is the father of five, three daughters and two sons. Under the old regime he worked as a reporter for state television. After the U.S. invasion he became a producer for Fox News in Baghdad and sometimes worked on the side for an Iraqi channel. The family lived in Adhamiya, a mainly Sunni neighborhood in northern Baghdad that became home for a number of Sunni militant groups during the height of the sectarian violence.

IT ALL STARTED with a shooting incident at the school near our house in February of 2006. The country was in chaos then, but we kept sending our children to school each day in Adhamiya even so. Either my wife or I would drop the children off in the morning and pick them up ourselves in the afternoon. Occasionally Abdullah, my youngest, would get a ride home from one of the guards at his school. There were three altogether, but he was especially fond of two, Hayder and Uday. Abdullah kept pictures of Hayder and Uday in a photo album of his. He was six years old then.

I remember I was home the day of the killings. We got a call saying we should come to the school right away to get Abdullah and his older sister, Zahra, who was above him at the same school. They were not there when we arrived. What happened, we later learned, was that a car had pulled up to the school with four men in it. Two of the men emerged with guns and went to kill the guards, who were unarmed. It was not a sectarian killing. It was just insurgents targeting these guards because they were technically employees of the government. In any case, Abdullah had been eating a chocolate bar and having milk with Hayder and Uday when the attackers appeared. He apparently hid behind a door and overheard an exchange between the attackers and one of the guards, who urged the gunmen not to shoot, saying they were all Muslims. The attackers shot Uday and Hayder to death, and the third guard got away by jumping over the wall.

Abdullah ran from the school at the sound of the shots and made his way to a nearby house where a family friend lived. He banged on the door and asked to be let in, but the woman inside was too scared to open the door and told him to go away. You can imagine what this was like for a six-year-old. He had just run from the scene of the death of his friends at school and now this. Luckily his sister found him, and the two of them made their way home. My wife and I found them there.

Abdullah looked changed when I saw him. I had never seen my son like this. He was not the same boy who had gone off to school that morning. His face was pale, and he wore a dazed expression. He had cried his eyes dry, and he was shaking. I didn't talk to him about what happened at the school in the days that followed. I was hoping he might calm down and begin to forget.

About a week after this, three Shi'ite men were murdered in our neighborhood. Their bodies were left very near our house, and they remained there for three days before anyone came to pick them up. Finally an Iraqi army patrol came to collect the remains, and a crowd from the neighborhood gathered outside to watch. Abdullah was among them.

It's no secret that Adhamiya was an insurgent neighborhood in those days. There was a house very near ours they used. Everyone in the neighborhood knew quite well the place was a terrorist safe house run by an insurgent leader named Abu Zaynab. But we did not dare say anything about it to the army or the police, because we knew we'd be killed if we did. Abdullah decided he wouldn't be silent anymore though. He had grown very angry about the death of his friends at school. He knew, like we all did, that the men who did the shooting at the school lived in that safe house, and he pointed it out to the Iraqi soldiers. He told them simply that the terrorists lived there, and the Iraqi soldiers immediately raided that house. They found a large cache of weapons and arrested a number of men.

I was taking a nap as all this was happening outside, because I had to work a night shift at Fox that evening. Suddenly a neighbor of mine burst into my room, a woman. She was frantic, telling me I had to hide Abdullah immediately. He's created a disaster, she said. She had heard what Abdullah told the soldiers and knew what was coming. I did too as I began to wake up. I quickly gathered up some clothes, grabbed Abdullah, and headed to the hotel Fox was using as its bureau at the time. I took a room in the hotel for Abdullah and me. The hotel had good security, and I thought we would be safe there while I figured out what to do next. We slept for several nights there in the same bed together. At night he would use my arm as a pillow.

Initially Abdullah denied saying anything to the soldiers. Eventually he confessed what I already knew. I could not help being upset with him. I tried to explain that he had probably put the whole family in danger. I already knew we would likely have to flee, which meant I would lose my job and my home. He couldn't understand how huge his act was, and he wasn't sorry for it. He was like, So what? Those people killed my friends. Let them get what they deserve. He was just too young to understand. He was six, after all. Just six. Basically he was telling me to go to hell with all my worries. He would never use such language with his father, but that was his state of mind. My friends are dead, he reasoned. To hell with the people who did it and to hell with anyone who would protect them. To hell with us all, was his attitude.

We had been in the hotel for less than a week when I got a call from a neighbor of mine. He had a message from Abu Zaynab. Word had spread through the neighborhood that Abdullah was the one who tipped off the Iraqi soldiers about the safe house, and Abu Zaynab's men knew I was Abdullah's father and that we had fled. Abu Zaynab, in asking around about me, told this neighbor of mine to tell me that Abdullah and I would be safe if we came home. And Abu Zaynab wanted to meet me.

I went back to my house the next day, and I took Abdullah with me. I had to go. My wife and the rest of my children were still there, and I was afraid something would happen to them if I didn't show for Abu Zaynab. I got the house ready for his arrival by taking out all the copies of the Koran I had and setting them around on the tables. I got rid of all the beer in the refrigerator. I turned on the television to a religious channel, and I had my wife and daughters put on *abayas* as we waited.

Abu Zaynab is a redhead, medium build, maybe 45 years old. I used to see the guy riding around the neighborhood on a motorcycle wearing blue jeans and sandals, but I didn't know who he was until he showed up at my house that day. He came in with about eight men, bodyguards. They were all men from the neighborhood. They carried pistols. They didn't act like bodyguards, however. They acted like they were just joining him for a friendly neighborhood visit. But we all knew who they were and why they were there. Nothing needed explaining. We were at their mercy. They made that clear to us without saying a word, and we made it clear we understood. We knew very well that Abu Zaynab could do whatever he wanted to us with a single word. We were entirely in his hands.

When he came in, I greeted him with a big smile and offered him a seat. He sat on a couch, and I took a chair off to his left. We served tea as we would with any guest. After a moment he asked where Abdullah was. I called Abdullah into the room, and Abu Zaynab motioned for him to come over. He put Abdullah on his knee and gave him a kiss on the cheek. And then he said, Why, my son, did you bring the military to my men? Don't you know that they are holy warriors fighting for the sake of the country? Abdullah said nothing. Then Abu Zaynab turned to me and said, Look, men I can replace. There are a lot of fighters. But what about the weapons we lost? We need those. I told him he could take whatever of mine he wanted. I offered my car. I offered my house and all its possessions. Abdullah remained sitting silently on his knee as I spoke.

Abu Zaynab waived away my offers almost as if they annoyed him, and after a moment he got up to go, saying he had other matters to attend to. He was in the house for maybe ten minutes. Before going he told me to consider the matter closed. But I could tell by his attitude toward us that he was unhappy, and I knew it would be only a matter of time before someone from his bunch came for us. We could never feel safe in that place again.

Khail Ibrahim al-Nasir fled with his family to Damascus, Syria, shortly after the visit from Abu Zaynab. Fox gave al-Nasir $5,000 upon departure as a kind of severance pay, but otherwise offered no help, he said, as he joined the throngs of Iraqi refugees moving across the border to Syria. Al-Nasir had returned to Bagh-

dad alone as of May 2009 to try to find work and perhaps lay plans to bring his family back, but he was not having luck finding employment. Abu Zaynab had disappeared from Adhamiya, al-Nasir said. Conflicting rumors in the neighborhood put Abu Zaynab either in prison or living in Syria.

☀

UM OMAR

She comes to the interview wearing a black abaya and carrying all her important documents, which amount to a clutch of tattered papers stuffed into a plastic grocery bag. Born in 1952, she is a mother of eight and the matriarch of a large, very poor Sunni family who found themselves under threat in their predominately Shi'ite neighborhood of Huriya as sectarian violence swept across Baghdad in 2006. She speaks in a trembling, raspy voice as she recalls the days when she was forced to flee.

I DID NOT HEAR THE BREAK-IN or the beating. I did not even know about it until the morning after the night it happened. I was in the house but sleeping with a daughter-in-law of mine who was recovering from the birth of one of my grandchildren. She had not been feeling well, so I had stayed with her through that night. When I woke up, I found my husband on his feet covered in blood. He had blood coming from his nose. He had blood on his nightclothes. There was blood on the floor. All he told me was that men in masks had come into the house during the night and threatened to kill the family if we did not leave. Outside, on the door, we found a threat letter saying the same.

That day we rented a small truck and packed up everything we could. There were fourteen of us living in a rented house together then. We took everything we could manage and drove to the house of one of my daughters, who was living with her husband in Bayaa, a neighborhood by the airport. We stayed there for about a month. Some in the family fled to Syria or went to stay with other relatives. The rest of us had to find a new place to live. Finally one of my sons found another rental house for us in Abu Ghuraib.

Six of us settled into the house in Abu Ghuraib. We were completely wiped out financially by then. My husband had a heart attack during the collapse of the old government and had not worked since then. We had to sell almost all of our furniture just to eat even before we were displaced. By the time we were moving into the new house we didn't even have bread. Our new neighbors were so good to us. They knew what had happened and welcomed us. They brought rice, bread, and blankets. They offered us money. We lived off their charity.

My husband's health began to get worse very quickly around then. We took him to the doctor, who said he had an advanced case of liver cancer. The doctor said there was nothing to be done and that I should take my husband home, make him comfortable, and wait for him to die.

His last days came soon after. By the end he got so weak he could no longer eat on his own. I had to feed him by hand myself. On his last day he asked if he could sleep in my lap. It was nice outside, so I helped him into the garden and let him put his head down in my lap. That is where he died.

I took him inside and put him on the bed and kneeled over him crying for some time. Then, suddenly, one of my daughters burst in shouting something about her uncle, my brother. He had been killed. Murdered. We don't know exactly what happened. As best we could understand, he had been targeted by the Mahdi Army because they saw him helping us move that day in Huriya. After abducting him they had broken his neck and shot him several times in the chest before dumping his body.

My brother went to the morgue to get him. Since we were burying my husband that day, we decided to bury my brother with him. So they brought his body to my house, and on the same day under my roof lay my husband and brother dead.

She begins to sob heavily. After a moment she is able to speak again, through tears that have been flowing intermittently throughout the interview.

It's all because we were Sunnis. Just because we were Sunnis.

Um Omar, who requested an alias for the safety of herself and her family, was still living in Abu Ghuraib as of February 2009 with no plans to return to Huriya. The family remained desperately poor. For a time, one of her sons was bringing in a little income by selling kerosene lamps, which sold well when Baghdad ex-

*perienced regular, prolonged blackouts. But sales of the lamps were falling, she
said, as power supplies in the city improved along with the security situation.*

※

IBRAHIM ISHMAEL KHALIL

*Before the invasion he made a good living installing and repairing air condi-
tioners. A Sunni, he was living with his wife, five children, and elderly father in
a predominately Shi'ite area of northwestern Baghdad, the city where he was
born in 1964. He has a booming, raspy voice and chokes back tears throughout
the interview, recalling how the months and years unfolded for him and his
family after 2003.*

THERE WAS AN ACCIDENT during the bombardment before the invasion. A man on a motorcycle was racing away from an area being bombed,
and he struck one of my sons, Mohammed, who was about ten years old
at the time. Mohammed's head hit the curb, and his skull cracked. He was
lucky to survive. It was a bad injury that left a visible scar on his head. But
after that he was always getting fevers. The doctors we took him to said he
had Red Wolf syndrome, which weakens the immune system. So he was
always getting sick. I was constantly taking him to the hospital for treatment. The bills became so high. I had to sell everything I owned just to pay
for his care. Almost all the things I had collected during my life I sold. I
sold our two television sets. I sold our refrigerator and freezer. I sold the
bedroom furniture I bought for my wife and me.

During this time the sectarian violence was rising. Three of my brothers were killed. One was strangled on the west side of the city. Two others
who ran a generator shop together were shot to death when Mahdi Army
men tried steal their generators. After the killing of my brothers, being a
Sunni in a Shi'ite area, neighbors who meant well started coming to me
and advising me. They told me there was no point in staying. They told me I
should move for the safety of my family. Where should I go? The only thing
left I owned was that house. We stayed because we had no place to go.

The neighborhood was becoming so unsafe then that we had to lock ourselves in our house. We almost never went out. The Mahdi Army was always on the street, gunmen dressed in black everywhere. One night in the fall of 2006 Baghdad was under curfew for some reason. I don't remember why. Suddenly a very bad fever came over my son, worse than usual. I had to take him to the hospital. At this time the sectarian killings were at their peak, and I had to go out into the streets after dark, breaking curfew to try to save him. I carried him in my arms to the hospital. The police allowed me through the checkpoints after seeing how bad Mohammed's condition was, and I was able to make it to the hospital along with my daughter, Wallah, who was a little younger than Mohammed at the time.

At the hospital, I saw three guys with guns roaming the halls. This was during the time when Shi'ite militiamen would kidnap visiting Sunnis from the hospital and murder them. The doctor treating Mohammed even told me that the men roaming the halls were asking about me. I had to run, right then. I left Wallah to stay with Mohammed, and I went out of the hospital, jumped the fence, and took off. Not far from the hospital I saw a guy I know on a bicycle. He took me part of the way home, and I walked the rest. I was scared, really scared, going through the streets after midnight. Sometimes I ran. Sometimes I walked. I remember it was very cold. My feet were killing me.

I finally reached home at four in the morning. I rested for just a little while and then got up for the morning prayer. As I was praying I had a vision of my son lying dead. The moment I finished praying, my daughter called me on the mobile. She said, Dad, come quickly, my brother is dead. Apparently the doctor had given Mohammed too strong a dose of medicine when trying to break the fever, and it killed him. When I heard that, I was on the verge of collapse. I was screaming and crying like a baby.

We had some good Shi'ite neighbors who helped us with the burial, since it was unsafe for us to move about. But the incident had drawn attention to us. Those men at the hospital had seen me. An ambulance brought Wallah back with Mohammed's body to our house, so other people at the hospital knew who we were and where we lived. After that we were fairly sure the Mahdi Army knew we were a Sunni family living in their area, and we grew more afraid.

Seven days after my son died I decided to go out, even though everyone was telling me not to. I wanted to see the situation. I took a motorcycle I have and drove to the nearest police checkpoint. I was stopped, and the police asked where I was going. I told them I was out to do some shopping. They let me through without any other questions, but I saw that someone was following me in a car as I drove away. The police of course at that time were working with the Mahdi Army, and I knew whoever was following me would probably kill me if they could catch me. I kept riding trying to lose them, and thankfully I saw an American convoy. I went full speed toward it. They might have shot me. They usually did shoot people coming straight at them. But if I didn't reach them, the men following me would kill me. So I went at them anyway, hoping the car would not follow me past if I made it. Somehow the Americans understood that I was being chased and they didn't fire. They let me approach them, and the car following me fell away.

I did not dare go home after that and knew we had to move. I went that day to Ghazaliya, to try to find a house to rent. I managed to find one that day, actually, and stayed there for three nights before my family joined me. My father decided not to move with us to Ghazaliya and went to stay with another family in Baghdad. But my wife and children eventually brought what little we had left in the house to the rental I had found. The Mahdi Army watched over them as they packed up our things.

As my wife and children were arriving with our things in Ghazaliya, suddenly a group of armed men appeared. Sunni gunmen of the neighborhood. They asked who we were and what we were doing there. I explained to them the situation. I think they must have not believed I was a Sunni because I had come from a Shi'ite area. In any case they said we could not stay in the house I was renting. They made us leave, and we were just wandering the neighborhood as it got dark. We had nowhere to go. We could not go home. We could not go to the house I had paid for because of these men. We roamed around Ghazaliya until we found an abandoned place, a shack really. We put our things inside, and I told my wife we should stay there for the night and figure out what to do in the morning. It was dark, and we were settling in for the evening when two cars approached. The men who chased us from our rental must have followed us. Armed men in masks got out of the cars, ordered me into the back of one, and took me away to a house in the area.

I remember it was the fifth of December 2006 and very cold. I don't remember much about the men who took me. They were always in masks. Two of them were very big, I know that. And I don't remember much about the house where they were keeping me. Only the bathroom. When we got to the house, I was beaten, stripped down, tied up and placed in the bathtub. Then they filled it with freezing water and left me there. I was in the bathtub for three days like this. They kept telling me I was a Shi'ite and a spy. I told them over and over again I was a Sunni, but they would not believe me. During the three days in the bathtub I was given no food. The only water I had was the water I was in. Of course I had gone to the bathroom in it. Eventually I was so thirsty I began to drink it and it made me so sick that I vomited in the tub as well. Throughout the time I was in the bathtub, men would come in and use the toilet. After using the toilet, each one would dump more water in the tub to keep the level up.

After three days of this they took me out, and they poured salt all over me. You can imagine the pain of having salt put all over your skin after three days in water. I could not take it anymore. I told them, Look, if you're going to kill me, please just do it. Don't put me through this anymore. Just please let me pray before I die. They gave me some clothes and left me alive for three more days. The questions about whether I was Sunni or Shi'ite continued. And then, suddenly, they became convinced I was indeed a Sunni and decided to let me go. Without any explanation they put me in the back of a car and drove me toward the area where I had left my family. The car came to a stop, and one of them asked me if I could find my way from there. I said yes, and they released me and drove away.

Ibrahim Ishmael Khalil reunited with his family and was still living in Ghazaliya as of February 2009. His life was gradually regaining a semblance of normalcy then, even though his father was murdered as the sectarian violence continued. After a period of desperate poverty, he managed to resume work installing and repairing air conditioners. He said business had gotten good enough for him to hire two laborers who helped him with various jobs.

YOUSEF ABOUD AHMED *AND*
ANHAM MUHANA HASOON

They have been married nearly twenty years. He is a Sunni. She comes from a Shi'ite family. He drove a taxi to support her and their three children, two sons and one daughter. They were living in a rented house in Huriya, a mainly Shi'ite neighborhood of Baghdad where her family also lived. Theirs was a poor but largely untroubled life before the war. They sit close together on a couch for the interview. He touches her knee gently whenever he mentions her. She sometimes pauses to cry.

YOUSEF: Things started to change in our neighborhood as soon as 2004. People started to look at us in a strange way. Even before the bombing of the shrine in Samarra in 2006 we could feel suspicion and hostility toward us growing where we lived.

ANHAM: I noticed a change in the way people were toward me when I was out shopping day to day. The way people would say hello was a little bit different, a little colder than it was before. Neighbors who had visited us frequently came less often. Our children complained about harsh teasing. We stayed in more and more as we sensed these things. The few other Sunni families around us began moving away after the bombing of the shrine. They were getting threats, and eventually we got one too. Someone threw a grenade over our fence and into our yard.

YOUSEF: It was not a big grenade, and none of us were hurt. But it blew out the tires of my car and broke windows. We could not just move like some of the other Sunni families did, even after that. We had no money. I had been working less because driving was becoming more dangerous. In some areas around our neighborhood the Mahdi Army was burning down Sunni houses. They would strap a grenade to a can of gasoline and throw it into a Sunni house. With all this going on we were basically just hiding in our house waiting. Then one evening they came to kill me.

It was November of 2007. I was at home in an upstairs room. I looked out the window and noticed a number of men hanging around the gate of my house. They were armed. And elsewhere along my street I saw other armed men going around to the shops, telling them to close. There were about twenty-five armed men altogether.

ANHAM: I was visiting my parents who live just a few doors down from us. I went to go home, not knowing what was happening outside. As I walked into the street, someone pointed a gun at me and told me to go back inside. He said there was about to be shooting and that I should stay in the house. I thought there might be some fighting between the Mahdi Army and a Sunni group. Some Sunni militant groups had been coming into our area to attack Shi'ite families, and there had been such fighting between them and the Mahdi Army. But that's not why these men were on the street. They were there to get us. I did not realize this at the time, and they did not know who I was coming out of my relative's house. I begged them to please let me pass, saying I lived just there and would have time enough to get in my own house if they let me through. When I told them where I was going, they realized who I was. They let me walk toward my house, and as I went I began to understand why they were there.

At the gate of my house there were four armed men standing. They asked who I was, and I told them. They asked me where my husband was. And my son. I told them both were out, which was a lie. They were both inside. They told me we had two days to leave our house, or we would all be killed. We could not stay in the neighborhood any longer. I begged them not to evict us, but they would not listen.

YOUSEF: When she came in I stayed hidden and decided I would wait until they went away to try and leave the house. But they stayed there in the street waiting for me to arrive at home. They stood out there for hours and seemed ready to stay until dawn. I could hear them talking and clacking their guns. I hid inside for about four hours, listening to them on the street. I wanted to spare my family the scene of me getting killed right in front of them, so I decided to try and risk running away that night finally. Shortly before midnight I managed to slip out the back unnoticed, hop the fence into a neighbor's yard, and make my way out of the neighborhood.

ANHAM: Somehow they figured out that he had been inside and ran away. I think one of the neighbors saw him leaving and told them, because shortly after he left they pounded on the door. They knew he was gone and not coming back, but they wanted to see Murad, our oldest son. He was twelve years old at the time. I think they had some misinformation that he was older, big enough to be a fighter. When they saw he was small, they didn't say anything. They just left without taking him and went to stand in the street some more. They remained there through the night and left in the morning. I did not recognize any of those men who came. They were not from our neighborhood, but they must have known someone in our neighborhood. It was like they had spies watching us in the neighborhood before and after that night. Yousef called me the same night he escaped and told me to leave with the children the next morning, not to delay. I could not get everything together that quickly. It took me about three days to get ready, but then we were gone.

YOUSEF: Our life curse really started then. That night when I escaped I went to my cousin's house in Adhamiya, a mainly Sunni neighborhood not far away. He was not in a position to take in me, much less my whole family. He advised me to go to the big Sunni mosque in the area, where a lot of Sunnis in the same position as me were seeking help. I went, and the men at the mosque arranged for me and my family to have two rooms in a dormitory building very near the mosque. It was meant to house the mosque's religious students but had been empty for some time.

Initially we slept on the ground in those rooms. There was no furniture, and we had brought no possessions with us except our clothes and a few small things. At least we had a roof to sleep under. When we moved into that building, there were only two other families. We were the third. But day after day more displaced Sunni families came. The building had three floors with fourteen flats. Displaced Sunni families filled all of them in just a short time after we got there.

Gradually we began to gather some things. Some of the other displaced families in the building donated blankets and cushions. So did the mosque. We made some simple furniture from refrigerator crates we found. With what little money I had left I bought some plates that we could both eat off and cook with. It was a horrible time. In addition to all this suffering of ours, many of the people in the building were suspicious of us. I don't blame them. We were strangers. There was a lot of sectarian killing going on at this time, and it was hard to know who to trust.

The neighborhood where the mosque and our building stood was not safe. There was a lot of fighting going on there from the time we arrived. The Mahdi Army was shooting mortars into the area in the hopes of hitting Sunnis they knew were gathering there. Sunni fighters calling themselves mujahideen were attacking the Americans and the Mahdi Army.

There was gunfire, roadside bombs, car bombs, mortars. We faced trouble on all sides.

ANHAM: Most of the Iraqi security forces were Shi'ites. So, when they came to raid something in Adhamiya, they did not just raid. They attacked. They destroyed buildings instead of searching them for people to arrest. If they came to our area, they came as though they were going to war.

YOUSEF: The Mahdi Army tried many times to enter Adhamiya to kill all the Sunnis there. The Sunni fighters were tough, though, and managed to hold them back. So, the Mahdi Army hit again and again with mortars from their areas nearby instead. Mortars fell somewhere in our neighborhood almost daily. It was one of those mortars that killed my son.

It was about two months after we had moved into that building, and late one afternoon we asked Murad to go get some bread. There was a baker who had a place inside the building on the ground floor, and Murad often went to get bread for us because it was so close. This day he went with two of his little friends from the building. The baker told the kids that a new batch of bread was just about finished and to wait a few minutes. So the three of them sat on a curb just outside the building. The mortar fell right in the middle of them.

I was on the second floor in a room almost directly above them. I saw flames shoot up past the window as the glass shattered. When I looked down from the balcony I could not see because of the dust. Then my wife started shouting, My son, my son! She had seen him sitting there in the minutes before, but I had not.

I ran downstairs barefoot. There were a lot of injured all over the ground. Someone, I don't know who, had picked up Murad. I took Murad from him. His head was split open. Most of his brain was outside his skull. A large piece of shrapnel had hit him in the cheek, and many other smaller fragments had gone into his chest. Both of his arms appeared broken. I knew he was dead as soon as I saw him. I knew I could do nothing, except bury him.

Yousef Aboud Ahmed and Anham Muhana Hasoon lived in the mosque dormitory for roughly eight months before they were able to find another home for themselves in Adhamiya. Yousef later joined the ranks of the Awakening, a movement of Sunni volunteer fighters who worked with U.S. forces against insurgents in western Iraq, parts of Baghdad, and areas just south of the capital.

✳

ALI IBRAHIM BAHER

He comes from a large, wealthy Sunni family who lived together in a house in the western Baghdad neighborhood of Ameriya. Ali was earning his master's degree in political science at Baghdad University during the time of the U.S. invasion and went to apply for a job as a staffer with the newly formed Iraqi parliament in 2004.

SOMEONE MUST HAVE SEEN ME going into the Green Zone when I went to apply, because a friend of mine in Ameriya shortly afterward told me that people in the neighborhood were talking about how I had been there. He told me not to go the Green Zone anymore, because it could cause a lot of trouble for me and my family if I were involved in any work there. I made some excuse, saying I was just visiting a friend. After that I dropped the idea of going to work for the parliament. Even if I got the job, I would be under threat and maybe bring troubles to my family. I would have to leave my neighborhood. What kind of job would pay for me to rent another house and move? And even if I were safe, my family in Ameriya might not be if word got out that I was working in the Green Zone.

In our house in Ameriya at that time was me, my father and mother, and my five brothers. Two of my brothers were married then and had their wives living there as well. I was single. Our family has some business interests that kept me busy and brought in cash for us. We have a small cinderblock factory that's belonged to us for a long time. We have a small car dealership. We trade in building materials, too. We were doing alright financially in the years after the invasion even while the situation grew worse.

Things in our neighborhood started getting bad gradually. First came the bodies. We began finding unidentified corpses in the road periodically. Rumors surrounded the bodies. For example, people would say that dead guy was working for the police and this dead guy was in the army or working in some government office or was a member of a certain political party. But you never really knew who the victims were.

I personally saw killings in the neighborhood. I was in the house one day when I heard shots in the street. I ran out along with a bunch of others on the block who heard the commotion. And there were three gunmen who had just killed a shopkeeper and neighbor of ours, a Shi'ite named Sallah. He was a close friend to one of my brothers and had come by just earlier that day to invite us all to his upcoming wedding. The killers were wearing blue jeans and baseball caps. They looked like teenagers. The oldest of them could have only been twenty. They left casually, as if they had all the time in the world, and no one tried to stop them. We were all too afraid.

More bodies began to appear in the streets as time went on. For a while whenever you went out you were sure to see a body in the road, or in the garbage or sitting in a car still running after being shot through the windows. These became everyday sights. By 2006 it got so bad that all of us in our family were afraid to go on the main street in our neighborhood. There were no Iraqi security forces at all in our area in that time. They did not dare come, because the place was totally under the control of al-Qaeda. Only American troops would occasionally enter.

We never came under threat, but we were worried nonetheless. Our neighborhood was so overrun with al-Qaeda that we knew either the Americans or the Iraqi security forces would attempt a crackdown. We had a family meeting one day. My father said, Look, you are six men of fighting age. For sure some of you will wind up arrested if we stay here. We had a place to go. My family has roots in Hit, and we have a small house there that's been in the family for years. My father figured we could all go there for a while until things cooled down. We knew our house in Ameriya would probably be looted once we left. We didn't care. We all knew we had to go. Most other families in our area had already gone. On our street alone there were about thirty families. All but five wound up leaving.

In Hit, we were there for about a year. Of course, as you know, the place is mostly Sunni, and al-Qaeda was there too. The al-Qaeda fighters were very open in their presence around Hit. They distributed leaflets advising residents to stay away from American patrols, because they were targets likely to be attacked at any moment. These fighters made it clear the town belonged to them. They did whatever they wanted.

Hit is a very small place. There's only one gas station in it. Twice a week, Mondays and Thursdays, a tanker came to refill the station. Huge lines of cars would appear on those days to get gas because there was such a shortage. The al-Qaeda fighters needed gas too, and they would roll up in their trucks, cut into the line, and fill whole barrels while everyone watched. One day there was a guy refilling his car when al-Qaeda came. He had just started pouring gas into his tank when one of the fighters ripped the hose from his hand. The man said, Listen, please let me just finish before you begin filling your barrels because it will take you so much longer than it will me. The fighter who grabbed the hose slapped the man. The man began shouting in anger, and a moment later he was shoved into a car by other fighters and driven away. Two days later his dead body was dumped on his doorstep.

The al-Qaeda fighters were not the only ones we were afraid of in Hit, however. We worried about the Americans, too. There was a shop in front of our house. And there was a big hole in the road right next to the shop. One day a man came and dropped a huge sack in the hole. The shopkeeper asked what was going on, and the man told him flatly that it was a bomb meant for the Americans. The shopkeeper was advised to close up for a while until the fighters had a chance to set the bomb off. The shopkeeper did and came and told us what was going on. Of course we did not dare try to remove it in case someone was watching.

About three days later we heard the sound of American vehicles approaching. They were heavy vehicles on treads. When the convoy was very near, the bomb went off. The blast was big enough to blow out all the windows in the area. The Americans did not appear hurt in the explosion, but one of their vehicles was disabled. They went about trying to clear it off, taking about two hours to get the thing out of there. Those two hours passed like two years for us in the house just across the road. We were so scared. We knew the Americans had gone on a rampage in Haditha after a similar bombing against them. As far as we knew, they were capable of anything in that moment. Maybe they would come and arrest all of us in the houses around the area, knowing that we must have known about the bomb. Maybe they would kick in the door and kill us. Maybe they would take some women and rape them. In the end they didn't do anything. They just left. But my blood pounded through my veins until they finally went.

Ali Ibrahim Baher and his family remained safe during their yearlong stay in Hit. They all eventually resettled in the family house in western Baghdad, where Ali remained living as of May 2009.

❋

KHALID ADNAN KHALID

He grew up an only child in the western Baghdad neighborhood of Saydiya, near the airport. Married in 2004, he and his wife began a family while still living with his parents, who kept a flat in Saydiya.

I GOT A CALL from my mother-in-law one day in July of 2005. She had gotten word that her husband had been shot near where I live and was down at the police station. My father-in-law was a former officer in the army, and he had gotten involved with the National Iraqi Accord party after the invasion. He worked as a liaison for the party to military men like himself, enlisting support where he could find it among his old colleagues. The role made him a target for Sunni insurgents. Anyone working in politics officially then was.

My wife and I got in the car and headed to the police station. Initially we all thought he had just been injured. I kept calling him on his cell phone as we drove but got no answer. Then about halfway to the police station I saw his car on the side of the road. He was inside, not moving, and there was a lot of blood. My wife of course became hysterical.

I pulled over, left my wife in the car, and went to check things out. He was finished for sure. There were at least nine bullet holes in the car, and I could see three wounds on him. There was one on the neck that must have killed him. He had one in his back and one in his shoulder. From what I could tell, a car must have pulled up alongside him as he was moving. Gunmen inside shot a burst with a Kalashnikov and then sped away. He appeared to have survived long enough to pull the car over but then passed away, probably only a short time before we got to him. There was no saving him. I called my mother-in-law right away and told her. A friend of hers quickly came. We decided it would be best for him to take my wife away in my car, while I dealt with the body. I managed to get him into the backseat, and I drove the car to the police station.

At the police station, I sat for questioning, and things began to get weird. Right away the police took note that I was a Sunni, and as you know at that time Shi'ite militias were working with the police in a lot of places. There were a lot of questions about where I was from and my family background, things that had nothing to do with the incident. They seemed to be growing hostile toward me the longer the questioning went on. At one point they asked me to wait outside. Things were getting busy at the police station, because American troops had just brought in two unidentified bodies found in the area. I went outside as they said, but I did not wait for them to call me in for more questioning. I ran. I had the feeling that if I stayed there any longer, something bad would happen to me. Maybe I was wrong. Maybe I was being paranoid. But I had heard so many stories about the police and the militias working together to kill Sunnis, and I was getting a really bad feeling from those guys at the station.

About two days later a threat came to my father-in-law's house in Ghazaliya. One of their neighbors quietly passed on a message that the family should not hold a wake, because it might be dangerous. It was a subtle threat to the remaining sons of the family. My father-in-law had five boys of his own plus me after I married into the family. It was clear he was murdered by al-Qaeda, which was in complete control of Ghazaliya at that time. And it was clear that we his sons would be targeted as well eventually. We knew we could not be safe. It did not need to be spelled out in a letter dropped on our doorstep. We understood.

I had two uncles living in Egypt, and my parents urged me to go and stay with them. They were so worried, you know, because I am their only son. For the next two months I stayed mostly at home, afraid to go out as I waited on my visa application. It was a horrible time, just sitting all day and all night bored and fearful at the same time. I passed endless hours with games on Playstation, reading books. My mood was always dark. My mind began to fill with a kind of waking nightmare, a vision in which I would be killed the moment I set foot out the door after getting my visa for Egypt. My wife Noor was so brave through it all. She had every right to be in worse condition than me. She had lost her father, and she was caring for our newborn daughter. But Noor through those days was always telling me to be patient, that things could get better once we were out of Iraq, that God would provide.

I had never been to Egypt before. I had never even been outside Iraq except once as a child in Jordan. It was really hard to go, but by 2006 we had made it to Cairo. We found a flat to rent. We got some furniture.

Through my uncles we began meeting a lot of Iraqis who had fled like us, and we began to get to know the city. In some ways it was nice at first. The newness of everything quickly wore off, though, and we fell into a bleak routine. We would sleep all day in our flat and drift around at night, afraid to spend money because we were running low. There was no aim in our life, no purpose for our being there except to be away from Iraq. Hope of returning home seemed to fade every day as the news from Iraq got worse all the time. Each day we heard on the television about how thirty bodies had been found in Baghdad, sometimes fifty bodies in a day. I got to the point where I could not sleep because of the stress of our situation and all the bad news we heard from home. I would close my eyes for only an hour or so at a time before waking up with my head filled with worry and images of dead bodies on streets I knew.

Khalid Adnan Khalid and his wife had another baby in 2007 while living in Cairo and eventually returned to Baghdad shortly thereafter. The family settled again in Saydiya. Khalid was looking for work without luck as of May 2009.

The Price of Sons

※

ZAID ALLWAN JAFAR

He was born in the northern city of Kirkuk but raised in Baghdad, where his father served as a high-ranking member of the Ba'ath party until 2003. The family managed to hold on to some of the wealth they earned under the old regime, however. He was attending college at a private school in Baghdad in 2005. At that time, elements of the burgeoning insurgency had begun to organize kidnappings in order to kill suspected American collaborators, extort ransoms, or settle scores.

IT WAS MARCH 25 OF 2005. As I left the college that afternoon, I was walking through a back alley toward home, the route I usually take. I had almost reached my house when I saw a white Oldsmobile with three men in it. I immediately got a strange sense about the car. I don't know why. I walked past them, trying to act nonchalant. One of the guys in the front seat I noticed was talking on a satellite phone. I got maybe eight meters away from them. Then suddenly the guy sitting in the backseat shouted out to me, telling me to come over. I did not look their way and kept walking. Then I heard the car start, and I broke into a run.

I made it to a nearby intersection, where suddenly a black BMW shot in front of me and blocked my way. The back door opened, and a guy in the backseat brandished a machine gun at me. The Oldsmobile was still coming, too. I was trapped, so I stopped. The guy in the BMW motioned for me to get in the car, and I walked over calmly and climbed in.

As soon as I was in they put a cloth bag over my head, tied my hands in front of me, and made me lay with my head in the lap of the man with the gun so I could not be seen. No one in the car said a word. My heart stopped. My brain stopped. Everything about me stopped, and I just waited for what would happen next.

Time wasn't making sense to me in those moments. I can't say exactly how long we drove, but it must have been more than an hour. I felt the car stop. I heard a gate opening. The car entered and moved up what seemed like a long driveway. The car then came to a stop, and all of us sat there for at least fifteen minutes without moving or saying anything. Nobody said anything, and the car kept running. I heard a second car, what I think was the Oldsmobile, enter the gate. That car stopped, the people inside got out. Then I heard someone say, Yes, bring him. Bring him.

They led me out of the car and into a house, still hooded. I remember I went up five steps then down two. I heard voices. I heard a television. Then I heard someone unlock and open a door, and someone shoved me. I hit a wall, and slid down it until I was seated. Then I heard the door close and lock.

About an hour after that, I heard footsteps in the hall of what sounded like at least three people. The door opened, and they entered. One of them took off my hood, and I saw the faces of four men from where I sat on the floor. I didn't recognize any of them, but none of them were the ones who grabbed me off the street. These were different men. I took them to be Sunnis. They all had heavy beards, but their faces were the faces of sophisticated men. I mean, they did not look like thugs or hard men. They looked normal, ordinary. None of them said anything to me. They just looked me over and kept the door slightly open, as if they were waiting for someone else to join them. Then I heard someone in the hall say, The sheik is coming.

The sheik was a young guy, maybe 23, and short. He wore a white dishdasha without the black headband the way Wahabi imams do. He said hello to us all as he entered, and all of us replied together. The sheik looked at me for a moment. One of the guys standing next to him said, Yes, he is the one. Then the sheik said to me, Why is your father working with the Americans? I said this is not true. My father was not. He starts lecturing me about how the Americans are occupiers. I started to feel relaxed, actually. I was thinking that these guys are insurgents who have got the wrong person. Once they figure it out, it will be no problem. I started explaining who my father was and how he had worked for the old regime. They asked me if I was a Sunni or a Shi'ite. I told them I was a Shi'ite, and they seemed puzzled by the idea that my father as a Shi'ite man could have been a part of the old government. Then the sheik said simply, Leave him. And they all turned and walked out leaving the door slightly open.

I didn't dare move, even though the door was open. A little while later a guy came in with a leg of chicken, some bread, and some juice. My hands were untied. He left me and locked the door. I couldn't eat. I just had a sip of juice. After an hour the same guy came back and was annoyed to see I had not eaten. He cursed me and left. About three hours after that, the guy who told the sheik I was the one came in and asked me for the phone number of my father. I gave it to him. They kept checking in on me as the hours passed but didn't say anything. At one point they made me take off my shirt and vest and put on a black shirt with a white stripe. No one was saying anything to me through this time, but I could hear a lot of movement in the house.

I began to lose track of time. I don't know when it was but some time later the guy who gave me the shirt came in and got me on my feet. I thought they must have gotten ahold of my father and figured out that none of us were collaborators and all was solved or soon would be. The guy did not put a hood on me as he led me through the house. It was a new, nice home. As we walked through the rooms I saw a guy sitting in a chair. He shouted at the guy leading me, Hey, jackass, put something on his head! So the guy leading me went and got a hood, and they tied my hands again.

The next thing I know I am in a car again. We drove a short distance to another house. I was placed in another room, where I was left hooded and bound. I stayed like that for hours. Sometimes I would doze off lying on my side. Sometimes I would stand and walk around the room a little. I could tell this house was old. The pavement of the floor was uneven like it is in old places. After a while I was falling into exhaustion, and I pretty much passed out.

I woke to the sound of the door opening. A guy I had not seen before pulled my hood off and started asking me how I was doing and what I had been up to. I didn't answer him. After a moment he said, Don't worry, relax. We're going to let you go. He said it with a laugh, as if I were being let in on a joke. I learned later that around this time they were negotiating a ransom with my father. They were talking prices for me. But I didn't know anything then as this guy was talking to me.

I passed what must have been a whole day without food or water. Then they were moving me again. I think I was in some kind of four-wheel drive vehicle this time. Again I was hooded and bound. This time I was allowed to sit up.

We drove for about an hour then came to a stop. One of the men in the car said to me, When we lift your hood, tell us if the man you see is your father. The car pulled up a little from there, and someone lifted my hood. The windows of the truck were tinted in a way that no one could see in from the outside, which is why they let me sit up. Looking out, I realized I was on Haifa Street in downtown Baghdad, and I saw my father's car. I told the men that my father's car was there. They put the hood back on me, and I sat there. Someone got out of the car. Then someone's mobile rang, and the guy who answered said only, Good news. Then he hung up. Seconds after that they took the hood off again, untied me, and opened the door. They told me to get out of the car and walk without looking back. I kept walking as I heard them pull away. I walked a block, and then I saw my father waiting for me. I hugged him, and we both started crying. The whole thing lasted three days.

I learned later talking to my father that the kidnappers originally demanded U.S.$100,000. They threatened to cut me up and send the pieces to my father if he did not pay. He did not have that much, of course. He convinced them of this and vowed to raise as much as he could for the ransom. He managed to get together just $4,000 and offered that. They accepted without argument for some reason, and that was it. He bought my life for $4,000.

Zaid Allwan Jafar returned to his studies and graduated in 2008 with the equivalent of a bachelor's in criminal justice.

SALIM KAMEL SHAWAL

Born in 1971, he is a longtime Shi'ite merchant and shopkeeper in a mainly Shi'ite area of northern Baghdad, selling women's underwear wholesale. He lived a fairly prosperous life as a local businessman in Baghdad before the U.S. invasion and afterward. But rampant crime and rising violence following the collapse of the Saddam Hussein regime began to affect him and his family despite their relatively good fortune.

BUSINESS WAS VERY GOOD just after the invasion, actually. There was so much money around. A lot of people who had never had money before in their lives were suddenly walking around with loads of cash, some of it gotten in the looting no doubt. They had little idea of the value of money and spent like crazy. New money, know what I mean? That year, 2004, was a golden year for us. I never dreamed I'd be doing business like I did then. We felt safe. We had plenty of cash. We were traveling for the first time in our lives. It was 2005 when our troubles started. My son, Yousef, was kidnapped that summer.

I was in my shop as usual when my phone rang. A neighbor of mine called saying I should come home immediately. When I got home I saw a scene on the street in front of my house. All my neighbors had gathered. My wife was there in the street screaming and hitting herself in the face and pulling her hair. They told me he had been taken. Yousef was only eight at that time.

What happened apparently was that Yousef and a friend of his about the same age were going together to a shop near our house. A car pulled up, and someone inside said, Yousef, come with us. Your father wants you.

Yousef told them that he could not get in a car with strangers. That's when one of the men in the car jumped out and grabbed him but left the other boy.

He begins to cry. He continues talking, waving away an offer to pause. He strains to force the words out, choking on sobs as his face reddens. He begins to regain his composure as he talks more.

I asked everyone to please leave us, and I took my wife inside and tried to console her. Then I picked up my phone. Some months prior, a friend of mine had had his son kidnapped, and it was solved with a ransom payment. So I called him for advice. My friend came over after an hour or two and advised me to simply wait and get in touch with no one, especially not the police. They will call, he said.

About two hours later the phone rang, and I picked up: Hello? Hello. Are you the father of Yousef? Yes, I am the father of Yousef. We have something that belongs to you.

I had never harmed anyone or been involved in anything bad in all my life. I went to my shop, and I came home to my wife and son. This was essentially my whole life, until now. I tried to sound relaxed. I wanted to keep things calm. So I talked to the man on the phone as though he were my friend. He was a Shi'ite, I could tell that. He sounded like he was from Sadr City. I told him that as long as Yousef was with him, I was not worried. I considered Yousef to be with cousins, I said. The whole time I was speaking I felt like I had a block of ice sitting in my chest. It was sweet talk, of course. My friend advised me to take that approach. I had to, anyway. He was holding my son. What else could I do? That first conversation was short. After hearing me sound calm, the caller asked if I was willing to make a deal. I said yes. He said he would call back.

Half an hour later he called again, the same guy. He said my son was wanted by people I had supposedly hurt in the market. I said, Look, I sell underwear for women! How could I hurt somebody selling underwear? He said these people were demanding U.S.$50,000. My entire business is not worth that much, and I told him so. He asked me how much I was willing to pay then. I told him that when my neighbors first called me, I thought Yousef might have been involved in an accident. So I took all the money out of the register in the store, in case I needed it for hospital charges or transportation or whatever. I told him that I wasn't going to pay a ransom for my son. But I would offer this money, since it's what I thought I might spend before I knew he had been taken. It was about $200. I told him I could maybe throw in another $200.

He asked if I was crazy, and then he got nasty with me. He said I must want my son dead. I said, If you are going to kill him, please leave him in front of the house so we can bury him properly. I just did not have the kind of money they wanted. I could not get it. So, there was no use pretending along those lines. Many of my friends and neighbors began offering money to help raise the ransom, but I refused it. Because even if I could get all that money, why should I give it to them? He is my son, and he should come back to me. My son. My son! That's it.

The caller told me Yousef would be dead by morning and hung up. I didn't sleep that night. I stayed up praying. I asked God again and again to let this thing please be over. At six the following morning, the kidnappers called. I saw it was them on my mobile. I didn't pick up. The phone rang again and again and again. Finally I picked up, trying to sound like I was just waking from a deep sleep. The caller asked me, How can you sleep with your son missing? I said, I told you, he's with family as far as I am concerned. When you are done with your visit, just bring him back. Then he told me that he was willing to drop the price, to $30,000. I told him that I already explained how much I could pay, the money from the register plus another $200 or so. He grew angry, told me again I was crazy. Before hanging up he said he would not call again since it was clear no deal could be reached.

I knew he would call back though. I felt it, and my friend whose son was kidnapped said the same. Sure enough he did. He called again and again, and we began having the same conversation over and over. Sometimes he would talk in a polite way, telling me that Yousef was a good boy and eager to come home, as if he were staying with a relative. Sometimes he would threaten to kill Yousef. Sometimes he would put Yousef on for a moment to let me know he was alive. They were even letting Yousef talk to his mother for long conversations. Sometimes another guy would call, a different negotiator. The ransom demand kept coming down a little with each conversation, but my reply was always the same. Sometimes they would suggest ways for me to raise the money, urging me to borrow from this person or that person I knew. Whoever they were they must have known people close to me, because they seemed to know a lot about me. I was on the phone so much with the kidnappers that they began complaining about the phone charges and asked me to reimburse them by sending them phone credit from scratch cards via text message. Fine, I said, and I did.

I could tell they were getting really sick of dealing with me. At one point the original caller had me talk to his wife, who was in charge of taking care of Yousef from what I could tell. She complained about how much he ate, saying she could barely afford to keep him fed. My answer was simple: bring him back to me if he is too much trouble. In one of the conversations the original caller grew really angry with me for refusing to budge on the ransom. He asked me how I could be so unfeeling toward my own son. Didn't I care if he wound up dead? I said to him, Look, I am young. My wife is young. If you kill Yousef, I will get her pregnant again and have another son. I will name him Yousef, and it will be just like he never left.

I think this really shocked them. I don't think they were expecting to hear me say such a thing. After that, I think they thought I really didn't care whether Yousef lived or died and decided to get whatever they could for him from me rather than just kill him and get nothing. Suddenly the ransom price dropped way down, until they were offering to hand Yousef back to me for about $6,000, which is roughly what my car is worth. So in one negotiation I offered him the keys in exchange for my son.

In the end that's what we settled on, about $6,000. I hid the car, so in case they were watching me, they would think I sold it. I got the money together. We negotiated in dollars, but they were willing to accept Iraqi dinars as payment. They knew the exchange rate. They gave me instructions on where to deliver the ransom. They ordered me to take the money and go alone to a junkyard. I did, the day after we struck the deal. It was so hot that day, I remember. They kept me waiting and waiting in the sun. I never even saw the person who took the money. I was standing in the junkyard when I heard a voice behind me. I was told to keep looking forward while emptying my pockets. I did as I was told, and when I felt I was finally alone I went back to my house.

The kidnappers did not say how or exactly when Yousef would be handed over. They only said that Yousef would be returned the day the ransom was given. We didn't know whether we would get further instructions on where to get him or what. My wife and I and some family and friends waited there in the house as it got later in the day, just wondering. Each hour felt like a week.

Sundown was coming, and still no Yousef. I phoned the kidnappers and talked to the original caller. He told me not to worry, that Yousef was coming. The drivers were probably just stuck at checkpoints, he said. As it got dark my wife and I were left alone in the house. Everyone else went out into the street in case the kidnappers dropped him on a corner or something.

Then, all of a sudden, Yousef just walks in the room. I have no idea how he got to the house without being seen by anyone looking for him outside. He just appeared. When he saw me he said, Papa, I thought they were going to kill me! Then he hugged his mother like he was never going to let go.

Salim Kamel Shawal heavily considered fleeing Iraq with his family after the kidnapping but in the end could not bear the idea of leaving his country. So he remained in Baghdad with his wife and son. About three weeks before sitting for the interview, burglars posing as police forced their way into the family home, he said, and robbed them at gunpoint. He believes the thieves were somehow connected to the kidnappers.

Questions and Answers

❉

MOUSTAFA AHMED AL-TA'EE

In Baghdad a lot of young men take care to dress smartly and look sharp, even in the hottest, dustiest weather. The city's stylish young men often wear short-sleeved dress shirts neatly pressed and open at the collar. Mustaches are grown long. Slender leather shoes are worn with a shine, and heavy gold watches are a favorite accessory. Al-Ta'ee, poised and handsome, looks the part exactly. He comes from a modest Sunni family who owned a shop for spare car parts in western Baghdad. He was nineteen when the United States invaded, enrolled in his first year at college and helping out at the family business when not in class.

AFTER THE COLLAPSE for the first few years, business at the shop was good. Everything was going well. I was in college. I had work. My family had money. What else do you want? But in 2006 the sectarian violence began to take hold of the street where our shop sat. A Shi'ite guy who worked in a juice stand a short ways from our shop was shot to death. Another guy nearer to us who sells cigarettes and stuff got a death threat, a bullet in an envelope, and he closed up his shop. Most of the shops in the area were run out of rented space owned by a local businessman known to work closely with the Americans in supplying the U.S. bases. So, we took the threats and the killings to be a message to him, not necessarily to us, at least in the beginning.

Next door to our business was a produce store run by two brothers, Sadeq and Nabil. They were Shi'ites and longtime friends of our family. In between our two shops there is a tree that gives a little shade. One afternoon that summer it was very hot. Sadeq and Nabil had put chairs between the two shops and were relaxing in the shade. About this time I was pulling up after running an errand with my car. I tried to go to my usual parking space, but I found a white Toyota there with three guys in it. Normally I make a scene when someone takes my spot, but that time I did not for some reason. I just found another spot nearby, parked, and got out.

As I moved up the street toward our shop, two of the men in the car got out while the driver remained. They were just two normal-looking young guys, dressed nicely much like me, clean shaven. You wouldn't think anything of them. I was only steps away from them on the sidewalk when both drew pistols as they headed toward where Nabil and Sadeq were sitting. They walked up on them totally cool and took aim, one at Sadeq and one at Nabil. Then without a word they started pumping them full of bullets.

Each of them must have shot six or seven times point blank into Sadeq and Nabil. Sadeq fell to the ground in the first shots and tried to get up but couldn't as more bullets hit him. Nabil remained in his chair, unmoved. He was sitting with his legs crossed smoking a cigarette when they came up. He remained like that, with the cigarette in his hand still burning, when the bullets stopped. I remember the blood pouring out of them didn't look red. It looked black like oil for some reason. The killers were completely calm when the shooting was done. They didn't run away or anything. They just walked back to the car, got in, and drove away. After that we closed the shop, and I decided to go to Syria some months later just to get out of the country for a while.

It was November of 2006, and I went to catch an early morning bus in Baghdad headed to the border. The bus was full, with probably forty people altogether on it. I was in a chair right next to the door. We drove the first leg out of Baghdad no problem and went on past Fallujah. Then as we neared Ramadi people started looking anxiously out the windows, and there up ahead of us was a checkpoint. There were three cars with three armed men standing around each, and a guy in a mask was motioning for the driver of the bus to pull over. When the bus came to a stop, two of the men, both in masks, flung the door open and climbed up. One of the guys was tall and the other one a bit shorter. The tall guy came in first and spotted a woman who didn't have her head covered. He hit her hard across the face and ordered her to cover up. Everyone on the bus began gasping and moaning with fear. And then the tall guy said to everyone, Don't worry. We're only here for a few people. We'll just take them and let the rest of you be on your way.

The two of them started moving down the aisle, asking people who they were and where they were from. The guy next to me said he was a Christian, and they left him alone. But they told me to get out my identification. I told them I didn't have it on me, which was true. My passport was in my bag in the luggage compartment. They asked where I was from, and I told them my tribal name, al-Ta'ee, and mentioned the name of the sheik from our area. That seemed to satisfy them, and they moved further down the aisle.

They seemed to be looking for Shi'ites, but they didn't reveal this. Then they came across a guy who said he was from the al-Janabi tribe, which is mostly Sunni. And the tall one said, Ah, a Janabi, today I will skin you alive. But it was a trick. They were trying to flush out the Shi'ites by making people on the bus think they were Shi'ites out to kill Sunnis. I don't know why anyone would think that Shi'ite militants were setting up checkpoints near Ramadi, which is a Sunni area. But in any case it worked. Some idiot hearing this suddenly jumped up saying, I'm a Khafaji! That's a largely Shi'ite tribe. Then the tall guy, speaking real smooth, said, Yeah, you're the one I'm really looking for.

They hauled him out of his seat. The man next to the Khafaji started begging the guys to leave him alone, and they hauled him up too and marched both down the aisle and out the door. With the two of those guys outside, they asked around a little more before moving back toward the door of the bus themselves. Then the tall guy looked at me again and said, Where did you say you were from? I said what I told him before. After a moment he said, You're a fucking liar. Get up.

The moment he said that, I lost all feeling in my legs. My head started ringing so loudly with fear I could barely hear anything. All I could think was, This is how I'm going to die? I managed to stand up and walk down the steps. I even carried with me a little handbag I had. I don't know why I took it. Outside the other two guys from the bus were being made to crouch in a ball with their hands on top of their heads. The men in masks ordered me to do the same. I told them no. I got a punch in the face and two kicks in the stomach from them, but I didn't feel anything. It was like I had no blood inside me at that moment. I managed to stay on my feet, and I started shouting at them. I said, I'm a Sunni! I'm a Sunni! Since when do you hit a cousin like this? They started punching me again, but I managed to get them to stop for a moment by saying that I could prove I was a Sunni if they let me get my passport out of the luggage compartment. I yelled to the driver to come down and help me find my bag, because I did not know where it was in the compartment. He refused, saying he was not going to get involved. I started screaming frantically as I searched the compartment, saying over and over again: I'm a Sunni! I can't find the bag! I'm a Sunni! I can't find the bag!

Suddenly the leader of this bunch came over because of all the fuss. He was the only one unmasked. He was young with light brown hair. He wore a gray tracksuit, and the others called him Haji. He stopped me from searching, turned me around, and put a gun in the back of my head. Then he said, I'm going to ask you a series of questions very quickly. If you have to think for even a second to answer any, I'll kill you. You just answer. You're a Sunni, he said, so tell me some people you know. I started saying the names of everyone I could think of in all the Sunni areas of Baghdad I knew. He let me go on for a minute then told me to shut up. Then he said, Okay, one last question. Get it wrong and you'll get slaughtered just like these other two sheep over here. Where, he asked, do you live? Without a pause I said Mansour. He said, Get back on the bus.

Once I got inside again I was shaking. All I wanted to do was sit down and smoke a cigarette. I went to settle back into my seat, and then I heard the guys outside calling for me to come back out. I waited for only a second before getting back up and going down the stairs again, thinking the same thing I thought when I went down the first time. At the bottom one of them was standing there with my handbag. You forgot this, he said, handing it over to me. I took the bag, and then, I don't know why, I started hugging each one of them and giving them each a kiss. As I was saying my goodbyes and getting back on the bus, I noticed that the other two guys had been tied up. And one of them was being stuffed into the trunk of a car as the bus began to move away.

The gunmen who released Moustafa Ahmed al-Ta'ee stopped the bus once more before it got fully away. They freed the second passenger ordered up, who turned out to be Kurdish, and allowed him to retake his seat. The passenger who gave himself away as a Shi'ite remained captive, however. Al-Ta'ee made it to Syria without further incident and eventually returned to Baghdad, where he got a job as a driver for Time *magazine's bureau in the summer of 2007.*

PART FOUR

The Mouths of Soldiers

※

SAJAD AL-HAKIM

Born in 1980, he was a student at Baghdad University in 2003 studying graphic design. The early days of the U.S. occupation opened something of a boom industry for young men like al-Hakim who were eager to work and spoke a reasonable amount of English. The U.S. military and defense contractors such as KBR were in desperate need of translators.

AT FIRST I DIDN'T EVEN CONSIDER working with the Americans. But after the invasion, the situation was bad for us financially. My family was never rich. I always had to work as a student. I needed to work even more after the collapse. At first I worked for KBR. But the pay was bad, and I didn't like the way they treated me. So I applied to be a translator for the Army in 2004, and I was accepted.

The first place they sent me was Forward Operating Base Falcon, in Dora. At that time, the translators were starting to call that base the interpreter graveyard, because so many translators who went to work there died. The base was right in the middle of an area controlled by insurgents then. The Mahdi Army was in control of another neighborhood nearby. Both groups were out to kill interpreters. It was like a contest between the two groups to see who could kill more. They seemed to think that if they killed all the interpreters, American soldiers would be blind and deaf in Iraq. It wasn't true. We didn't guide troops around Baghdad. With their satellite maps, they knew the streets better than we could a lot of the time. We didn't produce intelligence for them. They already had intelligence. We were just with them, interpreting, as they worked on the street. That was it. The militias and the insurgents seemed to hate us more than they did the American soldiers even so. I heard seventy interpreters from Falcon wound up dead. I was to be there for one year.

We started doing patrols immediately in Arab Jabour, Dora, and all the other shitty areas around there. Basically we went to all the bad neigh borhoods in the southern part of Baghdad and all the shitty farming areas to the south where insurgents liked to hide. Anyplace the Army thought there was AQI. That's what they called al-Qaeda in Iraq, the insurgents. A lot of translators were afraid of going on patrol, because it was so dangerous. A lot did what they could to avoid going on patrols and tried to find work that allowed them to remain on base. I decided early on that I was not going to try to avoid patrols. I was scared, sure. But that was the job, and I could not afford to quit.

The first day was scary. It's hard to describe how I was feeling, actually. I had seen American convoys of Humvees in the city, but I had never been in one before. I had never been in any kind of fighting before. I wasn't in the army or anything. All of a sudden I am on the streets in the worst areas of Baghdad with American soldiers, who were for sure going to be hit in the areas we were in. Small arms fire. Sniper fire. Roadside bombs. Rocket-propelled grenades. All this was coming at us. There was no way we were going to be left alone where we were going.

Usually we went out in four Humvees. On my first patrol, nothing happened. I was surprised. But on the second patrol we lost two soldiers. A suicide car bomb rammed the last car in our convoy as we were moving through Arab Jabour. I was in the second to the last car. The bomber seemed like he was trying to destroy two Humvees, but he only got one. One of the surviving soldiers lost a leg. And another one went crazy after that I heard.

On one of our patrols in 2005 we were on foot in Latifiyah, and we noticed some graffiti on the wall of a house warning people not to participate in elections. My captain asked me what it said, and I told him. So, he decided we should go knock on the door of that house. We knock. A man answers. I'm translating for the captain, who asks the man inside who wrote on the wall. The man says, I don't know. We heard that all the time—I don't know. No one ever seemed to know anything when we were out asking questions. The guy in the house was flip with us. He asked if he should be outside watching his wall all the time when the situation was so bad. He was complaining that he had not been able to work for two months because the situation was so bad. It was bad. Latifiyah was one of the worst areas for both insurgents and militias.

We talked to him for a little longer and then decided to go. As I turn to walk away, the guy says to me, If I ever catch you alone, I will kill you. I ignored him, pretending like I didn't hear at first. But then he went on. He said, I'm going to cut your head off from behind. I couldn't ignore that anymore. That was the first time I got really angry. I turned to face him. What did you say, motherfucker!? What the fuck did you just say to me? He said he was not talking to me, that he was talking to his son. Bullshit. I told the soldiers what he was saying, and they went to arrest him. Then the wife came in crying, and some old woman, and the kids, everyone crying, all this drama. They were begging us not to arrest him, saying he was a poor old man with nothing. The soldiers left it up to me whether or not to take him. In the end I left him there. He was just a normal guy for that area.

Sajad al-Hakim, who requested an alias out of concerns for his family's safety, continued working as a military translator with various units after his year at Forward Operating Base Falcon. He always concealed his work from all but his closest friends and family to avoid threats.

WISSAM AL-RASHIED

Born in 1977, he and his family were longtime residents of Sha'ab, a district north of Baghdad not far from Sadr City. He was pursuing a master's degree in software engineering in 2003 as the war began, going to class by day and doing computer repair and maintenance at night to earn money.

BOTH MY PARENTS had good educations in which they learned English. We spoke it a lot in the house, and I learned more on my own in school. My father always said, One day you will need this language. He was right.

An American patrol came to our neighborhood one day shortly after the invasion. They did not have an interpreter with them, so I volunteered to work with them. Our neighborhood was peaceful then. Militias had not really formed yet. They were too busy with the looting I guess to bother us then. The soldiers I worked with that day suggested that I apply to become a military interpreter at the Green Zone, so I did. I believe that it is my duty to help myself, help my family, and, if possible, help my nation. I was accepted, and by March of 2004 I was working with those same Americans I first saw in my neighborhood.

The base I worked at was called Forward Operating Base Gunslinger. It was in the north of Baghdad, not far from my home. There were only about nine hundred soldiers there and a few interpreters. A lot of interpreters just translate. I tried to help the soldiers understand Iraq better as well. I wanted to bridge the gap, if you will, between the two civilizations. I spent many nights trying to explain to the American guys Iraqi traditions and customs, why Iraqis act the way they do. There were still some misunderstandings. I had some trouble with the military terms. And there were other problems with translations. Once on patrol we went into an area, and the captain wanted to know if anyone had magazines, the bullet clips for automatic weapons. So I started asking everyone in Arabic in the area to bring out their magazines. They did. I collected a huge stack of old printed magazines and brought it to the captain, who was like, What the hell?

The income was very good, I have to admit. It was more than $1,000 per month, and that's good pay in Iraq. Also, I felt like I was doing something good. But the work was very dangerous. My worst nightmare was that killers would come for my family because of my work. If I die, okay, that's the job. But I worried for my family. I took a lot of precautions to conceal my work. I wore a mask when going on patrols and raids. I wore sunglasses with my mask so no one could see even my eyes. If you were ever caught, you knew you would be killed in some savage way, because you would be considered a traitor. These fanatics would do worse to an Iraqi than they would an American. They wouldn't blame an American soldier for being in Iraq because they would only expect it of him. But an Iraqi working with the Americans?

There was a female interpreter at my base. She had to be extra cautious, because she was a woman. You know, in Iraqi society there are a lot of restrictions on females. It is not acceptable for them to just be with soldiers, especially foreigners. But she was doing the work anyway. Only her sister and her mother knew about her work. She kept it very secret. Some other relatives of hers found out eventually, and they killed her.

We did an investigation at the base after she was murdered. We learned that the driver who had been taking her back and forth to the base for her work tried to sleep with her at some point. When she refused, he went to one of her cousins and told him everything about her work with the Americans. Then they made a trap for her. She apparently did not know that the driver had told her cousin anything and kept using him to go to the base. On one of the trips he stopped the car, saying he needed to do something with the engine, and then some in her family appeared and dragged her away. She was found with her throat cut in a remote area. The guy who discovered the body went through her pockets and found her military badges and brought them to the base hoping for a reward. Some soldiers went out and got the body and brought her to the base. I was one of the few interpreters who looked at the body to identify it. Most couldn't bring themselves to look. Seeing her there I could not help but think my turn was next, even as I was filling with sadness. We grew to be very close friends as interpreters, because you share such unique experiences. I had only known her about three months, but it felt like I had known her for thirty years. After a moment of looking at her body I could not take it, and I threw up. I had seen many bodies before that, but no one that I knew. That was the first friend I lost after 2003.

Wissam al-Rashied worked as a translator for U.S. forces for roughly two years before quitting. He later went on to pursue a doctorate in business administration.

***

SAIF MAJEED AL-TA'EE

He is thin with a dark, ruddy complexion. He is a dapper dresser and wears a fulsome, well-groomed mustache. He began working with U.S. forces as an interpreter shortly after they appeared in his neighborhood in 2003 and served off and on as a translator for many years before deciding finally to quit for good. He speaks smooth, quick English.

I WAS ON DUTY at the base one night when the unit I was assigned to got an emergency call to assist a patrol that had come under attack. Apparently

Shi'ite militiamen had shot at a passing Humvee convoy from a mosque, and we went to offer support. By the time we got there, the shooting had stopped, and no one was hurt. Everything was quiet, and the convoy that had taken the fire had left for some reason. So, that meant we needed to find out where the shooting had come from and if possible who had done it. It was a pretty routine deal. We had to search the buildings in the area and arrest anyone who looked suspicious.

There were only three structures in the area. There was this very large mosque. Across the street from the mosque was a largely abandoned apartment building. Adjacent to the apartment building was an open field. At the edge of the field was a small outpost used by the Iraqi security forces in the area, police and army. You know, this was the time when many in the security forces were working heavily with the militias. So, we could not really trust any Iraqi security forces in this area. And the patrol was not certain they had taken fire from the mosque. They might have taken fire from the building.

In any case, we went to search the building. Some Iraqi army guys had come along with us but did not enter the building. Inside, there was a family keeping watch over the building, and we began questioning them. An old man, a woman, and two young girls. They said that fifteen minutes before we arrived they heard shooting but did not know where it was coming from. That's what they all said. But in talking to them, I began to suspect that the gunmen had either shot from this building or shot from the mosque and were now hiding in the building.

I told the American captain that I thought the family was hiding something, and it turns out they were. Initially the family led us to believe that they were the only ones in the building. Then suddenly as we were talking a young man entered and sat down, and the old man pretended to have forgotten to mention there was someone else in the building. Then I noticed a pair of muddy boots that did not look like they belonged to the old man. So there was probably another man in the building we were not being told about as well.

I was getting worried. The guy who came in spoke a little bit of English, so I did not feel comfortable saying anything about all this suspicious behavior to the captain in front of him. So, I went down to the Humvees to speak in private with the soldiers about all this. In the time I was gone, the soldiers discovered someone hiding under the bed where the woman was sitting and arrested him.

On top of this, earlier when we first arrived at the building I saw someone on the street who seemed like he was digging by the curb. At first I did not think much about it. But now after all this other suspicious behavior in the building, I was wondering whether someone had been trying to plant a roadside bomb to go off on us as we left. I asked to see the guy hiding under the bed to see if maybe it was the same guy I saw fooling around in the road. He looked to be the same guy. I explained all this to the soldiers. They were annoyed with me for not mentioning earlier that I had seen someone digging and had me point out where the spot was.

Then the soldiers called in the bomb squad, and these two special vehicles designed for removing roadside bombs arrived and started working. In a short while they discovered that there was a bomb there, and they exploded it. The blast was big enough to break some windows around the area and bring some people into the street even though it was after one in the morning. After that things got quiet. The people who came out of their homes at the sound of the explosion went back inside. The Iraqi army guys with us went to the nearby outpost. And the people who we had been questioning in the building went to bed.

The soldiers decided they were going to stay there for the night. I don't know why. They don't tell me everything, I'm just the interpreter. So, they take the four Humvees and drive them into the open area. They park them as you would on the points of a compass or a cross, with all the fronts facing outward in order to keep watch around us. Behind the Humvees there's a space in the middle, and some soldiers took turns sleeping in shifts on the ground while others kept watch. I decided to get a little sleep. I took out my sleeping bag, found a spot on the ground, unrolled it and climbed in. I put earphones in and closed my eyes.

When I woke up, it was daylight. Six fifteen exactly. They were gone. I looked around for a second, wondering if it was a dream. It wasn't. They had left me alone there in the field sometime in the night.

I was terrified. From where I lay I could see the mosque, which might be housing gunmen. I could see the building where at least two suspicious guys had been. I could see the Iraqi security force base, where the people inside were likely involved in some way or another with the militiamen we knew were around in the area. In other words, any one of those buildings could have had someone in it willing to kill me. There I was alone, unarmed, and in U.S. military fatigues.

Luckily it was cold weather, and I had on a track suit beneath my fatigues. Without sitting up or getting out of my sleeping bag, I took off the fatigues and left on the track suit. I had been wearing U.S. military boots as well, and of course I had all my U.S. identification badges with me. I left all my identification and the boots with my fatigues in the sleeping bag and began walking through the field barefoot. I had to find a ride back to the base, but I could not risk being picked up by someone who might realize I was working with the Americans. I would be dead if the wrong person found me walking around there with U.S. badges and combat boots. It was bad enough that many people in the building had already seen my face, as I was working without a mask.

I tried not to be seen the best I could as I made my way across the field, and toward a main road there was some early morning traffic. I jumped out at the first car I saw and flagged it down. I told the driver I had been robbed and asked if he could please give me a ride.

The guy was nice and let me in. Naturally he offered to take me to the Iraqi security force base right there. No, no! I said. I want to go complain to the Americans. The guy started badmouthing the Americans, saying they were the cause of all the troubles and so on. He didn't quite understand why I would want to be dropped at an American base after being robbed but agreed to do so anyway. He was complaining more about the Americans, and I was agreeing with him, when suddenly we saw my patrol passing us on the other side of the road. I guess they had realized they had forgotten me and were going back to look. As the Humvees went by, the guy in the car started cursing them, You bastards! Fuckers! And I cursed them too. Both of us called them names as they went by.

Eventually after a lot of trouble I got back to the base and was let inside. I was really shaken up and spent much of the morning just trying to calm down. It seems kind of funny talking about it all now, but it was not funny that day. Not at all. I was shaking by the time I got back to the base. Really shaking. I had been working as a translator with the Americans for a long time. I had been on so many patrols, seen shootings and bombings, just like they had. And they just left me out there. I could have very easily been killed. They would have never forgotten one of their own like that.

I saw a bunch of guys from the patrol later in the day, in the mess hall eating lunch together. I walked up to them and said, Fuck you. Fuck you guys, I am never going out with you again. They all started apologizing and kind of laughing. They had heard I made it back okay and were thinking it was all kind of funny. I was not. I quit after that. Fuck them. Fuck. Them.

Saif Majeed al-Ta'ee became a flight attendant for a Turkish airline.

A Visit to the Temple

✳

HUSSEIN RADHI ZUBOON

He is a community leader among Iraq's Mandaeans, monotheists who believe in spiritual purification through ritual baptism. Mandaeanism is one of Iraq's earliest religions, predating Christianity. Adherents, who've lived mainly in areas of southern Iraq for roughly two millennia, look to John the Baptist as the faith's great teacher. According to Hussein, roughly 15,000 Mandaeans were living in Iraq at the time of the U.S. invasion. They were a relatively wealthy community. Many Mandaeans worked as goldsmiths. Criminals began targeting Mandaeans because of their wealth in the lawlessness following the U.S. invasion. Further threats came in later years because of their faith, as minority sects drew the attention of Islamic militants.

I WAS IN OUR MAIN TEMPLE one afternoon in the spring of 2007 with the head sheik of our order when three men visited. They were clearly conservative Sunnis by the way they dressed, and wanted to talk to us, the leaders of the temple. They were not armed as far as I could see, but they told us they were with the holy warriors fighting the occupation. They were very direct and did not take long to say what they had come to relate. They told us that they knew we were good Iraqis and would want to help our fellow countrymen in a time of need. They said they needed our support in their fight. We could offer either men or money. They were not asking. They were demanding. They said plainly that if we could not offer help to the holy warriors, then Hell's doors would open onto us.

We told them respectfully that we could not give them what they wanted. We don't believe in violence of any kind, so there was no way we could offer fighters. And because we're basically pacifists there is no way we could give money knowing it would fund violence, no matter what the cause.

They didn't like our answer, naturally. They began accusing members of our community of being involved in witchcraft and other evil practices forbidden by Islam. They said at the very least we had to call together a meeting of our congregation and tell those among them practicing black magic to stop. I argued with them a little bit, saying to call such a meeting would suggest that some Mandaeans were in fact doing such things, which was absurd. They did not budge on this last demand. Before they left they said we'd be dead if we failed to call the meeting or if we told anyone about their visit. And they promised to send spies among us to ensure we did as we were told.

Once they were gone I discussed what to do with our sheik. He was very scared. He had already been beaten up badly in 2006 by the Mahdi Army, who mistook him for a radical Sunni because of his long hair and beard. Now the actual radical Sunnis were visiting our temple with threats. He didn't want anything to do with any of it. He fled to Syria shortly after that visit, and I was left to deal with the situation.

I didn't inform the Iraqi government or the police. There was no point. All order had broken down at that point. I did inform the U.S. embassy, and American forces would sometimes visit our temple after that. That was the only help we could really hope to get, and it would not be enough to protect our followers. I decided to call a meeting as those men had demanded. I did not believe doing so would satisfy them enough to withdraw their threats, but I had to try. Roughly fifteen days after that visit I summoned about one hundred followers to the temple. I gave a speech saying that, if any Mandaeans had been tricked into believing superstitions and such that we should help them back onto the right path. In a roundabout way I delivered the message I was told to give by those men without directly accusing anyone of being involved in witchcraft.

I had only called males from the community to that meeting, but one girl appeared and slipped in. I noticed her and recognized who she was. She was the daughter of a family in our community who had married a man from Ramadi and converted to Islam. She and her husband had lived together in Ramadi for many years during Saddam's time, but had moved back to Baghdad shortly before the collapse. Throughout the meeting she was discreetly taking pictures and video with her mobile phone. I assumed she was the spy they had promised to send. Seeing her there for that meeting made me remember that I saw her hanging around the temple the day we were visited, too. I think she must have brought these men to us through ties of hers or her husband's back in Ramadi, which was a base for many Sunni fighters then. I didn't throw her out or anything. She was welcome to hear what was said. The followers who came to the meeting were told to spread the word among the rest of the community about the message as they left.

The day after the meeting we got word from these holy warriors. They called us and said they were satisfied with what we had told our congregation. They had clearly been listening either with this girl or some other way. We were left to believe after that call that we were no longer under threat. But of course you cannot trust such people. They are terrorists, killers. We knew they would still be after us.

Within a week of that meeting, three members from one family in our congregation were murdered together in their neighborhood. That was the first in a string of killings. Within a month fifteen members of our congregation were dead, all murdered. Also, around this time strange lists started appearing in different neighborhoods where members of our community lived. The lists had the names of people who were supposedly victims of black magic by Mandaeans. They were mostly Sunni names. I think they were fake. In any case the lists were meant to incite our neighbors against us, all of us. Our community had already suffered a lot before this episode. We had been heavily targeted because people wanted our money. But after this, things got much worse. We were now being publicly denounced by so-called holy warriors. It was open season on us. None of us could feel safe in Iraq anymore.

Hussein Radhi Zuboon saw the Mandaean community quickly dwindle as thousands fled the country shortly after the ominous temple visit by Sunni militants. Hussein remained in Iraq out of a sense of duty to lead the remaining congregation. As few as five thousand remained in Iraq as of 2009, he said. There was little hope of seeing the Mandaeans return in significant numbers. Hussein said most of those who had fled remained wary of coming home, as violence appeared to be rising in the summer of 2009 ahead of the U.S. troop withdrawal.

House to House

※

CAPTAIN EMAD

Married with six children, he was born in 1971, in Sadr City, where he has lived his entire life. During the last years of the former regime he served in the army as a radar technician. He was overjoyed at the downfall of Saddam Hussein, even as the family fell on hard times once his military job was lost. He sold household possessions and worked as a bodyguard to make ends meet until 2005, when he decided to join the Iraqi National Police.

A LOT OF MY FELLOW SOLDIERS from the old days were doing the same, rejoining the police or the army. Anyone looking around could see the country was clearly in so much trouble then. Iraq was falling apart, piece by piece, day by day. Things were getting worse and worse all the time. People like me with military experience had an obligation, I felt, to do something. We should not just let all our military expertise go to waste when the country is in such a situation. My primary goal, in all honesty, was to serve my country. I wanted to see the nation back on its feet. I wanted to be a part of that. I could not just sit and watch on the sidelines.

I signed up for the national police and joined a group of trainees stationed near Kut who got two months of basic instruction. The whole recruitment and training process was overseen by the Americans. It was good experience, even for those of us who had served in the military before. We were nine officers and about a hundred enlisted men in that training class. We learned new combat tactics like counter-insurgency strategy and got familiar with modern weapons.

After training, our unit operated in different areas of Baghdad for a while before taking a long-term post in Madayen, a small town just south of Baghdad. The place had been home to terrorists for a long time. Roadside bombs went off there two or three times a day for a time early on. We first got there in January 2007. I was a first lieutenant in a brigade of roughly 420 men. We saw a lot of fighting, and our brigade had a lot of martyrs as we tried to police the place. But perhaps the hardest day came when we went with only two platoons to raid a terrorist safe house in town.

That day was like any other, until about mid-afternoon. I made my rounds at various checkpoints, inspected my soldiers, the normal duties. Then suddenly a civilian showed up at our base near town. We had a good relationship with residents of the area, and occasionally they would supply us with intelligence about terrorist activities. This resident who came to us said he had heard that terrorists in the area were gathering at a certain house for a meeting that day. The purpose of the meeting, he said, was to plan an attack on our base. We trusted this guy. We had dealt with him before and found he had reliable information. So, we wanted to act on his tip and hit these guys before they hit us. It was a preemptive attack. We called the American unit in the area we often worked with and asked them to come, but we got word back that they were busy. They were on some other mission at that time, so we had to go it alone.

We decided we would strike at dusk, so we could get a view of the place in the last light of the day but then fight in the darkness, which was better for us. We went on foot. We decided not to take vehicles because a convoy would surely be spotted. We figured we had a better chance of surprise if we walked in. We took about thirty-five men. That was it.

The information we had said that all the terrorists would be gathered at a specific house owned by a known insurgent leader in the area. When we got near the place, we didn't rush right to it. We decided to first search some houses around it and leave some men in position. We quietly went through about ten homes before we approached the target house and left one or two guys in each of the houses we entered. In one of the houses we found a large amount of ammunition. No guns, just bullets. We grabbed them up, not knowing at the time what it meant. It was only after the battle that we figured what the enemy fighters had done; they had stashed bullets in several houses on this block, so they could fight house to house carrying only their weapons and not run out of bullets.

The target house where the meeting was supposed to be was empty when we burst in. Nothing. And the street outside was empty then too.

We had not seen anyone or anything suspicious except those bullets as we exited the house. That's when they opened fire. Fighters seemed to be everywhere all at once, in doorways, on rooftops, crouching in windows up and down the street. We all took cover. There was so much firing, none of us could get up. We were totally pinned. Looking around, counting muzzle flashes, I guessed there were at least twenty-five of them firing on us at once. They had roughly the same number of men we did but were in a far better position.

There was a new guy in our unit, a private named Hayder. He had transferred in just a short time before this. Hayder was young, just eighteen. But right away I noticed a sense of maturity about him. He was in every way an adult in how he handled himself among the other men, most of whom had known each other since training days. Everybody liked Hayder right away. He was quickly a favorite among a lot of us. He was one of those men everyone seems to like and respect right away.

Hayder was crouched with me and some others on one side of the road in front of the target house. Another group of men was crouched on the other side of the street. I was trying to figure out what to do, honestly. I was really concerned about running out of bullets. It was clear now what that stash of ammunition meant. I knew their bullets would outlast ours, and I was shouting to my men to conserve their ammunition. Don't shoot unless you think you can kill, I said. Suddenly, without saying anything, Hayder grabbed one of the heavy machine guns and dashed into the street, firing toward the rooftops. He didn't get far. All of the enemy fighters turned their guns on him, since he was the only one in the open, and they cut him down with an uncountable number of bullets. But in the few moments when all the guns were on Hayder the rest of us were able to lift our heads and see exactly where their positions were. Hayder's move unpinned us, and we were for the first time able to take the offensive. He must have known he would die before he stood up. I'm sure he understood that he would be giving his life to buy us those few moments. We were totally pinned down. Probably, if Hayder had not done that, we would have stayed pinned while they maneuvered in and finished us off. I think the other men understood all this too. As it was, Hayder opened the battlefield for us, and we all went into the street fighting all the harder so that Hayder's sacrifice would not be a waste.

The gunfire lasted for roughly two hours as we fought house to house. The terrorists, stupidly, actually helped us find them at some points in the battle. They would shout insults at us from their positions, calling us Shi'ite dogs and sons of bitches, things like this. We didn't mind the insults, because it let us know where they were hiding. In the end we killed six of them, wounded two, and sent the rest fleeing. They had good escape routes and got away quickly as the battle turned our way. They fled to the edge of the town toward the banks of the Tigris River, where they had hidden boats. They slipped across the river to the other side, where they could easily slip on foot into the southern outskirts of Baghdad. We saw some of them even swimming away.

We lost two other men besides Hayder in that battle. But the men took Hayder's death especially hard. Many of them were openly upset about it. I remember after the battle was over, we were searching the houses and came across the bodies of two of the terrorists we'd killed. One of my men became enraged looking at the corpses. He started firing into the remains. He emptied his gun into one lifeless body. Then he reloaded and turned it on the other corpses and began doing the same. He was hysterical with grief and anger. I had to stop him. It wasn't right to do that to a body. Such things are against Islam.

Captain Emad continued working in the Madayen area for about a year and a half. After that he began serving as an officer in the National Police in central Baghdad.

ZAHRA ECH'DAF SANGUR *AND*
FACKRIA ZUGAI'ER KHATA

The middle-aged women, who appear together for the interview wearing abayas, are longtime friends and neighbors in the Jihad neighborhood of Baghdad near the airport. Both are mothers to large Shi'ite families who lived in the mainly Sunni district for years before the invasion and remained during the period afterward for a time.

ZAHRA: My husband worked as a warrant officer for the police before the war, and he was able to rejoin the police again in time in the years after the invasion. The oldest of my four sons, Ryad, also joined the police force, and another boy of mine joined the new Iraqi army. The other two boys were working as day laborers in the years following the collapse. Our situation was good. We had three government salaries to support the family, and we were doing okay even through 2006 when things in Baghdad started getting bad because of the violence.

Jihad as an area was affected by the violence. We heard about killings and roadside bombs in the neighborhood. But our immediate area, our block and the ones around it, had not seen trouble even through the end of 2006. There had been no killings that we knew of, and only one family had moved. But we could tell this probably would not last. We could not remain safe forever as a Shi'ite family in such a place. We decided to go stay with relatives outside the city for a while, in Diyala province.

It was early December, and we had just settled with our relatives in Diyala when my husband got a call from a Sunni sheik in our neighborhood, Sheik al-Sali Hamdani. He lived close to us, just a few doors down. We had known him as a friendly neighbor for about nine years by then and never had any reason to be suspicious of him. There had been rumors around that time, however, that one of the sheik's sons, Tahar, had been involved in some sectarian killings. And about two months prior to this a group of armed men had driven through our neighborhood and passed close to our house before moving past the home of the sheik. Like a gang on patrol. Al-Sali was outside when they passed, and he waved. They fired two shots into the air, a kind of salute.

Al-Sali urged my husband to bring the family back from Diyala. He told my husband that something bad might happen to our house if we left it empty. My husband told him flatly that we had left because we were worried about our safety in the neighborhood. Al-Sali told my husband not to worry, that he would never let anything happen to us. My husband later told me that al-Sali said to him on the phone, Your sons are my sons. We decided to trust him and follow his advice to come home for the sake of our house.

We had been home for three nights when there was a knock at the gate leading to our front yard. Looking outside I saw four men standing there.

I knew them. They were from the neighborhood. I told my husband we had company, and he let them in. I made them some tea as we usually do for guests. They sat with us for a bit, asking if we were all okay and if everyone had come back with us from Diyala. They acted like they were concerned for us, like neighbors checking in. They even urged us to keep our boys off the roof. They sometimes go up there, but the neighbors said they shouldn't anymore because there was a sniper about. They finished their tea and left. I didn't think anything of it at the time, but I believe now they were sent by al-Sali to make sure we were all at home for what he was planning.

The following morning, a little before dawn, we were just beginning to get up when we heard a knock at the gate. I went to look, and there stood a party of what appeared to be about twenty heavily armed men. About half of them were wearing masks, and the others had their faces showing. I recognized Tahar among them, as well one of al-Sali's brothers. They said they wanted to come in and go up to the roof of the house to have a look around the neighborhood. We let them in, and they all went up the stairs to the roof. They came through the house respectfully and quietly, not threatening, as if they really did just want to take a quick look around, like neighborhood watchmen might.

We were all gathered at the foot of the stairs as they came down from the roof. When the last one of them was off the steps, all their guns suddenly went up at us, into our faces. They ordered my husband and our boys outside. In the yard they lined them up against the wall. One of the gunmen turned on a video camera, and some of the others started shouting, Allah is Great! Allah is Great! And then they opened fire. They cut them all down with a burst of gunfire. It all happened so, so quickly. I was in shock as I stood in the doorway watching it all. I remember seeing how one of my sons threw his arms up as the shooting started, and I saw bullets enter his hands and then his body. I remember seeing my husband running toward me through the gunfire. He was covered in blood even as he ran. At least three bullets entered his back as he came toward me, and he fell before he reached the door. I looked toward my sons again, and they were all on the ground. At least two of them were still alive but covered in blood. One of the gunmen then shouted, Finish them! You would not believe the amount of bullets they fired in that second burst.

She begins to cry but continues talking steadily and softly, standing at one point to show me how people were situated when the killing began.

There's no way I can describe what it was like to see what I saw then. How do you describe the sight of all your sons' arms, legs, faces, and bodies being cut apart right in front of you? As the gunfire died down I heard the killers screaming: Allah is Great! Rejectionists! Rejectionists! That's what Sunnis sometimes call Shi'ites. Rejectionists, for not believing in their version of Islam. They screamed as they left, all of them filing out the gate.

When they were all gone, I went over to where my sons were on the ground. I started yelling, Are any of you alive!? Is anyone alive!? And then very faintly I heard the voice of my youngest, Mohammed. He was nineteen at the time. Mohammed was murmuring, I'm cold. I'm so cold. I managed to drag him inside and get a blanket over him. He was breathing, but he was badly hurt. He had two severe wounds on his head and several on his arms and on his body. Blood was pouring out of him from everywhere. My husband as a police officer had kept a handheld radio for communicating with the police station in the house. I left Mohammad for a moment to go and find it. When I pressed the thumb button, I just started screaming.

FACKRIA: I could not hear the screams from my house, but I did hear the gunfire moments before. But there was a lot of gunfire around Jihad in those days. You heard bullets rattling every night usually, so I did not think much of it. It was a normal morning for us too in our house. My husband and I had eight children together, five boys and three girls. We were all in the house and getting up ourselves as usual when there was a knock on our gate. It was them. As I peered through the gate, one of the men said, We are searching for weapons. One of my sons, Hussein, came forward to open the gate for them. I told him not to, but he said it was okay to allow them to search. He took them to be guards for the neighborhood, I suppose.

Once inside they did the same thing. A group of them went to the roof, while a few remained downstairs. My three girls are small, and they were nervous at the sight of all these armed men in the house. A few of the gunmen tried to sooth me and my daughters, saying, Don't worry, it's just a search. Don't worry. We're all brothers and sisters.

After they had a look around the house, the gunmen turned to my sons and said, Okay, guys, let's go and talk outside. They said it in a nice, polite way, nothing threatening. My husband lingered inside. He had had a stroke a while back and was struggling to move and talk as he once did. As my boys stepped into the yard one by one, the gunmen started shoving them in a rough way. As soon as the last of my sons was through the door one of the gunmen stood in front of it to block my way.

I began to realize what was happening then, and I forced my way into the yard, leaving my husband inside. I began begging those men to leave us alone. I went around on my knees kissing their hands, telling them we are all neighbors, telling the young ones they were like sons to me. We are like family here in Jihad, I was saying. We will give you anything you want. What do you want from us? I recognized the ones without masks. They were all men from our neighborhood. One of them carrying a heavy weapon looked at me as I pleaded and said, If my own mother was a Shi'ite, I wouldn't think of her as family.

Once all the boys were lined up against the wall, one of the gunmen yelled, Brothers, start firing! My two youngest tried to run and actually made it out of the yard, but some of the gunmen chased them down and shot them just outside our house. My other sons fell in front of the guns together. The killers started calling to my husband to come out once all the boys were down, beckoning him. He remained inside, and they did not go in after him. They suddenly began rushing to go, and wound up leaving him alive.

I didn't know what to do when the gunmen left. I couldn't bring myself to touch my sons, because there was so little left of their bodies. They were just heaps of torn flesh, piles of brains, blood, and eyes. I was hysterical, and I started running toward Zahra's house. I found her there and saw it had happened to her too, and the two of us sat on the ground together screaming and beating our chests.

Zahra Ech'daf Sangur managed to get her injured son Mohammed to a hospital after the massacre. He survived despite severe injuries and made a full recovery. Zahra abandoned the house in Jihad that day without taking a single possession and settled with in-laws living on the northern outskirts of Baghdad. Fackria Zugai'er Khata also abandoned her home without taking anything the day of the attack. She managed to find the family a house to rent in Sadr City, where she settled with her husband and daughters. Both women were surviving on family support and charity as of May 2009.

Paths to Safety

※

MAYSOON MAHDI

A mother of three, she had worked since 1986 as an expert on livestock in the Ministry of Agriculture but was fired for alleged political dissidence in 1990. The entire family was blacklisted by the former government and struggled to survive financially through the years up to the invasion, which brought hopes of a normal life again for a time. The family home, however, sat in an area of northwestern Baghdad that grew notorious as a killing ground for Sunni militants during the ensuing sectarian violence.

I SAW MORE KILLINGS than I can count. There were hundreds of violent attacks in our neighborhood. Armed men would walk the streets freely every day. It became common to see random gunmen stopping cars in our neighborhood and abducting people. They would take out the passengers, blindfold them, and beat them there in the street. Then they would force those they had beaten into the trunks of cars and drive them away. A few days later the bodies of the people who had been stopped would turn up on the street. I would see these abductions happening around me three or four times a day, sometimes in daylight hours.

I even once saw a beheading in front of my house. My children came inside suddenly in the afternoon looking pale and frightened. When I asked them what was wrong, they said there was a man outside with a sword. I went to my roof and looked into the street. From there you can see the surrounding streets well. Down below, not far from the gate of my house was a group of masked men surrounding someone they had captured. One man had a sword. Another had a video camera and was recording, and several others were standing guard over the scene. As I watched the sword fell, and the captive lost his head. My children had come to the roof with me and saw it all too. They were horrified of course. I tried to calm them down, telling them not to worry, that we were right with God and nothing like that would ever happen to us.

Why did you continue to live in this area?

Where were we supposed to go? We didn't have another place to live or enough money to move away. And my husband and I mostly believed what I told my children. We were not involved in political parties or militias or anything like that, so we thought the violence would not touch us. It was all around us, but we didn't have anything to do with it. As long as we weren't involved in these political troubles, we figured we could remain safe.

I began working again in 2004 at a charitable foundation dedicated to helping poor Shi'ite families. I worked on promoting agriculture projects like increasing farmers' crops. But I wanted badly to return to the Ministry of Agriculture. So, in 2005 I began applying for a position. I needed to get some papers to one of the ministry's satellite offices in Abu Ghuraib as part of my application one day. I went that morning by myself to the office, dropped my paperwork off, and met with some people there. I had finished all my business a little before noon. It was slow in the office that day, and three ministry employees who also lived in Baghdad said they would go with me back to the city. The four of us went to catch a minibus at a nearby stop. In addition to me there was a woman from the office and two men, one junior official and a more senior one. At the stop we found our bus and got aboard. I went with the woman toward the rear, and the two men sat near the front. I didn't know any of them so well. They weren't friends of mine or anything. Just people from an office where I was putting in an application.

I don't remember anyone else on the bus besides us, so that would make five of us with the driver as the door closed. The bus never had a chance to move. Just as we were getting ready to go, two armed men in masks appeared at the door. They burst in, and the one in the lead took aim at the junior ministry employee seated ahead of me. The gunman looked ready to shoot him, but suddenly the one behind him shouted, No, the other one! So the first gunman hauled the junior employee out of his chair and forced him off the bus. Then he turned to the senior employee and shot him. Just like that. I don't know how many times the killer shot, but at least one bullet struck the senior employee's head. Blood and brains flew everywhere inside the bus. The seats were covered with it. I was covered. Then the gunmen got off the bus and left us sitting inside with the driver.

We sat there terrified not knowing what to do. We didn't know whether they would kill the driver or us next. They had seemed to be looking for that particular ministry official for whatever reason, but who knows what else they had in mind. It's hard for me to describe to you how those minutes went. It's difficult to remember because of the shock. But at some point I noticed that there were not just two armed men. Another four were with them outside the bus keeping watch. After a few minutes of being left alone inside the bus, the other woman and I guessed they did not intend to kill us too, and we figured we might be able to try and get away calmly. We considered going back to the office, then thought better of it. We decided to walk instead toward Baghdad and home and hope they would let us pass.

We stood together and walked out past the driver, who said he was staying with his bus to deal with the situation. He seemed to think he would be allowed to live. Climbing out the door and off the steps we found the gunmen still in their masks milling around. They were still holding the junior ministry official but appeared ready to let him go. We did not stop. We walked through them quickly, not knowing what would happen. Not one of them said a word to us, and we didn't look at them as we went. We kept our eyes straight ahead.

There is a verse in the Koran that is sometimes said when you wish God to keep you safe. It comes from a passage about walking the right path and goes, We have put a barrier before them and a barrier behind them and covered them over, so that they cannot see. The other woman and I both began saying this softly as we walked farther down the road, chanting it together. We did not know whether they would come after us or maybe just shoot us in the back as we went. Anything could have happened in those moments. But those men just watched us walk away.

Maysoon Mahdi and the woman she was with walked only a short distance on the road after the shooting before a passing car carried them both safely to Baghdad. She managed to rejoin the Ministry of Agriculture in December of 2005 and remained working there, mainly promoting chicken farms, as of April 2009. Her family was eventually forced to leave their longtime home under threat in 2007 and settle elsewhere in Baghdad.

❋

USRA J'BARA HADI

She is a mother of six sons and the matriarch of a Shi'ite sharecropper family who lived on a plot of land near Salman Pak, a rural area south of Baghdad. Date groves sprawl across the farmlands of the region, which became a haven for Sunni militants as violence rose across Iraq.

UNTIL 2006, there was no trouble in our area that I knew of. But then in June of that year the sectarian violence began to reach our community and touch my family. A cousin of mine was murdered. Someone just walked up and shot him as he was shopping in the market one day. There was no explanation for it. The killers were never captured. Then in July two young men from the farm next to ours were kidnapped while they were out working in the groves. They were Shi'ites too. I realized then that the violence had come to us, and we decided as a family to remain at home as much as we could and wait until, hopefully, things calmed down. I thought this period would last a short while and then pass.

In the weeks afterward things began getting bad in our area very quickly. A husband and wife from our village were killed together, and we heard about many more murders. More time passed, and our living situation got difficult because no one was working. The men stayed at home, because they could be killed at any moment if they went out. We had to have something to live on, though, so I started doing some farm work around the area. I thought as a woman I was less likely to be killed or kidnapped.

One day I had gotten some work harvesting dates at a nearby grove. I got up early to join a group of pickers who were supposed to be working together in the grove that day, three other women and two young boys. I was running a little late that morning and trailing behind the rest of the group as they went to the grove. When I arrived, I could tell there was something weird right away. The place was totally quiet. No one was in sight, even though the other workers should have been just a little bit ahead of me. I got scared and decided to go, but just as I was turning around a group of armed men popped out from hiding places in the bushes. I was trapped.

There were four of them, and they were heavily armed. One was even carrying a rocket-propelled grenade launcher. They ordered me to come with them deeper into the grove. I started begging them not to take me, saying, Look, I'm an old woman, you don't want anything with me for God's sake. One of them said to me, May God help you, now move. And then they forced me down the path. We walked for a while before coming to a spot between two farms where a little road runs. Sitting there was the rest of the group under watch by at least eleven other armed men. They seated me with the rest of the workers, and then the leader of the group, one the others called emir, ordered his men to bring a vehicle.

I thought we would be driven to another place to be executed. That's how it often happened. People would be kidnapped from one place and then taken to another location, where they would be killed. A minibus pulled up. All the chairs had been taken out except the driver's seat. There was a heap of blankets in the back. All the women started to cry at the sight of this, except me. I don't know why, but I was feeling very strong in that moment, and I stayed composed. One of the crying women, Um Mohammed, asked them where they planned to take us. One of the kidnappers replied, To the eyes of Hell. Then the gunmen huddled to discuss something just out of earshot from where we sat. I think they were debating whether to kill us there or drive us someplace else for execution.

They had seated us all together in a ditch along the side of the road with some branches overhanging it. From where we sat we could see them, but they did not have a good view of us. It was enough cover to make a run for it, and I decided to go. I told the others I was going to try to escape. They urged me not to, saying I would be shot. They were right. I knew I probably could not make it. But I wanted to try anyway, because if I were shot there while running at least my family would be able to recover my body. If they drove us away, we might just disappear. I wanted to be found if I died. I didn't want to just vanish. I took one final look at the men to make sure they weren't watching, and then I ran.

I made it to a nearby fence and hopped over without looking back. No shots came. Then I ran in the opposite direction of my house. I figured they would learn from the others in which direction I lived and try to trace me directly. I ran through three farms going in the opposite direction and then began circling back toward my home. Eventually I passed a house that belonged to the father-in-law of one of the women who had been kidnapped with me. I went up to the house and told all inside what was happening and where, and they quickly got together a group of about fifteen men with guns and headed in that direction. I collapsed from exhaustion and remained in the house as the rescue party set out. I learned later that the kidnappers fled as the rescue party approached, and everyone was freed.

In the weeks after that incident, our house started to come under attack on a regular basis. Gunmen would fire at our place with pistols and rifles, hoping to scare us off. They would creep to the edge of our land and shoot into the house. We would shoot back whenever they attacked, but the gunmen kept returning for more. It was the same for the houses around ours. Most of the families in the area lived like we did, in houses on small plots of land. There were about eighty such families who formed a kind of village around us. One of our neighbors lost two of their boys in an attack around that time. Another was injured. And people were disappearing all the time during this period. At least nine people from the group of houses closest to us vanished. I think there must have been more than fifty cases in all throughout the village in the months afterward. Most were killed and dumped into a river with their bodies found downstream from us.

These terrorists were trying to do whatever they could to displace us. There were Sunnis in our village as well, by the way. About half the families were Sunni and the other half Shi'ites. We all banded together against these terrorists, because they seemed to be out to kill just everybody. When we stayed, the terrorists brought in heavier weapons. They started firing mortars and anti-aircraft cannons at our house and others in the area. They had stolen these weapons from the police force after killing them off. Eight or ten people died in homes around us as the attacks grew more intense.

As the months passed we came to live in a state of siege in our own houses. We organized defenses and patrols for the village, and the fighting came daily. We were trapped there, and we were running out of food and ammunition. We were going to die unless we did something. We regularly called the police and the army to come and help us, but no one ever came. The Iraqi army was in the area, but we could not convince them to help us. Many families wanted to flee. I was against this and urged people to stay. This was our land, our home. We should not be chased away. At the same time, life was impossible. We needed the army or the police to come to the area and remain to ward off attackers. So, we decided to stage a kind of demonstration in order to demand security forces for our village.

Sometime in the fall of 2006, nearly a hundred of us walked together from our houses one day in a group, made our way to the main road and sat down in the middle. We could stop all the traffic through the area that way. We flagged down an army patrol, and soon the Iraqi commander for the area arrived to try to sort out the situation. They wanted us to disperse. We refused. We wanted the army to come right then in force and protect us. After a lot of arguing the commander split our group in two, with the men on one side of the road and the women on the other. He began talking directly to the men, and it seemed like they were negotiating some kind of solution. The commander was saying he needed some time to make arrangements for a full-time army presence in the area, and the men in our group seemed okay with a promise from the commander to return in three days.

I had heard enough. I crossed the road alone and in front of my father and my husband told the commander in essence, No way. You don't leave us here for three days. If you think we can stay safe for that long, then send your family to stay with us. At the very least, I said, if you are going to leave us today, give us your guns and ammunition so we might have a chance. And then I walked away from him. The commander followed me after a minute. When he caught up he said, Okay, where do you suggest I set up checkpoints? I suggested a spot, and he left six or seven men there that day.

Things were quiet for a little while after that, but it was not enough. The attacks started again on our plot and homes around us. The security forces were gradually overrun all across our area, and we had no choice but to flee. By December 2006, we were in Baghdad looking for someplace safe to live.

Usra J'bara Hadi and her family eventually settled in Zafaraniya, an area on the southern outskirts of Baghdad that became home to many displaced Shi'ites. The family was living off the earnings of a makeshift stand selling snacks and cigarettes as of May 2009.

The Face of a Savior

※

ALI MOHAMMED HIAL

He is from a Shi'ite area of northwestern Baghdad. He has a handsome face, the kind of good looks you see in the leading men of movies playing on television sets around the Middle East. His left arm is missing, and his right hand is badly scarred with burns. What's left of the skin is so papery thin you can see the bones of his hand moving as he gestures.

I WAS WORKING at a vegetable stand before the war. Things were okay for us then. We were four brothers and four sisters, ten of us altogether including my mother and father. Everybody in our family was financially okay, you could say. As the war drew nearer, we were all happy inwardly even so to see the end of that regime, which had been like living with something heavy on our souls and hearts.

The years after the invasion were not good for us financially, however. By 2005, working at the vegetable stand was not enough to live on. I had married, and my wife and I were raising three young children in a rented house. So I decided to volunteer as a fireman. I went to apply one day in April of that year. I woke up that morning wondering whether I would be accepted or not. My whole family had been praying for me, because it was difficult to find work at that time. We really needed the money.

I went by taxi with two friends from my neighborhood to the recruitment center in Khadra, a bit south of our area. We left early and were there by nine in the morning. We all filled out forms and sat for interviews. I was told on the spot that I would be accepted. I was supposed to report back and get ready to attend a training course in the United Arab Emirates.

All three of us were heading back to the neighborhood together around three in the afternoon. Two of us got out at the edge of the neighborhood. My friend Abid and I lived near each other and decided to walk home together and let our other friend take the taxi the rest of the way. As Abid and I walked into our area together, we heard an explosion and saw flames and smoke rising. A car bomb had gone off about one hundred meters from us. We rushed to help. At the site of the blast, we saw a woman lying on the ground, all her clothes on fire. Abid went to her and tried to put the flames out. I ran toward a minibus burning in the street. There was a kid in the back, maybe three years old. He was on fire but looked alive. I tried to open the door of the bus but could not. So I grabbed something off the ground, I cannot remember what, and smashed open the window. I managed to reach inside and grab him.

He was in fact alive. I felt his pulse as I gathered him up. Inside the bus many of the passengers were on fire, and everybody else appeared to be dead. I pulled the kid close to me and began moving away.

Suddenly the police started screaming: Another car bomb! Another car bomb! I turned my head. About five meters away from me I saw a red Volkswagen Passat. Smoke was starting to pour out of it.

I cannot say exactly what happened next, because the explosion knocked me out. The next thing I knew I felt myself on the ground. Smoke was everywhere, and my side was on fire. I could barely move. I looked down and did not see my arm, and there was nothing left of the child's body. Only his head remained, and I was cupping it with my right hand as I had been when the second bomb went off.

I blacked out. Moments later I was awake again and able to look around. There were body parts on the ground all around me. The child's head was there, very close. I had dropped it I guess when I fainted the moment before. I wanted to push it farther away from me. I wanted to get it away. I tried to, but I couldn't. My good arm was too badly hurt to work properly. Then I fainted completely. I don't remember any more moments from the street. The next time I woke up I was in the hospital. I later learned Abid had died in the second blast.

When I think back on it now, I realize I was saved by the kid. His body absorbed most of the blast. I wound up with a lot of small pieces of shrapnel in my body. But his body took all the big pieces, which is why it was dismantled. That kid saved me, even though I was trying to save him. I never learned who he was or anything about him. I'll never know. A lot of minibuses pass along that road carrying people from all over. I can still remember clearly looking into his face as I lay there on the street. The image comes to me sometimes now when I put my head down on the pillow.

After a long and difficult recovery, Ali Mohammed Hial established a nongovernmental organization dedicated to helping civilian victims in 2006.

Waking Up

SHEIK HAMID AL-HAIS

By 2006, insurgents under the banner of al-Qaeda in Iraq controlled whole swaths of territory in Anbar province, which covers Iraq's western deserts. Dozens of tribal sheiks in the province had supported the insurgency either passively or actively in the years since the U.S. invasion. But turf wars and other disputes caused friction between many of the Anbar sheiks and the insurgents, whom the sheiks referred to simply as al-Qaeda even though Iraqis, not outsiders, made up most of the insurgent ranks. Sheik Hamid al-Hais is a tribal leader with land just outside Ramadi, which in 2006 was effectively occupied by insurgents who came to consider al-Hais an enemy to their cause. He was among the first of the Anbar sheiks to take up arms against insurgents in the province and was a founding member of the original Awakening, a band of tribesmen who began fighting alongside U.S. forces against insurgents in the latter part of 2006.

AL-QAEDA STARTED HANGING BANNERS saying I was a collaborator with the Americans and the new Iraqi government, and soon after that they tried to kidnap me. It was May of 2005, and I was on the road just outside Ramadi when we were ambushed. There were five of them with a vehicle, and they managed to force our car off the road. They pulled us all out of the car and disarmed my bodyguards, who were let go along with the driver. But they began pulling me toward their car. They meant to take me. I had managed to keep a pistol on me hidden, and I decided to try and shoot my way out rather than get in the car with them. I knew what was coming if I was driven away. They would behead me. I figured it was better to die there on the road than under one of their swords. So, I drew the gun and started firing at the two men closest to me. I managed to kill them both before the other three could act. In the shooting that followed I managed to kill one more and badly wound a fourth. I took four bullets myself and fell to the ground with blood all over me. The two survivors left, thinking I was dead.

After that incident, al-Qaeda began targeting my family, abducting and killing people related to me. And we began doing the same toward them in retaliation. They would abduct and murder someone from my family, and then we would go and capture a fighter of theirs and kill him. Every day was a life-or-death struggle with these people in that time. It kept going like this for months. I lost eight members of my family this way, including my brother. No matter how many of theirs we killed there was no solution. There was no peace to be had. Either you armed yourself and fought or you and your family would be slaughtered. The killing just seemed to go on and on. There was no end in sight. Finally we decided to get more organized and form a proper armed group so that we might kill them off or drive them out.

Initially there were around ten of us sheiks in my area who got together to discuss forming an alliance against al-Qaeda. We managed to form a group of about fifty people willing to fight. I have a farmer on my land who has two sons. His boys became part of my fighters along with others we gathered. With fifty fighters, we were able to secure our homes. Gradually we were able to start establishing checkpoints on some of the roads, just as al-Qaeda did in areas they controlled. We were holding some ground, in other words. As we started to hold ground, more people began to step forward supporting us. Our numbers grew, and soon we began to go on the attack against their hideouts. We started raiding their safe houses and kidnapping the fighters we found there. We decided we would kill them just like they killed us. We dressed like them, wearing all black and masks. We used the same kind of cars they used when we came. We were going to slaughter them. That was our goal, because we knew they would do the same to us. We even used roadside bombs against them. Why not? We would terrorize them. They never thought anyone would do to them what they did to others.

The first major battle we had with them was in a village not far from my land. The insurgents had taken over a clinic and were using it as a base. We surrounded the clinic and torched the place. Al-Qaeda fighters started jumping out as the flames rose. As they ran, we cut them down. I don't know exactly how many we killed that day, but I can assure you it was a lot. A lot. By May or June of 2006 we were getting some financial support from the Americans, who had heard of what we were doing and wanted to help. The Americans had tried to work with a lot of different tribal leaders in the area for a long time. Many of the sheiks they had dealt with since 2003 had taken the money offered to them and fled the country. We were willing to stay. Our fighters needed salaries, however. The Americans began offering each of our fighters $300 per month and we added to that $200 per month.

We fought like outlaws, and that's why we began to beat them. America is a country of laws. You have to abide by the law if you're an American, even if you're an American here in Iraq. We were not bound by any laws in the fight we started with al Qaeda. If the Americans found people from al-Qaeda, they arrested them. We killed them. That's the difference. That's why we were able to start defeating al-Qaeda in a matter of months where the Americans had struggled to beat them for years. These people, al-Qaeda, are not human. You cannot deal with them according to laws. The law is for people who make mistakes but can be reformed. These people cannot be reformed. There's no cure for these people. The only way is to kill them.

I would say my group killed more than 300 al-Qaeda fighters in the first year of the Awakening throughout Anbar province. Another 300 gave themselves up to us. I wish I had killed more, believe me. I've wanted to kill them all since the day my brother was murdered. That was in May of 2006. I don't want to talk about how he died. But I'll tell you that from then on I was out to kill as many of them as I could. I was ready to kill them even if I would wind up hanged for doing so. I could kill a thousand of them, and it would still not be enough for me.

Sheik Hamid al-Hais remained a central figure in the Awakening movement through February of 2009, when the interview was conducted in Baghdad. He was visiting the capital often then and planning to go back to school to get a master's degree in political science. He already held the equivalent of a bachelor's in criminal justice.

SHEIK AHMED BUZAI ABU RISHA *AND*
SHEIK ABDUL SATTAR ABU RISHA

The two brothers formed a center of gravity for the burgeoning Awakening movement. The younger Abdul Sattar perfectly played the part of a swaggering Arab chieftain. His older brother Ahmed earned a reputation among U.S. commanders who worked with the tribesmen of Anbar as being the brains behind the leadership of the Awakening. Both spoke with Time at the Abu Risha compound just outside Ramadi in December of 2006, when the Awakening was beginning to have some success against insurgents.

AHMED: The reason why the movement started was because al-Qaeda was intimidating the people and interfering in their daily lives. They began killing our sheiks, killing our teachers, killing our people. Civilian life stopped. So, we decided to reach out to the various sheiks in Anbar and try to turn them against al-Qaeda.

There are thirty major tribes in Anbar. Initially we approached eighteen tribal leaders, hoping to bring them to our side. We reached out to them individually in May of 2006. We drew up a list of all the crimes al-Qaeda had done to our people and put that to the sheiks we contacted. We also drew up a list of what the Americans had done to our people. They had been trying at least at building the country since they came. We wanted to further that endeavor. And the Americans had a plan to get rid of al-Qaeda that we all might join. Fifteen agreed with the way we were thinking. That left seven tribes who were with al-Qaeda, and about eight who were neutral or sitting on the fence as we called the conference together in September of 2006. At that meeting, all the sheiks publicly declared their tribes to be at war with al-Qaeda, and that's how it began.

Why did it take three years for some tribal leaders to break with al-Qaeda?

AHMED: Al-Qaeda claimed in the beginning they were defending Islam, and people believed them. But the true Muslims began to see that Islam was under attack not from the occupiers but from al-Qaeda. Crimes against the country were being committed in the name of Islam by al-

Qaeda. They were ruining the country in the name of Islam. The real Muslims knew this was a danger to the whole religion. The sheiks gradually came around to this idea, and that's how we got to where we are.

When we told the Americans about what we were doing, they seemed really excited. They were ready to help. Al-Qaeda was preventing anyone from joining the police at that time. Anyone who joined the police would be captured and beheaded. So, we first tried to get a new police force ready from among our tribesmen with help from the Americans. We rounded up 4,000 police volunteers from men in our tribes. The various tribal leaders each brought recruits by the hundred.

How did you get so many?

AHMED: You have to understand how a tribe is formed. A tribe at the center is a family and those loyal to it. It's a family network. And the sheik stands as the most trusted person in that network. That's why they call him a sheik. He should be a moral man. His credibility comes from his morals, and when he has that people listen to him. They will obey him. They'll do what he says. They trust that he has their best interests in mind. These are old traditions. This is our culture.

The men who answered the call to volunteer from the sheiks had different backgrounds. Some had been police before. Some of them were uneducated and jobless and needed the work. Others had jobs, like driving trucks back and forth to Jordan, and they quit in order to fight al-Qaeda. There were some shepherds who signed up. Educated men who held law degrees volunteered to fight as well. All sorts came to volunteer. There were many people who were earning more in their regular job than we could pay them as policemen, and they joined anyway. They came because of the tribal ties and because the situation had gotten so bad that they wanted to fight.

Some say the Americans drew al-Qaeda to Iraq by invading. Do you blame the Americans for the presence of al-Qaeda even though you are now working with them?

SATTAR: Yes, they are to blame. The first thing the Americans did when they entered Iraq was to disband the Army. They opened up the borders and allowed people to come in. They did not work with us, the people, in the beginning. Al-Qaeda was able to come in and gain influence with the people instead. I don't think there is any American who can deny that, because that's the truth.

Sheik Ahmed Buzai Abu Risha emerged as the senior leader of the Awakening movement after assassins killed Sheik Abdul Sattar Abu Risha in September of 2007. Sheik Sattar died in an explosion near the family compound just ten days after he met President Bush, who posed for pictures alongside Sheik Sattar during a brief visit to Iraq.

SHEIK MUSTAFA KAMIL HAMAD SHABEEB AL-JABOURI

He was a retired brigadier general as of 2003, living on family land in Arab Jabour, a predominately Sunni rural area south of Baghdad where some of the earliest resistance to the occupation took shape. He appears for the interview in business attire but carries a long-barreled Smith & Wesson .38 revolver tucked into the waistband of his pressed gray slacks. He thumbs orange prayers beads as he talks.

IT'S OUR RIGHT AS IRAQIS to fight occupiers. In the beginning it was a clean, honest resistance movement among the men from Arab Jabour. Our only aim was to fight American troops, not Iraqis. I believe even the American troops respected that. We were honest men trying to defend our country from invaders. We simply did not want foreign troops on our lands.

To tell you the truth, I did not participate directly in the early resistance movement. I couldn't. The U.S. troops based in my area knew quite well I was a former general and a tribal leader and someone likely to be involved in insurgent activity. They had come one day to my land early on and confiscated my old uniforms and some guns I had. After that they kept coming back for searches. I lost count of how many times they came to my land. More than three hundred. Sometimes they would come twice a day, once in the morning and once at night. Sometimes a few soldiers would stay overnight on my land, watching my house and listening with their instruments. I knew who the resistance fighters in the area were, it's true. One of their commanders had actually served under me in the army for a time. I respected them and what they were doing. And I would have probably gotten more involved if I had not been so closely watched by the Americans. As it was, I kept my distance.

In 2005 the resistance began to change. It grew corrupted by outsiders and fanatics, people who were totally opposed to any involvement with the new government. Many Iraqis like me did not like the occupation but knew there was no going back at the same time. We could not drive off the occupiers and bring back the old government. Nor should we. The country needed something new. I was eager to support a new government, but I wanted the invaders gone at the same time. So, I was encouraging toward people in my family and my tribe who wanted to get involved in the new government even while being sympathetic to the insurgents. But fighters with al-Qaeda in Iraq hated the government and the occupation all the same, and they began killing any Iraqi from our area who took an official job.

Around the middle of 2005, it seemed like anyone who tried to go to work for the government wound up killed. So many men from Arab Jabour wound up murdered soon after they found work as a policeman or a traffic cop or a bureaucrat at some government agency. When that began happening, we knew the honest resistance was gone. It became clear that al-Qaeda fanatics had taken over the movement. The insurgency had become something else.

In October of 2006, one of my nephews was murdered. He had been working as an investigative judge at the Ministry of Justice. Gunmen had dragged him from his car one day and shot him execution style in our area. Two others with him managed to get away, and there were a number of witnesses around too. Within hours we were able to figure out who was likely behind the killing. It's a tribal society and a very small community. Everybody knows everybody. People talk. It was al-Qaeda. That was clear from the start. And within a few days we were able to get the name of the guy who pulled the trigger.

I sent four men to get this guy and bring him to us. Our four wound up killing that guy and wounding three other al-Qaeda fighters in the process. This was the first time anyone from Arab Jabour dared to challenge these people at all, and they were enraged. Very soon we got a demand from them. They wanted us to hand over the four men of ours involved in the incident for a trial in one of their Islamic courts. Al-Qaeda would just execute them if we agreed, so we said no way. Then we knew it was just a matter of time before they attacked.

About fifty tribesmen and family members of mine gathered on my land, and we formed defenses. I broke up the fighters into groups of three and four and put them in positions around the farm. We set up some ambushes and dug ourselves in very well. We did not have to wait long. They came the next day with more than a dozen vehicles and I would guess about 1,000 men. It was a real battle. There were a lot of them, and they had heavy weapons like machine guns mounted on trucks and mortars. We dealt them a heavy blow with our men on the main road as they approached, and the fighting went on from there for about three hours.

They started lobbing mortars toward the main house on my land where I lived. More than eighty fell on or around the house. Some of the mortars were badly aimed, however, and went in the direction of the American base about ten miles from my land. I guess the Americans thought they were being shelled, because suddenly they sent up a bunch of helicopters. The helicopters came swooping low over the area, scaring the hell out of the al-Qaeda fighters who all started running immediately. They abandoned many of the vehicles they brought and ditched weapons in the bushes as they fled.

The American helicopters did not shoot, however. I don't know why, but they did not fire a shot at anyone. I wish they had. They could have destroyed all their vehicles and practically wiped out the al-Qaeda contingent in the area. Instead they just roared over the area and then went away again. That was the beginning, though, the moment when we all realized that al-Qaeda had to be destroyed—and that the Americans could help us do it.

In May of 2007, Sheik Mustafa Kamil Hamad Shabeeb al-Jabouri met with U.S. and Iraqi commanders in Baghdad and struck a deal similar to the one the original Awakening leaders had made with U.S. forces in Anbar province in 2006. He said he survived more than fifty assassination attempts as he continued to battle al-Qaeda in Iraq fighters in his area with backing from U.S. forces.

✳

AHMED BASIM MOHAMMED AL-ABAJE

He's a Sunni born and raised in the central Baghdad neighborhood of Mansour. He made a living as a salesman for furniture and cars before the invasion and through the occupation until sectarian violence in his neighborhood got so bad he considered fleeing the country.

BY 2007 the violence in our neighborhood was so bad that people were afraid to be in the street even late in the afternoon. Just before dusk the streets would empty. You could not even see a dog or a cat in the open. My wife and I could not take it anymore, so we decided to go to Syria for a month to get a break from the situation and see if perhaps there was a way to live outside the country. I really didn't know how long we would be gone when we left in July 2007.

Not long after we got to Syria a friend of mine from the neighborhood called me and said the Americans were planning on forming an Awakening movement for our area. I had heard about the Awakening movement in Anbar province and what they had been doing there. Every Iraqi had heard of Abu Risha. You know, he was a wealthy man. He supposedly spent most of his time in the United Arab Emirates. He did not need to pick a fight with al-Qaeda. But he decided to do something for the country. So why shouldn't I? That was my thinking as I went back to Baghdad. I thought I would try it with the Awakening for a while to see if the situation improved.

I was very scared about the whole thing. The Americans had just established a combat outpost very near my house, and I knew signing up for the Awakening would probably involve coming and going from there. Anyone could see you. Our neighborhood was still mixed, with Sunnis and Shi'ites. Both the Mahdi Army and al-Qaeda operated in the neighborhood. Either one might come to kill you for working with the Americans.

By August the Americans were patrolling the area and reaching out to younger guys from the neighborhood like me. Just a few days after I got back from Syria I ran into an Iraqi interpreter who worked with the

Americans. Like most interpreters, he went by a nickname in public, Z. I was told by Z to get ready to join if I was willing, and he took my contact information. Pretty soon Z passed me on to a guy from the neighborhood the Americans had designated as a recruiter, Faris. I was told to put a file together containing all my information. Faris and Z told my friend and I to collect files from any others we knew who might like to join as well. We put together our own files and gathered others in secret through September. Then one day in October my friend and I went to Faris's house to hand over the files. We had collected more than one hundred.

I have to be honest, handing over those files to Faris then was scary. Faris had a good reputation as a secular Shi'ite, but we did not know who else would be looking at them. They contained everything about us. If someone from the Mahdi Army or al-Qaeda saw them, they could come to kill us so easily. A lot of us volunteers were really terrified wondering what might happen if we were found out. The neighborhood was still very unsafe then.

After handing over the files we waited as the Americans vetted the names of the volunteers. From what we heard, Faris and other Iraqi recruiters approved by the Americans for the area were discussing names of volunteers with local elders whom they trusted. If anyone was suspected of being involved with militias or insurgents, his name was thrown out. For example, we handed 124 files to Faris. He passed on 90 to the Americans, who checked the names in their system and ultimately approved 75.

In January of 2008, Faris got in touch with me with the names of 75 men from my immediate area. He told me to call them up and get them ready for training. I had been cleared as an officer, it turned out. Regular Awakening volunteers were getting $300 a month. Officers got $360.

Training was just two weeks of lessons in arms and basic police practices. Most of the guys didn't need it, since so many of us had been in the army in the years before the invasion. But a few of the younger guys got some good out of it. After training we went home and waited for orders. We were to begin setting up checkpoints at entrances to the neighborhood and go on patrols when the Americans gave the word.

I got my first threat even before the first orders came. It was a call to my landline. I picked up the phone one afternoon when it rang and heard someone switch on a recording. A voice read some verses from the Koran and then said, We know you are working with the infidel occupiers. Unless you quit, you will be killed. I called Z immediately and told him what had happened. He told me to relax, that the Americans didn't think the threat was very serious and to be ready to go about things as normal.

Not long after that we got our first orders. I led about twenty men in setting up a checkpoint at one of the entrances to my area. We stopped cars and pedestrians coming and going, searching and checking people's identification badges. At the same time, another group of us joined an American patrol through the area. You could feel a difference in the street immediately on that first day we all went out together. All the tough guys in the neighborhood with al-Qaeda and the Mahdi Army who used to swagger around acting powerful realized very quickly there was a new force in the streets.

Ahmed Basim Mohammed al-Abaje luckily faced no major confrontations with insurgents or militiamen in his neighborhood through 2008 as sectarian violence dropped. He remained serving as an Awakening volunteer as of April 2009, when the interview was conducted in Baghdad.

Laughing to Bucca

RA'AD JAMAL HABIB

Before the war he was a long-haul bus driver doing routes all over Iraq from Baghdad, where he has lived all his life. He continued working as a driver for hired cars running convoys between Baghdad and Damascus after the collapse, traveling the dangerous highway route through Anbar province on a regular basis beginning in the summer of 2005. In August of 2007, U.S. forces raided his home in northern Baghdad at night and arrested him. U.S. troops, often working with Iraqi security forces, at that time were arresting thousands of Iraqi men in an effort to thin the ranks of Shi'ite militias and Sunni insurgents. Most wound up in Camp Bucca, a U.S. military detention facility that was then the largest in the world. U.S. officials acknowledged that many Iraqis were likely detained

wrongly but considered the extrajudicial arrest sweeps necessary to quell vio-
lence. The average stay for an Iraqi in Camp Bucca was one year. Ra'ad Jamal
Habib was imprisoned from August 7, 2007, to September 25, 2008, according to
U.S. military documents handed to him as part of his release papers. He brings
the documentation to the interview.

I HAD BEEN IN BAGHDAD for about three weeks, which was rare for me.
Normally I was only at home for a night or two between trips to Syria.
But the car I normally drive was in for repairs. So I was mostly just at my
house, where I was living with my mother, father, three of my sisters, and
my brother.

On the night of the raid it was very hot, and I went to the roof to sleep.
It's cooler up there. I was alone when, at about half past two in the morning, I heard an explosion. It woke the whole house up. I called down to
my mother asking what happened. She yelled back up that it was probably just a roadside bomb going off somewhere. There had been a lot of
sectarian violence in our neighborhood. I had not seen incidents, because
I was gone so much. But there had been a lot of killing, and things like
roadside bombs had become common. So, I lay back down. Moments after
that, I opened my eyes and saw what looked like the entire American army
standing over me. U.S. soldiers were all over the roof, along with some
Iraqi soldiers. Apparently the explosion we heard was them blowing open
the gate to our house, and in the time it took me to go back to bed they had
rushed upstairs. I said to one, Yes? He pushed me over and tied my hands
behind my back and then sent me toppling down the stairs.

Downstairs another of them asked me through an interpreter, Do you
have a motorcycle? I did have a motorcycle, a very beautiful Kawasaki I
loved. I told them so. They led me into the street. I was only in my under-
pants. They picked up a dirty rag from the road and used it as a blindfold
on me. I felt myself being put into the back of a pickup truck.

Sometime later the truck came to a stop, and I was taken off the back
of it and placed in a room, where I remained blindfolded and bound. I was
there for three hours before someone came in and undid the blindfold
and the hand ties. I was handed some clothes taken from my house. My
mother had given the clothes to the soldiers as they were taking me away
in my underwear. I was told to put the clothes on. After I did I was bound
and blindfolded again.

I was led to another room, this one packed with people. I could feel people everywhere around me. I could not even open my legs without touching someone else as I sat. I managed to peek a little out from under the blindfold with my left eye. I could see people packed together in the room like sardines, sleeping curled up against each other all over the floor. I whispered to the guy closest to me, Why are you here? He told me that he had gone shopping. Outside the store he was loading groceries into the trunk of his car when all of a sudden he was grabbed by soldiers. Like me, he was not told why he was being arrested and did not seem to know. I asked him how long he had been in the room. He said three days. We didn't manage to say much else to each other, because one of the American guards came over and pushed me when they heard us talking. He said, in broken Arabic, No talking, head down. I have to tell you I was really worried. We had all seen the pictures of the abuse of Iraqis at the Abu Ghuraib prison. I didn't know what they would do to me. Anything could happen. You are in their hands. They could do anything to you. And they had been treating me very badly from the moment they took me. My back was hurt when I was pushed down the stairs. They kept pushing me when I was blindfolded, telling me to hurry up. How can I hurry up when I can't see? I was in that crowded room for at least two days and fed only bread and water.

Then very late on the second night of staying in that room an American soldier with a translator came and got me off the floor, led me to a small room, and sat me down on a stool. I was still bound and blindfolded as he talked to me through the translator. The soldier said to me, Sayed Munder, confess what you have done. I said, That's not me. I am Ra'ad Jamal Habib. He said I was not who I said I was and that I had forged my identification documents. I told him that he could very easily check who I was. They clearly knew where I lived. They had been through my house and had all my documents. There was a moment of silence, then the questions started.

The soldier asked, Where are the rocket-propelled grenades? I told him I didn't know anything about any such weapons. I'm not a military man. I was never in the army. He said, How can you not know since you are the one who attacked us with them? I said to him, Look, I dodged my military service during Saddam times. I have never wanted anything to do with fighting. The soldier started saying a list of names to me, asking me if I knew any of them. I didn't. He said, How could you not know them, since they are Mahdi Army just like you? I said, Man, I didn't serve in the regular army. Why the hell would I serve in the Mahdi Army? There was a really long silence. I had only heard the voices of the interrogator and the translator, but I could feel other people in the room. I cannot say for sure, but it seemed like at least two or three others were in there watching the questioning.

Then the translator said to me, Why did you just swear at me? I said, What are you talking about? I didn't swear at you. He said, I just heard you say something nasty about my sisters. And then he slapped me so hard I fell off the stool. I started crying. They got me off the floor and led me back into the crowded room.

The next day I was put in the back of a Humvee and driven to another detention facility near the airport. There I fell in line with a group of prisoners being processed for Bucca. Neither the guy in front of me nor the guy behind me knew why they had been arrested. None of us had a chance to talk much. Any time we spoke we were told to be quiet by American guards. A female translator went over a list of prisoner rules with us. I asked her what I had done. She said she didn't know, that I would probably find out the charges later.

Altogether I was at the airport camp for eight days. After that first day there I spent most of my time in a small hold with about six other prisoners. No one knew what the charges against them were. All the arrest stories were more or less the same. People going about their normal daily lives suddenly surrounded by soldiers and taken away. We were laughing, actually. Because that was exactly how Saddam used to do it. We used to hear about how America was a democratic country, a free country, that would never suppress people. I found the opposite to be true.

I was interrogated two more times in those days. They kept asking me where the rocket-propelled grenades were and about people I supposedly knew in the Mahdi Army. I said to them, Look, there is not an inch of my passport that does not have a stamp on it from coming and going across the border. I am a driver, and I am almost never in Baghdad. How could I have possibly been involved in militia activity in Baghdad if I was always on the road back and forth to Syria? I said yes, it's true, there is Mahdi Army in the neighborhood where I live. Everybody knows that. But I had never had anything to do with them. They didn't believe me. They told me I was a liar and that I would be going away for a long, long time.

Late one night guards came into my hold and took me, just me, out. There was another guy with them from another hold, and they took the two of us to a far corner of the base in a minibus. We drove a long way. I thought for a moment that they were going to let us go. It seemed like they were driving us to the gates. Instead the minibus pulled up to a building where soldiers were waiting. Two led us into a room and told us to strip. I was thinking of Abu Ghuraib as I took my clothes off. We stripped to our underwear. They told us to take that off too, but we both said no. We're people from the East, you know. It's not in our culture to just take off our clothes like that. We were told again to take off our underwear. When we didn't, one of the soldiers came and shoved me hard against the wall. Both of us started crying. We were terrified and humiliated. There was nothing we could do. We took off our underwear. The looked us over like a medical exam. We had to lift our testicles for them. They made us bend over so they could look up our anuses. Then we were given yellow jumpsuits and put into a room where there were roughly eighty other prisoners dressed like us, waiting to be flown to Camp Bucca. When it came time to go, they loaded all of us into the belly of a huge cargo plane. They lined us up and seated us on the floor of the plane with our backs against the hull. Then they strapped us in by stretching a long canvas belt across all of us that they tightened with a wench, just like we were a bunch of crates.

Ra'ad Jamal Habib, a Shi'ite, described narrowly surviving two murder attempts by Sunni inmates during his time in U.S. custody. Like most Iraqis imprisoned by U.S. forces, he was never given a trial. A military judicial committee at Bucca eventually cleared him for release after putting him through re-education courses designed essentially to deprogram militant thinking among insurgents and militiamen. As of February 2009 his efforts to find work again were unsuccessful, he said, because of his prison record.

Keeping to the Neighborhood

✳

ALI FAHED MAHMOOD

He has a beefy face, small hands, and a steady gaze, looking a bit like a boxer past his prime. He says he did indeed box as a youth growing up in Baghdad in the 1980s.

THE SECTARIAN WAR turned my area into a disaster zone. I have a small house in Mansour, a mixed area. Shortly after the U.S. invasion I joined a volunteer guard force established by the Americans to protect public buildings, and when the sectarian killings started I was in charge of security for forty guards keeping watch over sixteen schools. I would patrol all the schools twice a day, once in the morning and once in the evening, usually on foot but sometimes with a car if I could get one.

The threats started from both sides in our area as things got bad in 2004. Shi'ite militiamen with the Mahdi Army would paste warnings on the houses of Sunnis, telling them to leave. Sunni insurgents would post lists of names of people said to be working with the Americans, people who were to be killed. My name appeared on one of those lists, because I am a Shi'ite. So did the names of three people who volunteered at the same time as me, two men and a woman. All three were murdered. Someone threw a threat letter into my yard as well. Later they threw a grenade that broke all the windows in my house but thankfully didn't hurt anyone.

I thought about leaving, but it was impossible. My roots were there. I lived in a small house I inherited from my father. It was everything I had. A lot of people were urging me to come with them to Syria or Jordan to get away from the violence and try to find work. A friend of mine headed for Syria really pressed me hard to come. He was afraid I would be killed. I kept saying no. When he left he said to me, I am talking to a dead man. You will surely die if you insist on staying here.

I kept up my patrols every day during the height of the violence. I don't know how many bodies I saw on the street, heading out each morning.

Four or five a day usually, some on my street. None of us guards had proper weapons, because we were not an official force, just volunteers. But I had a personal pistol I always took with me on patrol, even though I did not have a license. I would walk with my arms crossed and keep the pistol in my hand. And I would jump and pull it out if I heard any sound, even someone calling my name. I was terrified!

I came home after my patrols one cold February Monday to find a gunfight blazing away very near my house. I made my way inside, and there was my wife, holding our three children and sobbing hysterically. She asked me, How long do we have to live like this!? How long!? What if you die? We will have no one! She was having a breakdown, screaming and crying and yelling at me as the bullets flew outside our house. The shooting was so, so close. Anything could have happened in that moment. If someone had burst through the door and killed us all, I would not have been surprised. I tried to calm her down. I joked with her a little, saying, Look, I will be the last one to die in Iraq. So don't worry. It was the worst moment of my life. That was the only time I seriously considered leaving Iraq. But no matter how I planned, there was never enough money. We just couldn't afford it.

Yes, of course more friends of mine died. So many. If I counted up all the family, friends, and friends of friends who died, it would be more than a hundred. I managed to keep my wife and children safe through the violence. They basically never left the house. And I am proud to say that none of the students or teachers at any of the schools I oversaw was kidnapped.

Gradually things settled down and began to improve. I didn't see too many U.S. troops fighting in our area during the surge, but the military came in and worked on the roads and the water system. Life slowly got back to normal as the violence lowered in 2008.

Life for me is okay these days, much better than during the time of Saddam Hussein. I have three televisions and a Jeep Cherokee. I've been able to get enough money to improve my house. I will never long for the old days, no matter what happens. Everything that happened to me since the invasion is easier than one day under Saddam. Look, I was forced to join the army at age 18 and spent six years as an infantryman in the Republican Guard. For nothing! I grew so poor after getting out that I didn't even have enough money to pay the hospital bill for the birth of my first son. I had to sell my television. There was no work. In order to survive I opened a falafel takeout stand out of a window of my house. It was the only income we had. And still the Ba'athists hounded me. When there was talk of an American invasion, party officials came and pressed me to rejoin the army. I argued with them, saying we should form an army to liberate ourselves from the inside rather than organize to fight the Americans. They detained me at a party office for days and beat me, but my family and people in the neighborhood managed to get me out.

I wanted the Americans to come, and I never doubted whether the invasion was a good thing. I'll always remember the first time I saw American troops with my own eyes. We were on the road into Baghdad shortly after the invasion. We left the city during the bombardment because my wife was pregnant, but came back right after it fell. As we neared, I saw them in the road at a checkpoint ahead of us. I was jubilant! I just knew everything would be better because they came. I started screaming when I saw them, actually. Saddam is through! Saddam is through! My nephew, who was 19 at the time, was with me in the car. He totally rejected the invasion. I said to him, Look, in one year's time, we will be like the United Arab Emirates. You will see.

Ali Fahed Mahmood was still patrolling schools in his neighborhood as of January 2009. The volunteer guard force was eventually incorporated into the Iraqi Ministry of Interior.

Less Than Whole

※

ALI'A ANWER MAJID

He is a taxi driver supporting a wife and four children. He had managed to keep himself and his family safe through the invasion, the looting, and the outbreak of sectarian violence until one summer day several years into the war.

IT WAS JULY AND VERY HOT. I went to buy some ice at a place a short walk from my rented flat. On the circle at the end of the street there were some American troops. As I approached, a roadside bomb went off. Everybody started running. The Americans started shooting as they normally do when attacked. Most people got away unharmed, but I had gotten too close and caught a bullet in the face. It went in my left cheek, cut through part of my tongue, and flew out the upper part of my right cheek.

It felt like my face was on fire, like I had flames all around my head in the seconds after I was hit. I really didn't understand what had happened in that moment. I just started running and saw as I went that I had a lot of blood coming from my face. I made it almost to my home. I could see the door of my building, but I collapsed before I could reach it. A neighbor of mine saw me fall in the street from his window. He came and dragged me inside. After that I fainted.

When I woke up I was in the hospital. My face was covered in bandages. My jaw was broken and wired shut, and my right eye was dead. It was destroyed when the bullet passed through my face. The doctors left the eyeball itself in the socket, but it was useless. They said the bullet had severed all the nerves. I was in the hospital for almost a month. I spent about another seven months recovering at home before feeling well enough to get around again.

The injury affected my health. I suffered dizziness. I struggled to remember much before the accident. Sometimes it is hard to breathe, because the bullet damaged my sinuses. Of course it changed the way I look. My children began to be teased in school because I only had one good eye.

There was a small American outpost in my neighborhood, very close to my building. The soldiers who had shot me accidentally were based there as far as I knew. A lot of my neighbors advised me to go to the base and explain my situation, tell them the problems I was having because of the accident and see if there was anything they might do. Perhaps they could give me some proper treatment to help my sinuses or some financial assistance for all the hospital bills I had. So, one day I went. I got to the gates of the base, which was an old bomb shelter in Saddam times. I was let inside and shown to an interpreter. Initially I explained my situation to him. He told me that the commander of the base was out on patrol and that I should return the next day.

When I came back I was allowed to see the commander. At least I think he was the commander. An officer, in any case. He did not give me his name or rank as I sat in his office. It was a small space without much in it. There were some couches. There was a desk with a computer on it. There was an Iraqi and an American flag.

I showed the American officer my hospital records, which had the date of my injury. When he saw the date, he said, Sorry, we cannot help you. The unit that shot you went home shortly after that incident. The officer was very polite to me that first visit, even though he offered no help. He and all the other soldiers treated me with respect, I have to say.

I left without an argument but kept coming back in the hope they would change their mind and do something. I went back more than six times, each time sitting again in that same office, explaining myself and my situation. Each time their answer was the same as before. Finally they got tired of me coming around. They began turning me away at the gate. On one of my last visits the interpreter told me that the Americans would begin to think I was a spy for the Mahdi Army if I kept trying to hang around the base and that I should not come back.

I was really angry at this. What about my rights? I had been shot on the street in broad daylight. That would be a crime anywhere. I decided to go to the police station in my area and file a complaint. They let me fill out the paperwork but were no help either. The police told me to let it go as well. They said if I kept harassing the soldiers, they would think I was Mahdi Army, arrest me, and send me to Bucca. So, I was never able to get any help from anyone for what had happened.

Ali'a Anwer Majid managed to resume work as a taxi driver but remained fearful of traveling too far from home given his limited vision.

⁂

RANA ABDUL MAHDI

She goes everywhere on two grimy wooden crutches. She is in her mid-twenties with a soft, simple face. She offers a shy smile initially when speaking alongside her mother, Kadhmia, both of them huddled in long, black abayas. She cringes when helicopters pass overhead.

I WAS NINE MONTHS PREGNANT in October of 2007 and feeling some pain one morning, and I thought the baby may be coming soon. We knew it would be a girl. We had gotten a sonogram the month before. I asked my husband to pack my things in case we had to go to the hospital quickly, and I thought I might go to my mother's house that day and wait for the baby to come there. We decided to have breakfast first, and I walked outside to get some things from the market.

We had moved to the edge of Sadr City just the day before. My husband and I had been living for about a year in central Baghdad, near Haifa Street, but there was too much fighting there. So we moved to Sadr City, where thirteen of us crowded into a two-room house. I've always been poor. Even before the war no one in my family ever had a regular job. My father and brothers always worked as day laborers earning what they could with odd jobs. Sometimes my mother sold fruits and vegetables on the curb outside the house where I grew up in Baghdad with twelve brothers and sisters. It was the same when I got married and started living with my husband's family. I moved from one poverty to another.

I still felt like a queen in that first year of marriage, though. We were young and in love. We had a child on the way. He found a job as a bodyguard with a British security company. Life for us was good, even though things in Baghdad had gotten very bad.

We heard a lot of helicopters and airplanes overhead that morning in Sadr City. I walked out onto the street, which was full of people even very early. I had walked just a short distance from the house when I saw a helicopter floating very high in the air away from me, and I watched as it fired a rocket toward me and my little sister, Zahra. She was eight.

I felt heat all over my body, and then I was on the ground as the street filled with smoke. There were bodies all around me, and I saw my sister with all her insides spilling out her front. She was reaching for me, motioning with her hand for me to come and help. She could not speak. I sat up and looked down at myself, and I saw my left foot was gone. It was sitting there in the street a little ways from me. I didn't feel any pain at that moment, except for in my stomach with the baby.

I started screaming for help. But no one from the neighborhood knew me, and there were so many other dead and wounded on the street. My family did not know what had happened to me. It seemed like half an hour before someone came to help. Finally some people started giving me first aid. I told them not to waste help on me and just try to save the baby. I wanted the baby to live even if I died.

They took us to the hospital, which was far away through traffic jams and checkpoints. I bled jugs of blood in the ambulance. It was almost two hours before I got to a doctor. The last thing I remember before passing out was being moved to the operating room. I begged the doctors to save the baby, but they told me she was already lost.

I spent two months in the hospital. They had to cut sections from my leg three times to stop the spread of infection, and I lost my knee as well. My other leg was badly wounded. Whole pieces were gone. They put skin from my thighs onto the wounds.

She shows me her legs. What remains of the left one is nothing more than a stump etched with the scars of dozens of stitches. The right leg has grayish, papery skin covering two areas as big as an outspread hand where flesh is missing.

My husband never came to visit me the whole time I was in the hospital, and I went home to my family's house, not his. They brought me home in an ambulance. I lay there for eight months. I could not even get up to go to the bathroom, and bed sores grew on my back. It was suffering, in every way you can think the word to mean. My husband came to see me only once in that whole time. He stood in the door, hardly looking at me. And he said, You were not this way when you last left me. You left me whole, and now you are in pieces. If you cannot come back to me the way you were, with my daughter, then don't come.

He hurt me so much, but I didn't blame him. I knew I was not useful to him anymore. Who would have me? What man would want such a wife? I cannot have children because of the injury. All his brothers have wives who give them children. This is what he wants. He does not want to be taking care of me, drawing baths and washing me every day, taking me to the bathroom, making all my meals because I cannot. Maybe he could bring himself to do it for a week or two, but no more. And whatever care he gave would just be pity, which I don't want. I didn't even reply as he stood there, and I never saw him again.

I started walking a little eventually just because I wanted to go to the bathroom by myself again, but I began passing every day in that same dark room. I took up smoking. Cigarettes were my only friends. What can I say? It is a miserable life. I would ask God why he did this to me. Why does God put so much suffering on poor people? Why not take legs from people who can afford to help themselves by getting new ones? No one ever offered to help me get a prosthetic leg. The Iraqi doctors say I am not their problem because I was hit by the Americans. Even if the Americans would help me, they can never bring my legs back. I had no money for any kind of treatment even if we could find some in any case. In the end I would always apologize to God for thinking such things.

Finally I could not take it anymore. I felt like a wall of locked doors stood in front of me. Life was so dark. So one morning after most had left the house for work I crawled on my stomach to the cupboard, where all the medicine was. The only people in the house with me were my mother and Gufran, one of my younger sisters. Gufran watched as I went. She knew what I was doing. I begged her not to stop me as I gathered up all the pills I could find. She tried to reason with me, saying suicide was against Islam and would make God very angry. I don't care, I said. I want to die. This is my only solution. Then suddenly she ran to get my mother. In the second she was gone I swallowed everything I could. I don't know how many pills I took or what they were. A lot, all kinds of pills and capsules. As they soaked in it felt just like the day I was hurt, sitting there on the street waiting for help. Everything grew foggy. I felt my heart slow. But this time I did not call for help. I was glad to be dying now.

They took me to the hospital. The doctors pumped my stomach, and I survived. But looking at me even the doctors said they would do the same if they were in such a condition themselves.

Your god must want you to live, I say.

God must hate me for leaving me alive! Now I ask God to give me one of his terrible diseases, like cancer, so I can die. Nobody understands what I'm living through. I wish I would get hit by a car or involved in some other incident somewhere, some fighting or an explosion, so I could be killed as I should have been. Whoever kills me should have a palace built for him in paradise. Why am I still alive?

Eight-year-old Zahra died in the attack that disfigured Rana Abdul Mahdi, who left the interview vowing to try to kill herself again. She was eventually persuaded to reach out to American and Iraqi nongovernmental organizations dedicated to supporting civilian victims.

Beloveds Lost and Found

✳

MAYSOON JAHIL OBEID

Jails run by Iraqi authorities overflowed as Iraqi security forces rounded up thousands of suspects amid uncontrollable sectarian violence. Conditions in Iraqi jails were grim. Abuse was common in many prisons, where detainees were often held without proper hearings on charges against them, owing to dysfunctional and overburdened courts. Arrests were often arbitrary as Iraqi security forces, sometimes working with Shi'ite militias, swept neighborhoods around Baghdad. Many families began a long nightmare in learning that a loved one had been taken away by Iraqi security forces. Maysoon began hers in the spring of 2007, when her husband Haytham Muzaham disappeared one morning on a street near the couple's home in Karada, a neighborhood in central Baghdad.

HAYTHAM HAD HIS OWN TRUCK that he hired out for various delivery jobs. That's how he supported me and our four children. We had been living a fairly good life through the years after the invasion despite some struggles. Haytham had lost a brother in an explosion. We were having a hard time financially, like many. Still, we had decided to have another baby and were feeling hopeful.

Haytham was supposed to help deliver government rations on the day he was arrested. He left for the job very early in the morning. It was barely dawn. About an hour after he left the house, I heard a commotion on the street. Outside we saw Iraqi security forces raiding residences and shops. They had a list of names of people they were looking for. I saw my husband's truck in the street, but he was not in it. I thought he might have been arrested, so I went down and began asking about him. One of the officers told me my husband was not on their list and so therefore would not have been arrested. They told me he had probably just stepped away from the vehicle for a moment.

I waited. I sat next to his truck. I was there for an hour. Then two. There was no sign of him. I found another police officer and told him what was happening. They told me the same thing as before. I went back to the truck and waited some more. I waited there until past noon. Finally I decided to go check at the police headquarters for our area. No one there knew anything.

I'll never forget the feeling I had that day as I began to know something was very wrong. I felt dizzy. I could not eat. I know my husband well. He would not just leave his truck sitting like that and give no word about where he was to me or anyone. But what could I do? I could only wait and hope he appeared again. After six days of waiting, my sister-in-law came to me and said it was no use hoping for him to come back. We had better start looking.

We began asking around at various police stations and jails. For nearly a month we searched. No one seemed to know anything. There was no sign of Haytham on any rosters at the jails. Then, all of a sudden, I got a call. Some clerk from the prison in Kadhimiya told me that I had a visit with my husband scheduled for that Saturday, as though I had put in a request that had been approved. I was told the visit would be only for immediate family and to be sure and come on time. That was the first I had heard anything about him since he vanished more than twenty days before.

I went to see Haytham that Saturday as told at the jail in Kadhimiya. He didn't even look like the same man. Haytham had always been a big, muscular guy. Now he looked like a skinny rabbit. He was scared, like a caged animal. He was turning his head nervously left and right, and there were clear signs of abuse on him. His arm was broken. He had been beaten. He told me that they had been shocking his genitals with electricity. And he said he was certain they would never let him out, unless we figured out a way to bribe someone. Haytham had in fact been arrested that day he disappeared on suspicion of some illegal activity. He had been held since then and even appeared before a judge, who ordered him released for lack of evidence. But the police kept holding him even so, and it was unclear how he might be released.

During that first visit Haytham gave me a phone number to call. At some point in his initial days in jail an American inspection team visited. An American officer noticed Haytham's bad condition and offered to move him out. Haytham refused. He was scared of the Americans after what he had heard about what happens to Iraqis in their prisons. So he decided to stay in the Iraqi jail, despite what was happening to him. The American officer gave Haytham his phone number and told him that, if he changed his mind or needed help, to call or have someone he knew do so. I called when I got back from seeing Haytham. Someone answered in English. I don't know what they said. Then an interpreter got on the phone, and I explained who I was and that Haytham needed to be gotten out of that jail. The interpreter said, Okay, we got your message. And that was the last I ever heard from the Americans about it.

Haytham had also told me that a man named T'aha could get him out if bribed. For some reason Haytham believed that only T'aha could free him, and he told me to find T'aha. According to Haytham, T'aha was among a group of civilians whom the Iraqi police allowed into the jail after hours, to torture the prisoners. They were supposed to be special interrogators who used special methods for questioning, but really they were just torturers. I actually knew T'aha. He was a young guy from our neighborhood. He and his family had a bad reputation. T'aha was rumored to be involved with the Mahdi Army. Some said he had been working with the militia to displace families. Some said he was dealing weapons. Still others said he had a hand in the bombing of a Sunni mosque.

I went looking for T'aha but could not find him. Finally my brother-in-law located him and brought him to our house. We told him our situation and what Haytham had said. At first he denied any connection to the police or Haytham's case. He told us we were mistaken about who he was. We kept begging him to help us. He went away without making any promises but left us understanding that he at least knew who Haytham was.

Three months passed, and we did not hear any more from T'aha. I kept visiting Haytham. Meanwhile, we were going broke. We had no money coming in, and every time I went to the jail, I wound up handing out bribes. For example, my husband smokes. If I wanted to bring him a pack of cigarettes, I would have to give a guard a scratch card for his mobile phone. It was always something like this at the jail. I was pregnant, too, and getting bigger all the time. It was getting harder and harder to go among the crowds at the jail in such a condition. I was at the jail often in those days, even when I was not allowed a visit with Haythem. I went frequently to check the jail's roster to make sure Haytham's name was still on it. Sometimes people's names fell off the jail registry, which meant they might have died or disappeared to another jail, so you had to check all the time. One afternoon I was at the jail checking the registry when I saw T'aha there with about seven other men. He did not see me, but I saw him. Later that day I went and found T'aha where he would sometimes hang out, a place in our neighborhood where you can play Ping-Pong and foosball. I told him I saw him there. He said, Why did you not say hello? I was there applying for a job. I told him, Listen, T'aha, I'm not a fool. I know what's going on. I want Haytham out, and I am ready to give you whatever you want. Then he said, Okay, look, I have been meaning to tell you that there is an officer there in the jail who says that for $10,000 he can have Haytham out in a week. I said, We barely have enough money for bread! But okay, fine, we'll get the money together if you are serious. He assured me he was. But he said the offer would not stay open. We had three days.

I took my mother-in-law, and we started begging from everyone in the neighborhood. We went to everyone we knew. We knocked on doors of strangers. I only managed to get $7,000 together in the end. Everyone was having a hard time financially in those days, and it was difficult to get money even for us, a family people knew and liked. I called T'aha. He came over. I handed him the money we collected, and then I fell to my knees and kissed his feet. My mother-in-law was there too, and she knelt to kiss his hand. I said, Please, I want Haytham back. Please. He promised I would have Haytham in less than fifteen days, and then he left.

Shortly after he left, I had a nervous breakdown. I was so exhausted from getting the money together and all the worry that I collapsed. I was taken to the hospital, where I remained for two days. While I was there I heard that T'aha had been arrested. Iraqi army forces had found him with a dead body in his car and had implicated him in a fake checkpoint used to abduct and murder Sunnis. T'aha was gone, and so was the money.

Some weeks after that I went into labor and gave birth to twin girls. Now we had six children and no father in the house and no income. About two weeks after the birth I was well enough to go visit Haytham. He had heard about his daughters already. When I asked him how he could have known, he said, Look, all the men from our neighborhood practically are here. We get all the neighborhood news. I heard about the girls the night they were born. Two or three days after that visit, someone called asking if this were Haytham's house without identifying themselves. I said yes. They said Haytham had been transferred to another jail and that I could visit him every other Monday. The prisoners could see male visitors on one Monday and then female visitors the Monday after that. Before hanging up, the caller asked me to deliver the same message to a family in the neighborhood who also had someone in jail with Haytham, to save them the trouble of making two calls.

My brother-in-law got to see Haytham first at the new prison. He came back after a visit saying Haytham was looking and feeling good. He said the new facility was much better than the other one. When I went for my visit on the next Monday, Haytham was indeed looking better, but his spirits were very low. He had tears in his eyes, and he seemed to be broken psychologically. He was despairing. He told me, I have done nothing, but I'm in here with the drug smugglers, the pimps, and the murderers. I told him to be patient and to be strong, that I would collapse if he collapsed. And I could not take care of all our children if he had lost hope for coming home. He suggested we hire a lawyer. He thought that might help get his case in front of a judge again.

I went looking for a lawyer and found one I thought could help. The lawyer asked for $300 just to read Haytham's file, and the price for services went up from there. I could not afford all his fees, but he agreed to reduce the rates if I handled much of the paperwork myself. He didn't want to be bothered bringing copies of documents to offices around the city. Getting the process started involved a lot of gathering, copying, and delivering documents related to Haytham's case around to various police stations and government offices. I kept working at things with the lawyer in the months that followed and continued visiting Haytham when I could.

The last time I saw Haytham alive was at the end of January 2008. He had developed some kind of skin condition and was not looking so good. And he was in very bad shape emotionally that day. He started talking like he was not coming out, telling me to say goodbye to his parents and the children for him and things like that. I asked him why he was saying such things. He said, I just have a bad feeling. I'm innocent, but I'm still here. I told him again to be patient. We were making progress with the lawyer. It could be any day now when he could go free. Just give it some time. You know how it is in this country. Everything takes a long time.

About two weeks later, at around noon, I got a call while at home. It was one of the guards I had gotten to know a little in my visits. He said he was sorry to inform me that Haytham had been dead for eight days and that his body was resting in the morgue. Haytham's family refused to let me see the body for fear I would have another nervous breakdown. To this day I do not know exactly how he died. I was only shown a picture of his face taken at the time of death for identification purposes, and I could not see anything unusual. At the morgue they said Haytham died from complications related to the injuries he got when they were torturing him heavily. Apparently a wound on his neck had gotten infected and poisoned his blood. But it could have been something else. They were forced to eat food with rodent droppings in the prison. Perhaps that gave him a fatal infection.

Around this time, ironically, all the work I had been doing with the lawyer finally began to pay off. Two days after I got the news of Haytham's death, a judge signed an order for him to be released.

Maysoon Jahil Obeid was making a living doing odd jobs at the main hospital in western Baghdad as of May 2009. She said most of the men arrested along with her husband Haytham in Karada were released about four months after Haytham died. T'aha, she said, had bribed his way out of jail and could be seen around Karada.

※

SHIEK JAMAL JASSIM SUDANI

He is a deeply religious Shi'ite from Sadr City. In the 1980s, he and several like-minded friends from his neighborhood began an informal charity meant to offer proper Islamic burials for families who had suffered a loss and were struggling with funeral costs. Out of their own pockets Sudani and his friends provided coffins and burial clothes. Sudani often allowed preparations of bodies in his home. Scores of poor Iraqis sought help from Sudani as the years went by and word of his charity spread. Eventually the government of Saddam Hussein even reached out, granting Sudani and his fellow volunteers access to the morgues in order to bury unclaimed remains. He continued with his work immediately after the invasion and throughout the sectarian violence.

WHEN I SEE A BODY, I think of them as a soul, someone born to a father and a mother and a family who was happy see him grow up day after day. Someone who carried a family's hopes until his life was cut short by a bullet or an explosion. I respect their lives and what they meant. I don't just bury Shi'ites because I am a Shi'ite. No, I bury Sunnis or Christians or Jews. They are all humans, and they are all souls.

In the years before the collapse, we were burying about thirty unidentified bodies monthly. Many of the people we buried then had clearly been murdered. I saw bodies of people killed by axes. Some were cut into more than a dozen pieces. Some were beheaded. We thought honestly that after the invasion our work would be less. There should be fewer bodies without the Saddam government murdering. Unfortunately, we were wrong.

During the initial days of the invasion, there were dead bodies all over the city. For weeks there were as many as 250 a day to be dealt with. We were overwhelmed. We could not figure out how to gather up them all. People began to help us, though, and we managed. After that initial wave of deaths, the appearance of unclaimed bodies slowed. I would say that through the first three years of the occupation on average we were burying between 75 and 100 bodies per week, taking them from wherever they were found in Baghdad to Najaf as we always had. Najaf is a holy place, and it's good according to Islam to be buried there. Also, the ground is sandy, so you can dig deep for a proper grave that won't be disturbed by dogs or animals.

I have a personal computer at home. I take pictures of each body brought to me, four or five images, which I store on the computer in a database. I take photographs of any tattoos, for example, anything that might help identify someone. I keep a map of where we bury each person in Najaf and give them a number in the database. That way anyone who comes to me and identifies a loved one by looking at pictures in the database can go to their grave and either exhume the remains for burial elsewhere or pay respects.

After the Samarra bombings, the unidentified bodies were everywhere in Baghdad, more than we had ever seen before. The ones piled up in the main morgue alone were enough to create a stench you could smell a kilometer away. In the early months of 2006, we started burying on average nearly 500 bodies per week. That's nearly 2,000 per month. I catalogued them all in my database. The condition of some was unbelievable. Many were without heads. Some were without eyes. It's difficult for me to describe for you what it was like to see so many mutilated bodies. It was very hard. Really, there is no way I can tell you what it was like to take in the smell of so many bodies day after day. There is no way I can describe the fear we felt so often when transporting dead as Shi'ites to Najaf from Baghdad when Sunni insurgents were doing so much killing.

And those thousands of bodies I mentioned were just the ones that came to us. That does not count the identified people who were killed and buried by their families or the unidentified bodies that were either dealt with by others or just never found. Who knows how many people were buried in mass graves that remain undiscovered or how many people were simply chopped into pieces and scattered. I would guess you could multiply the number of bodies we were burying each week during the sectarian violence by five to get an estimate of the real number of deaths in that period.

I'm sure one day when people feel totally safe they will point out where all the mass graves are. I don't know where in Baghdad they will be found, but certainly there are many. So many people came to me, thousands of them, and looked through all the pictures in my database searching for someone without finding them. So where did they go, these people?

After the U.S. troop buildup of 2007, Shiek Jamal Jassim Sudani said the number of unidentified bodies he helped bury per week went down to between 50 and 75. As of May 2008, when the interview was conducted, his work was increasingly focused on recovering bodies from newly uncovered mass graves.

※

RAJIHA   JIHAD   JASSIM

Her husband, Ghazi Swadi Tofan, was a watchman at a school in western Bagh-
dad. The two lived on the grounds with their five children, a common arrange-
ment for school watchmen in Baghdad. He disappeared one morning late in No-
vember of 2006. Wearing a gray tracksuit, he went out early to run an errand.
By noon his kidnappers were calling.

THEY WANTED $30,000. There was no way. We are so poor. He only ever
made about $100 a month, which was nothing. All five of us were living in
one room at the school. How could we possibly get such money? After that
first call, I ran into the street screaming, crying for help. I was hysterical.
I went to the police station and reported the kidnapping. The police did
nothing. They simply wrote up a report repeating what I told them. That
was it, and I went home. For the next ten days or so the kidnappers called
roughly once every forty-eight hours to see if I had arranged the money.
Of course it was impossible, and they knew this. The last time I talked to
them I asked if I could speak to my husband. Let us talk, I said. Let me hear
his voice. Maybe he knows someone who can help me raise the money.
They refused to put him on, and they never called back.

After that I started going to police stations and hospitals asking if there
were any word about him or his case. There never was, and eventually I
started going daily to the central morgue to view photos of the unidentified corpses brought there. The scene at the morgue was very bad. The
smell of bodies was overpowering. The corpses were scattered everywhere as new ones came each day. Many of the bodies were so mutilated
from torture that you could not recognize them by the faces. It was very
bad. Very bad.

Inside the morgue at that time was a large viewing hall with five
television monitors high on the wall. The room could hold maybe 300
people, and it was always full of women with more waiting outside, all
looking for husbands, sons, and brothers. Men would not come to the
morgue then, because someone wanting to kill them might be watching or

waiting. So the viewing room was always packed with women. We hardly ever spoke to each other as we stood looking up into the screens at pictures of corpses. Each monitor scrolled photographs of bodies grouped by the month they arrived at the morgue. For example, one monitor showed corpses from April, and the next monitor showed corpses from May, and so on. The scroll was controlled by a young man who sat at a desk in the hall. If anyone saw someone they knew among the pictures, the man at the desk would stop the scroll and give her a number from the picture that matched the storage slot holding the body so she could claim the remains.

Hundreds of pictures of bodies scrolled on the screens. Thousands. I lost track of how many pictures of bodies I saw looking at those screens for my husband. Only once did I see one that might have been him. One picture showed a body naked except for underwear without a head. The body really seemed like his, but I could not be sure without the head. As I looked at the picture wondering whether it was my husband or not I had a nervous breakdown. I went home in a state of shock and stayed there unmoving for days. The body looked so much like his, but I could not bring myself to get the number for the remains. I told myself it was not him, and managed to find enough strength to start going back to the morgue each day after a few days at home. Altogether I went virtually every day for six months to the morgue before stopping. Eventually I just could not afford the daily trips. The fares for buses and taxis became too much. We were allowed to remain living at the school but had no income with my husband gone. Thank God our neighbors offered some money, and I began baking bread in a small oven to sell on the street. This is all we live on now.

Ghazi was very good to us. We had been married since 1985, and he always worked hard to support our family. He would do odd jobs as a laborer in addition to his work as a watchman to bring in some extra money for the family. Anything he earned he spent it on the family, not himself. He was very sweet to me, and all our neighbors thought well of him. Sometimes I still let myself hope a little that he may come back.

Rajiha Jihad Jassim renewed periodic trips to the morgue but had found no trace of her husband as of February 2009.

⁂

ENTASAR ABUD TAHAN

She is the mother of seven, six daughters and one son. Originally from Baghdad, she had settled with her husband in Hibhib, a mainly Sunni village in Diyala province where insurgent leader Abu Musab al-Zarqawi was killed by U.S. forces in June of 2006. Her husband owned a car and made a living using it as a taxi for years around the area, which grew extremely violent during the sectarian bloodshed and remained so through the early phases of the U.S. drawdown.

IN 2006, as sectarian violence began to rise in Baghdad, an incident or two happened in our village. We heard about a kidnapping case and a murder in which the victim was hacked to pieces. People in Hibhib began to fear for their lives and started to move out. Initially I didn't think we should go, even though we're Shi'ites. Our family was well known and respected. We had a good name and had never faced any sectarian problems before. But I began to change my mind as things got worse. I urged my husband to move us. He didn't think we should. He kept thinking like I initially had, that we had no enemies and therefore nothing to fear. Also, we had no place to go, frankly. Hibhib was our home.

The stories of the killings and kidnappings in our area kept coming. I don't know how many I heard. A lot, especially after they killed Zarqawi. Things got much worse after that. Then one day in mid-July of 2007 my husband left for work and did not return. Apparently he came across a fake checkpoint shortly after leaving the house and was taken captive.

I got a call from the kidnappers shortly after he disappeared. They demanded $50,000. I told them I didn't have that kind of money, as they knew. Even if everyone in our family gave all they had, it would not reach that sum. Over the course of the next few days they called us several times, pressing for the money. Each time I told them the same thing, that it was impossible for us. Finally on the last call they told me that since I could not find the money I could go find his head under a bridge leading to Baquba.

I went to a friend of mine, a female neighbor, and we took a car and went together to the bridge the callers identified. We looked in the brush under the bridge by the river but didn't see any heads or human remains. We started asking passersby if anyone had found bodies or heads in the area, and we heard from people that someone had in fact found some heads under the bridge and had taken them to be buried at a nearby mosque. People told us that the person who found the heads videoed the faces before burying them. Gradually, after asking one person after another through that day, I was able to get the name of the person who found the heads, and I went to him.

He was a young man from the area, maybe 25. He told me that the only reason he videoed the heads he found was so that someone might be able to identify them later. As it was, the three heads he found were buried in a makeshift grave at a nearby mosque, but no one knew who the victims were. He had made three short separate videos of the remains before burying them and showed me each one on his phone. I didn't recognize the faces of the men in the first or second videos, but the third was my husband.

Entasar Abud Tahan never found the rest of her husband's body, but she managed to make a proper grave in the place where his head rested before fleeing Hibhib with her children for Baghdad. She hoped to exhume the remains at some point and rebury them alongside family members resting in Najaf. But as of April 2009, when the interview was conducted, she felt Diyala province was still too unsafe for her to return.

SALMA HAMID

Born in 1971, she lived her whole life in Mahmudiya, a small town roughly 50 miles south of Baghdad bloodied by successive waves of violence throughout the conflict. She is a Sunni but married a Shi'ite merchant from the town in 1997, and the two of them raised nine children together, five boys and four girls. The oldest, Hayder, had gone to college in Baghdad but returned home in 2002 to serve as a vice principal and a volleyball coach at a local high school.

I REMEMBER THE LAST TIME I saw Hayder alive with my eyes. He was getting ready to run errands. He had on tan slacks and a bright shirt with pink, yellow, and red stripes going up and down it.

The day he disappeared started normally. We all had breakfast. He was talking to his sister. Both of them were saying they could not sleep the night before. Something they could not put their finger on was making them nervous, and they decided not to go out of the house that day after all. Shortly after breakfast I left the house to pay respects to a family who had recently lost someone. I had a bad feeling the whole time I was gone and returned home quickly. In the time I was gone he went missing.

He decided to go out anyway to get a scratch card for his mobile phone, and one of his sisters needed to see the dentist, too. So they left together for their errands on foot. When his sister finished up at the dentist, she found Hayder on the street standing with some of his friends and putting minutes on his phone. Hayder told her to go ahead and that he would catch up. Then a white sedan pulled up, and some men emerged and beckoned him to get in. They said he was wanted for questioning by the local intelligence chief, whom everybody knew was working with the Mahdi Army. He got in without a fight.

We felt something was wrong and went to an Iraqi Army outpost in the area, because everyone knew the Iraqi army was working with the militias. We were told by people at the outpost that Hayder was there being held for questioning, but we were not allowed to see him. They told us to come back tomorrow. But when we went back the next day, we were told Hayder had been taken by another group of men because he was Sunni. No one would tell us who the men were or where they had taken him. No one there had any answers for us.

In the days that followed we began to hear rumors about where he was. We heard that he was being held by the Mahdi Army. We heard that he was being held by the National Police. Twice people claiming to have connections to the police and the militias came to me saying they would find him for a fee. I could tell they were swindling me. They would not find him, I knew. But what could I do? I had to pay them, just in case they might come back with some information. Nothing ever came of it.

In the months that followed I checked all the jails around Mahmudiya. I checked several jails in Baghdad. I even went to the American detention facilities hoping he had wound up there somehow. I never found any trace of him.

Throughout this time we were hearing whispers about mass graves around some houses in an area just outside town, where the Shi'ite militias were supposedly torturing and killing Sunnis they had abducted. It was an open secret. Everyone knew it was happening. But no one dared to talk too much about it, because the militias at that time were supported by the government. Anyone who talked too loudly about it would wind up killed, either by the militias or the Iraqi security forces.

For the next year I never stopped searching for him. How could I? Then, on the tenth of April, 2008, American and Iraqi military vehicles drove through Mahmudiya blaring an announcement on loudspeakers. They were calling anyone with missing relatives to a neighborhood just outside of town where they had found a mass grave.

American forces were at the grave site with body bags. Iraqi army forces were with them, and volunteers were digging up remains as others looking for loved ones stood around. The killers had thrown bodies, I don't know how many, maybe thirty, into a trench and poured cement over them. So the volunteers had to chip some bodies out of the concrete as well as dig. Unearthed bodies were taken from the pit and lined in a row on the ground above so people could look them over. Most of the remains were nothing more than bones.

Even as the bodies were being pulled out I could tell we were being watched by the Mahdi Army. We knew who they were, and they were there watching the whole scene. I pointed this out to some of the men from the Iraqi security forces on hand, and they told me they saw them too but not to worry. Things had changed, they said, and we would be safe from these men from now on.

I didn't see my son among the bodies being pulled from the grave. I was told that some bodies taken from the grave had been moved to the hospital, so I went there. At the hospital, the morgue trays were completely full, so they had lined up bodies on the floor. I don't know how many bodies there were. It was impossible to count, because most of the remains were just piles of bones and scraps of clothes. But my son somehow had remained whole.

I saw him there among the body parts, and I knew it was him because he was still wearing that brightly striped shirt I saw him in before he left the house the day he disappeared. I was surprised how clean the shirt looked, actually. How could it be so clean?

You know, when he was missing I would sometimes feel a sharp pain in my neck. I could never explain it. And then when we were looking at the body I saw that he had been shot through the head. The bullet had gone through the top of his head and out through his neck, at the same spot where I had been feeling pain in mine.

We took the body home, and I put him in his bedroom. We wrapped him in blankets and put lots of pillows under him. Family and neighbors gathered to help us put him in a coffin and take him to the mosque, where they would prepare him for the trip to Karbala. I'm a Sunni, but my husband is a Shi'ite. So we decided to bury him in Karbala, as many Shi'ites do.

We were very happy, actually. At least we found him and were able to bury him in a proper way. We consider him a martyr. We decided that we would make his funeral like a wedding day for him, because he had been wanting to get married when he died. So we organized a procession as you would for a marriage to carry his coffin. It was midday but dark outside because a dust storm had risen. We lit candles and carried him through the haze to the mosque.

Salma Hamid, who insisted on aliases for herself and her son out of continuing concerns for her safety, pressed local authorities in Mahmudiya to conduct an investigation into the murder. But she had seen no effort on their part as of April 2008, when the interview was conducted.

The Makings of Another Life

❋

HAMIDA RAHDI SALAH

She and her husband, Ryad Nima'a, were newlyweds eager to start a family in 2003. She brings to the interview two photographs to show me. One is of her and Ryad shortly after they were married. They smile in the picture, which is blurry, crumpled, and faded with tattered edges. The second snapshot shows Hamida with her son, Safah, born in 2005, and her daughter, Sandy, born in 2006. The children stand without expression on either side of their mother, who appears on the verge of tears. I ask her if she was crying when the picture was taken. She says no but that the whole family was sad because the portrait was taken a short while after Ryad's death in the summer of 2007.

AFTER WE WERE MARRIED, Ryad and I were living in Abu Disheer, southern Baghdad. Ryad owned a car and sometimes used it as a taxi service. He also fixed cars, working on engines in the yard of our house. Our life was quiet and simple up to 2006, when we began to grow worried about all the violence. Abu Disheer is a Shi'ite area, and we are Shi'ites. But the areas around it were mainly Sunni, and al-Qaeda was in neighborhoods like Dora, which is very near us. Ryad decided we should move to a safer area. We were fine to live in Abu Disheer, but he had to drive through Sunni areas when using his car as a taxi. That was not safe. Taxi drivers were always getting killed then because of random checkpoints. We found a rental house in Sha'ab, near Sadr City, and we moved there in 2006. That was better. We felt safer, and Ryad spent most of his days driving back and forth between Sha'ab and Sadr City, which was relatively safe as a Shi'ite. But the rent on our house was high, and after a while the money wasn't enough. So we eventually had to settle back in our old house in Abu Disheer.

On the eighteenth of June, 2007, Ryad left the house as usual at seven in the morning. He always got up early to go out for work. And he would always be back for lunch with me at exactly two in the afternoon. This was his routine. At about eleven that morning, I heard a huge explosion. Someone had bombed the gas station not far from our house. At noon one of Ryad's brothers came over asking for him. When I said I had not seen him or heard from him since he left in the morning, he said he thought he saw Ryad's car among the wreckage of the blast at the gas station. I told him he was probably mistaken. Ryad did not use that gas station precisely because it was dangerous to wait in line in that area. He often filled up in Sha'ab. His brother said he would go back to the gas station and make sure.

The hours passed without word from anyone, and the worries began to come. I called my mother-in-law, and the two of us went together to the hospital where the victims of the blast were taken to see if Ryad was there.

It was a huge explosion, and there were many bodies burned beyond recognition. Hospital workers were tagging the charred remains with the make and model of the car in which they were found, because that was the only clue for identification for many of those killed. There was no sign of Ryad among the dead when I was there, and we could still hold out some hope he might be alive. There was an American base in our area, and we thought maybe he might be there. Sometimes after such attacks the Americans would arrive at the scene and begin arresting people. Ryad might have survived the blast but then been swept up by the Americans. That's what I thought leaving the hospital. But his brothers went to the hospital after I visited, and they found what was left of him there. His body must have arrived some time after I was there.

For the next two months after his death I lived with my children in his brother's house. Of course he could not support his family and mine indefinitely, and he asked me to go live with my family. So then I settled with one of my brothers who also lives in Abu Disheer. He has family of his own too, a wife and four children. He had also taken in my mother before the three of us arrived. There were only two rooms and one bath for all of us.

Around this time the government issued a law saying victims of terrorism were entitled to about $2,000. It was a lot of money for someone like me. But it wasn't easy to get. The process of applying for the funds was long, tedious, and expensive by the time you added up all the transportation costs going back and forth to government offices. For a year I was going around to government buildings, filling out forms and trying to push my paperwork through the bureaucracy. I had to leave my children with my mother, who's almost blind, and brave the buses day after day to run errands related to my application. There was always something needed by this office or that committee. There were still explosions and killings all over the city then, too. It was dangerous to be moving about so much.

I finally got the money about a year after I started the process. I didn't have enough to rent or buy a home even with the payment, so I decided to build a room for myself attached to my brother's house. I hired carpenters to put up some walls and had a thatch roof made. I also put in a separate bathroom so we could have our own sink and toilet. After I did all that the money was gone, but at least we have a space of our own now. It isn't much, just one room and a bath for the three of us. The walls are white. I have a small table with a television on it. I have a sewing machine I keep in there. That's how I make money now, doing odd sewing jobs. We have a small wardrobe for our clothes. Safah has his own bed, and I share a bed with Sandy. That's how we live. It's a lot different than before. You can't even compare the life we had with the one we live now. The hardest moments I think come each time my brother arrives home. We watch each time as all his children rush to him as he comes through the door.

Hamida Rahdi Salah was still living with her brother in Abu Disheer with no means to get a place of her own as of May 2009. She doubted whether she would ever marry again. Most would-be suitors, she said, were not interested in taking in two children.

※

HASSAN RISN BADR AL-RUBA'I

He joined the medical division of the Iraqi army in 1985 and became a technician specializing in making prosthetic legs. Working at a military hospital in Baghdad, he treated patients who mostly lost limbs to landmines during Iraq's long war with Iran. The hospital fell under control of the Ministry of Health after the U.S. invasion and became known as the Baghdad Center for Amputees. Hassan stayed on and watched his caseload grow.

EVERYTHING FROM THE HOSPITAL was looted when we returned after the collapse. We abandoned it during the bombing and came back to find it virtually empty. There were about thirteen of us who wanted to get the hospital back in order. There was no functioning Iraqi government really at that time, so we managed to find some donors from the United Arab Emirates who helped us restore the equipment for making limbs and refurbish the place. We had just gotten everything more or less back in order in the latter part of 2003 when a huge bomb destroyed much of the place. We had to start all over again. Luckily we managed to salvage some of the workshop equipment, and we found some nongovernmental organizations to offer further funding. By the middle of 2004 we had the place operational again.

I specialize in cases where the amputation occurs below the knee. There is a wing of the center dedicated to just that type of injury with several technicians like me who make only that type of prosthetic. There's another wing for patients who've lost legs above the knee, a wing for patients who've lost hands, arms, and so on. The entirety of the cases just my wing handled in 2005 was about 18,000. That number included recent injuries and those going all the way back through the war with Iran. During the next four years that number more than doubled, and we became totally overwhelmed.

The injuries were almost all from the explosions and bullets. Rarely did someone come in with problems related to diabetes or something like that. On some days in 2006 and 2007, we would see sixty or seventy new amputation cases. This was just in my section. It doesn't count the cases that went to any of the other wings. And we were just one such prosthetics center in Baghdad. There were others in Basra, Hilla, Najaf. Who knows how many new amputation cases there were around the country when the violence was at its worst

The cases I see now are a lot different than the cases I saw earlier in my career, too. The old cases were mainly people who stepped on a landmine. We knew how to deal with that. It was a common thing. There were military medics in the field usually, with the soldiers, who could offer initial treatment to allow for a more successful prosthetic later. Now, someone loses a leg in an explosion on the street and then goes to a hospital with a civilian doctor who does not have experience in such cases. Often the doctors do damage to the residual limb in trying to give emergency treatment, so by the time a patient makes it to me they have an amputation with complications. And the injuries themselves are more complicated. The explosions from car bombs and roadside bombs tend to mangle people in unpredictable ways, at least compared to landmines. I have multiple cases now in which a person has lost one leg below the knee and one leg above the knee. That's a very difficult case to treat. I see cases in which the person has lost all four limbs. I've seen on average two or three of those cases a month from 2006 until now. New ones are still coming.

Let me put it to you another way. Basically, I'm a workman making prosthetic legs. I make about twenty-five a month these days. The other technicians working to make arm prosthetics or full-leg prosthetics make a similar number per month. The number each of us makes is limited because we are usually short of supplies. If we had all the supplies we needed, we could probably each make double that number and still not be making enough to meet the demand, because so many cases have backlogged on us in recent years. The violence has created an endless demand for prosthetics. We could never make enough. My appointment book right now at the center is full for more than the next six months. That means if someone loses a leg tomorrow and comes to me, I cannot do anything for them for more than half a year because there are so many in line for treatment already.

It has to be said that in Saddam times we never lacked materials. The military always kept our facility supplied. These days, getting what we need from the Ministry of Health is always a problem. And we are short on technicians. During the height of the sectarian violence, five of my colleagues were murdered. We mourned them as friends and really suffered in our ability to make limbs at the center at the same time. It takes a long time to learn how to do this work properly. People with experience are really valuable, and when you lose them it's a major setback to your ability to provide care. This job is like being a builder or a carpenter or an artist, some might say. Years of experience mean a lot. New people, even with training, can't replace experienced ones.

I've never turned anyone away despite the backlog. I could not bring myself to do that. I actually helped open a private clinic that makes prosthetics as well, in addition to my work at the center. I have a partner, an Iraqi doctor who specializes in broken bones. He has provided the money for all of the clinic's equipment, and I make all the limbs along with one other helper. We didn't have enough money to buy professional machines from abroad like we have at the center, but I know how to make them from my years of experience. I went around to the industrial areas in Baghdad and got the parts and materials we needed. You need some essential equipment to make proper prosthetics, an oven to bake the molds, precision grinders, hand drills, and so forth. I assembled the machines myself and set up a workshop where I make limbs and assess cases at night after a day at the center. On an average day I work a full shift at the center assessing cases and making legs. Then I go to the clinic in the evening and do the same. I work until I am too tired to do anymore, and then I go home.

Hassan Risn Badr al-Ruba'i remained working at the Baghdad Center for Amputees as of May 2009 while keeping up his work at the private prosthetics clinic as well. He hoped to see the clinic grow with the help of nongovernmental funding.

※

ALA'A ALZOBEIDI

He worked as an artist from 1998 until 2003, painting mostly portraits for income to support his wife and three children living in Kadhimiya.

RIGHT AFTER THE INVASION I got the idea to start a call center, a place where people could come and make long distance calls all over the world. There were so many people in Iraq with relatives all over the place who had fled the country over the years. Keeping in touch during Saddam times was difficult. There were no such facilities. We had been so isolated from the rest of world. The country was one big prison. But things were open suddenly, and I was able to set up phone lines without any trouble at all. My four brothers and I launched the venture together, just a simple office on the west side of Baghdad with a bank of phones able to make international calls. The place was a big success. In the early days we even had American troops dropping in to use the phones to call home sometimes. We kept the center open from eight in the morning until ten at night, and we were always busy.

The place was so busy in fact that I rented a house in Jamia near the center just so I could be closer to the business. I was working hard, and life was good. I would usually go to work early in the morning, take an hour break in the afternoon, and then go back and oversee the center until closing time. But I began to sense trouble just before the kidnapping. A neighbor of mine in Jamia was abducted, and I began to notice some people and cars who seemed to be watching me as I came and went.

It happened on a Friday in September of 2005. I went to run an errand and hailed a cab. As the taxi went, two cars moved to follow us. There were four men in each. The taxi driver noticed and told me. We didn't get far before they ran us off the road. Seven of them had pistols. One had a Kalashnikov. I thought they were going to execute us, but instead they dragged me from the taxi and put me in the back of one of their cars. They bound my hands with tape, which they put over my mouth and eyes as well. Soon I found myself in a house not far away, and they began torturing me, demanding to know how much money I had. They beat me with pieces of wood about the face and shoulders. They lashed me with electrical cords. They punched me. They kicked me in the stomach. After two days of this they brought in some kind of electrical device, a cattle prod or a stunner. I couldn't see. I was still blindfolded with tape. I could only hear the current sparking as they turned it on and put it to me.

I told them the truth about how much money I had from the beginning. I said I had about $30,000 in my safe, which was true. But they wouldn't believe me. They were talking about holding me for ransom for a half-million dollars at first. Who am I, Bill Gates? Finally after six days of this one of them put a gun to my head and said he would kill me if I kept lying. I told him that the truth was what I had been saying—$30,000. If they wanted some other figure, I said, I could make one up. But that was the amount they would find I had once they got their hands on it. After that they seemed to believe me, and the beatings stopped.

Eventually the kidnappers decided to move me to another safe house outside Baghdad, somewhere in Anbar province, while they negotiated payment of the ransom with my family. I didn't see where we went when they moved me. I was in the trunk for the trip away from Baghdad, which took a long time. But when they let me out I could tell from the accents of the people talking around us that we were in a village somewhere in Anbar. I thought for sure I was going to be executed out there, but the opposite happened. The kidnappers handed me to a family who was supposed to hold me until the ransom was paid. And the family turned out to be rather nice. They treated me with a lot of respect from the very beginning. I had not been able to clean up for an entire week. I had a cut above my eye that was getting infected and beginning to smell bad. I still had tape over my eyes. The guys in the house put masks over their faces, unbound me, and told me to uncover my eyes and clean myself up. They were almost apologetic about the situation, as though I should have been treated better by the initial kidnappers.

I was locked in a room for the entirety of my stay with the family at the second house. During the day I was left unbound. They tied my hands loosely at night before I went to bed. Before entering the room they would order me to put a scarf over my head so I could not see their faces. They allowed me to pray.

The final ransom price for me I learned later was $50,000 cash and one kilogram of gold, which my family got together by gathering up all the jewelry of the women. The day they released me, I was hooded with a scarf and driven a short distance, this time not in the trunk but in one of the seats of the kidnappers' car. They gave me a small amount of pocket money as the car came to a stop. Taxi fare, they said. I was ordered to walk ten paces from the car before taking off the hood. I did as they said and then removed the scarf. I found myself at an intersection on the far outskirts of Baghdad. I saw no car around, just people walking. No one seemed to think it was strange to see someone emerge from a car hooded and walk ten paces as his ride sped away. Everybody around was just going about their business. I guess that was a normal sight for people in that area during those days.

Eventually I made my way back to Baghdad. I had been held for ten days. Before being released, I was warned to leave Baghdad. I think the kidnappers figured I would be trouble for them if I remained in the city. I left within three days. I went to the United Arab Emirates via Jordan and settled there with my family in a rented flat outside Dubai. Our business in Baghdad was still running, and my brothers continued to send me my share of the profits. Thank God financially we were okay. But there were a lot of empty days to fill. I mostly drew and painted.

The years passed, and we remained safe and lived well there. You could even say we were happy. I probably would have kept living there if my residency had not been rejected. I went to reapply one day and was turned down without explanation. I think it was bad timing on the part of my application. My last name is clearly Shi'ite, and tensions were high then between Iran and the United Arab Emirates when I was submitting my papers that time. In any case, we were made to go.

We arrived back in Baghdad in July 2008. The moment I stepped from the plane I was thrilled, not sad. For me, nothing is as beautiful as Baghdad, even now. This city has been my whole life. I missed Baghdad the entire time we were away. I just love it. I love everything about the place. I even love the weather. Even those who kidnapped me, I don't hate them. They are from Baghdad, and so I love them too.

How can you say that? They were ready to kill you.

Look, I know. But I have a belief that everyone who deserves it will be punished in the end. I know who did it, by the way. At least I know the name of the family who held me at the second safe house. I overheard it while I was there. It would be easy enough to put the police onto them or find some other way to make them pay. I explained how I knew the family involved in the kidnapping to one of my friends. It turns out he knew one of the daughters from that family, and he offered to arrange to have her killed for me. I told him no way! That family had treated me with kindness while I was there. I cannot repay that kindness with an act of revenge. All those responsible for what happened to me I'm sure will pay for what they did one way or another, in time. So, let life run its course. Let them get theirs—but not from me.

Ala'a Alzobeidi got out of the phone center business to work on a new venture, prepaid credit cards. He and his family remained safe and living in Baghdad as of April 2009.

※

HAYDER MOHAMMED JODAH

He was born in Baghdad in 1985 and lived in various quarters of the city throughout his youth. When he was seven years old, agents for the former regime arrested his father on charges of political dissidence. He remembers watching men lead his father away in the darkness that night, never to be heard from again. He was the youngest of three sons raised by his mother, who sold off all the family's possessions piece by piece to keep the family afloat in the years after the father was gone. By 2003 the family was broke and homeless, forced to live with relatives in western Baghdad. That year Hayder turned 18. His brothers, identical twins Sermed and Samir, were older by four years and serving in the army at the time of the invasion.

WHEN THE BOMBING STARTED, the twins were by chance at home on leave for just a few days. They didn't go back to their posts. Throughout the next few months we had to keep them hidden in the house. They couldn't go out. If they were spotted by someone from the Ba'ath party, they would be executed for sure as deserters. All of us were fully supportive of the American invasion. We were glad to see Saddam go because of what he did to our family, and we were looking forward to a better life. When we saw the statue of Saddam fall on television, we were ecstatic. The feeling was unbelievable! But it didn't turn out the way we had hoped. We wound up suffering more as a family after the invasion than we did during Saddam times.

The main thing for my brothers and me in the time just after the invasion was finding work, so we could better our family's financial situation. I started studying in 2004 after high school at an industrial arts institute in Baghdad, learning pottery and other crafts. My heart wasn't in it. I really wanted to work to support the family. But my brothers insisted that I keep up my studies. They wanted me in school. My brothers meanwhile found work as guards at a children's hospital in Kadhimiya.

We moved to a rental house in the same neighborhood where we had been living with relatives, in Ghazaliya. My mother even got a job working in a date factory. We had income. Life was getting better. But you could tell things were getting worse all around. Bombs kept going off in the city, more and more with each passing month it seemed. My mother wanted us to flee in 2005. Let's sell everything we have and go, she said. My brothers said no. We were making a life for ourselves for the first time in years, and they did not want to give that up. They kept on working at the hospital. After the Samarra bombings, my mother and I pressed my brothers again to leave. We thought maybe Syria. We knew what was coming in Iraq. But Sermed and Samir still wanted to stay, because they figured we did not have enough money to go, and no way to earn if we made it out of Iraq.

I think my brothers did not sense what kind of danger they faced in their position. My father was a Shi'ite. But the twins and I were considered Sunnis, like my mother, because we had been raised by her and prayed as she did. All the hospitals at that time were under the control of the Mahdi Army. It's not so surprising they would be targeted by Shi'ite militiamen who saw them pray as Sunnis. At the same time, they might have been targeted by Sunni militants for working with the government. The twins had enemies on both sides. They never discussed this fact with me, and they never mentioned getting any threats or feeling unsafe going about their work. But they had a very close private relationship as twins. They were secretive with each other. I know there was a lot said between them that my mother and I never heard.

One day in the spring of 2006 they were late coming home. Every day they went to work together and came back by three in the afternoon, but this day three came, and they did not show. I kept calling and calling them on their mobiles. My mother felt that something bad had happened. She started crying and wailing even before we knew for sure. It was up to me to find out what happened. I called one of their friends at the hospital and learned that they had been kidnapped. When I was first told, you can't imagine the feeling. Sermed and Samir meant so much to our family.

I was expecting someone to call us demanding a ransom, but four days passed and the phone did not ring. The whole family searched for them all over Baghdad. Finally we found them on the second of April. It was their birthday actually. They were in the morgue. They had been executed, shot to death, and left on the side of the road by their killers. From what we could tell they were murdered within a half-hour of being abducted. We learned later that they had been stopped at a checkpoint in Shula, which was controlled by the Mahdi Army then. One witness who came forward said Sermed and Samir were talking and laughing with the men at the checkpoint as they were asked to get out of their car, as though they knew them. They probably did know them, since they drove through that neighborhood every day on their way back and forth to work. Apparently they went without question with the men who stopped them at the checkpoint and were killed a short time later.

My mother and I knew we were not safe even for one night in our house after that. We stayed for a while with relatives elsewhere in the city, and then I decided we had to leave the country and go to Syria. Six months later we were gone. We left everything behind. We only took our clothes. It was like our family was in some kind of downward cycle. First my father was killed, and we were left with nothing. And now my brothers were dead, and we were again left with nothing. It was hard enough to lose a father, and now this, just when we thought we might begin to have a normal life again.

I had only been to Syria twice in my life before my mother and I went across the border together. We settled in a rented flat in the north of the country, and we started again from zero. We hardly had any money. To make matters worse, my mother began getting ill and needed a lot of hospital treatment.

I wanted to find asylum somewhere for us. My father had been executed. My brothers had been executed. Our family could not be safe in Iraq. I got the idea to apply for asylum in Sweden. I heard they were accepting cases. I did not bother with any application. I had tried that with the United Nations and gotten nowhere. I thought if I could just make it to Sweden, illegally, then I could claim asylum and send for my mother.

It was late 2007, and I decided to make a go of it. I first flew to Turkey with a friend. We got in without any visa trouble. The idea was to find a smuggler there who could get us to Europe. We found an Afghan guy who said he could do it, and the two of us joined a group of about a dozen Afghans all headed to Europe. The smuggler had said we would go overland the whole way. But as we neared the Turkish border, the plan changed. We were to take a boat, he said. I got nervous. I had an Iraqi friend, actually, who had made it all the way to Sweden already with smugglers and was living there. I called him before getting on the boat and told him what was happening. He advised me not to get aboard. He thought we'd be robbed and thrown overboard. I decided to turn back. I left the group and made my way back to Istanbul, saying I had to tend to my sick mother and that I would try to make the journey another time. The organizer was quite nice about everything. I didn't expect him to give me my money back. I had given a down payment of $1,500. He gave me back all but one hundred, and I flew back to Syria. It turned out to be a wise move on my part. My friend stayed with the group and got on the boat. They were all captured by Greek authorities.

I was determined to try again. I called my friend in Sweden and asked him to please find me a smuggler who could get me into Europe by road, not boat. He found me an Iraqi who had been living in Turkey for five years. I called that guy from Syria. He said the whole operation would cost nearly $10,000, because I would have to cross so many borders in Europe. But he said that, if I brought more people to him, he would drop the price for me. I managed to get thirteen people together. We all got plane tickets and boarded a flight bound for Istanbul. We landed but were detained immediately. The Turks held us for five days and then put us on a plane back to Syria. They clearly figured out what we were doing there all together.

When I got home again after that second try my mother was crying with one eye and smiling with the other. She was glad to see me but sad I had not made it. She didn't want me to try again. I had already spent a lot of money in those two tries. She thought it was probably better to save what money we had left so we had something to live off. I still wanted to keep trying.

I have two uncles in Iran. I got in touch, and they told me I should come stay with them for a while and perhaps try to get smuggled into Europe from there. I went to Iran, but my uncles weren't able to arrange any trip to Europe. They urged me to settle there with them instead. Get married, find a job, start a life like they had. But I could not bring myself to live in Iran. We're too different, Iraqis and Iranians. About this time my mother went back to Baghdad to stay with relatives, because all the money we had been using to live in Syria was now gone. I went to join her.

I got back to Baghdad in March of 2008, almost two years since my brothers were killed. My mother was staying with a brother of hers, and I was taken in by an aunt on my father's side. Through some family connections I managed to get a job as a driver with a governmental office that works to restore Shi'ite shrines. And I found a wife. Three months after getting back I got married to a girl my mother picked for me, Samah. She used to work with my mother at the date factory. She comes from a good Sunni family. Her father was well connected with the old regime and loves Saddam to this day. But Samah and I never let any of that past or sectarianism affect us. It's been a good start for me. I'm hopeful now.

We recently found out that Samah is pregnant. It's a boy. I'm definitely going to name him after one of my brothers. I can't wait for him to come. I'm so eager for him to be born. I'm talking to him already. I tell him, I am your father. I hope that you will come to me. I want you to come to me so that I may have something for the loss of my father and my brothers.

Hayder Mohammed Jodah and his wife Samah had a baby boy, Sermed, in the spring of 2009. Hayder initially planned to name his son Samir, after the younger of his slain twin brothers. But then a close family friend came to Hayder and

Samah saying she had a dream in which the older twin Sermed appeared and asked for Hayder's boy to be named after him, so the couple did.

❋

SALAH HAMID JASIM

He was born in 1969 in Samarra, where his father had served since 1957 as the voice calling worshipers to prayer at the venerated Askariya shrine. Salah spent his childhood in Samarra before growing up to become a professional athlete, earning a spot on the Iraqi national soccer team in the years before the U.S. invasion. After that he worked as a youth coach and played for a Baghdad club. He lived mostly in Baghdad but visited the family home in Samarra often until 2005.

WE COULD SENSE WHAT WAS HAPPENING. You could feel the sectarianism as it rose. But our family is respected in that community. We felt for a while like we might go untouched. We began to think differently when some people close to our family were killed. My father wisely decided after that to move the family before something bad happened. He worried that something horrible would happen to our family if we stayed, something so bad that we might never be able to bring ourselves to return. He wanted us to leave on our own terms, in other words, so we might come back one day the same way when things had settled down. We abandoned the family home there in the summer of 2005.

I was already spending a lot of time in Baghdad then for my athletics, so life went on normally for me until February of 2006, when the shrine was bombed. I was in Baghdad when the news reached me. I was not surprised. That was not the first time someone had tried to destroy the place. There had been several bombing attempts previously. But I was surprised at the extent of the damage when I saw the pictures of the destruction later. I know that building by heart. I know which walls are thick and which walls are thin, and I know how sturdy the building is in the place where the bomb went off. The amount of explosives they used must have been enormous. Only a huge bomb could take down that much of the shrine.

Through the time that followed, our family settled into Baghdad and remained safe. We heard squatters overtook our family home in Samarra. I had never considered going back until 2008 as things got quieter. In December of that year, I set foot in the city again for the first time since our family left when I went with some friends of mine to see a soccer game. The difference between the city when I last saw it and the city when I arrived again was huge. The biggest difference perhaps was the mood of the place. Samarra used to be a city that welcomed everybody, a destination for pilgrims year after year. But now you could feel that anyone not a Sunni was seen as an outsider in Samarra. You could see it in the way people looked at you. They seemed afraid to talk to strangers. I don't remember the city like this. I always knew it as a place with an open heart. To me, Samarra had always been like a beautiful garden filled with all different kinds of flowers. There were Christians and Shi'ites and Sunnis and all kinds of people living together in Samarra when I was growing up there. Now the place is like a garden for just one kind of flower.

Samarra looked different too, with the shrine still in ruins. Every city in the world has some mark of distinction. For Samarra, it was the golden dome of the shrine and its minarets. When you neared Samarra by car in the past, you would see the dome of the shrine shining as the city came into view. When you arrive now, and see the shrine collapsed, what can you think about the city? That sight casts a pall over all of Samarra. The city didn't even look the same to me because the mood was so different. It was like all the color had drained away. Not to mention the signs of destruction all around. Buildings were scarred. Roads were cracked. Bullet holes and rocket craters could be seen everywhere. Wherever you looked there was some sign of destruction. The lack of visitors adds a lot to the sadness too. The city is a small place, and it thrived on the arrival of the pilgrims who visited the shrine. They gave the city life by filling the shops and hotels. Without the pilgrims coming through, life in Samarra stops. And none have been coming for a long time now. The pilgrims were really part of the city's soul. A part of the soul of the city is missing as long as they stay away.

I went to look at the shrine before leaving, to see the reconstruction efforts. A lot was still undone when I visited, so it was difficult to tell how the reconstruction would turn out. What I saw did not look hopeful. It looked shoddy, and it was hard to imagine the shrine ever being again like it once was. When I was in the shrine in years prior, everything about it felt so huge, so important. Seeing it again amid the destruction, the place felt so small somehow. Looking at what was left of the shrine that day, I found it hard to believe what all had happened and what it meant. Okay, fine, maybe you can rebuild the shrine. Maybe the rebuilt shrine will look great when it is done. But you can't erase the memory of its destruction among the people, no matter how good the rebuilding is. People will always remember what happened.

Salah Hamid Jasim remained living and working in Baghdad as of May 2009. His family had no plans to return to Samara.

※

HASSAN ALI

Born in 1972, he is a lifelong resident of Sadr City. A father of six, he made a living as a day laborer during Saddam times, usually mixing concrete. His brother had been a political prisoner of the former regime, so good work was hard to find because of his family name. After the invasion he worked as a cook, but gradually became more and more involved in charity efforts in the impoverished section of the city.

LIVING IN SADR CITY IS NOT EASY. The number of young unemployed people is unbelievable. What little work there is to be had is day labor stuff. You're lucky if you can work two days a week. It makes for a lot of poverty.

In 2004, I was seeing a lot of suffering in the community around me. I got this idea and discussed it with some of my friends, merchants and people with money. I went to them and said, Look, if you give me a little something every month, I will make sure it goes to families in need. That's how it started. Friends of mine who had money would make donations to me, and I would spend that money helping families I knew needed help. This went on for some time. It was just an informal charity. Then two friends of mine who had experience with nongovernmental organizations suggested we set up a foundation officially. So, we did. We established a small office, just the three of us initially, and called it the Bright Lights Foundation.

There are many people in Sadr City who have lost someone dear to them in the violence over these last six years. When I started the work with the foundation I would go around Sadr City on foot, simply asking about families and learning who needed help. I would do this all day while my other two partners at the foundation dealt mostly with funding and administrative things. There were so many cases and more all the time. There is a case I know of in which two brothers went out to work together one day in Baghdad. A roadside bomb exploded near an American convoy. The Americans began firing, and both these guys were killed. One of them had two wives. So now you have three families with no source of support. I arranged a modest stipend for all three of these families. It's all they have. Without that, they would be totally ruined. We pay the rent for some other people who cannot afford it in Sadr City. I have seven such cases. We offer enough to allow them to stay in their homes and give them a small amount of money to live on as well. Look, there are the poor who can get help from relatives. And then there are the poor who cannot get anything. These are the poorest of the poor, and we try to help them in Sadr City.

There's some unused land near my house owned by the Ministry of Transportation. It used to be part of the railroad system, but that's all gone now. When the violence was really bad in Baghdad, a lot of displaced people began settling there after being driven from their homes. There are all together thirty squatter families there. I went to the Ministry of Transportation and explained the situation and suggested they let our foundation organize the settlement so that people could have some services and order in their lives. I guaranteed the ministry that if they ever needed the land back, I would organize a dismantling of the settlement and find someplace else for the people to go. The Sadr Office backed me, and the ministry agreed. I went to the area and divided up the land in plots so each family had an even share. When it was all divided up, there was one plot left. I took it. I built a two-room house so I could be there in the community to help. The whole point is just to help people in Sadr City who are in trouble. And there are a lot of troubles in Sadr City because of all that has happened in the past six years.

I think the hardest day in Sadr City through the war so far was one in 2006 when five car bombs struck one after another. I don't even know how to describe that day to you. The first bomb went off, and the crowds rushed to the site in the hopes of saving victims. And the crowds were huge. This is Sadr City after all, the most crowded part of Baghdad. As soon as people gathered at one bomb site, another explosion nearby tore through the crowd. It went like this again and again and again. Five car bombs in less than fifteen minutes.

Despite all of the suffering that I have seen in the past six years, I believe life is better now than it was during the time of Saddam Hussein. You want to know why? I'll explain. I'll put it to you in very simple terms. You always had one thing over these past years since the invasion that you never had in Saddam times. Throughout all the violence of the last six years, all the explosions and all the murders every day for months all around, you could always go to your bed and sleep in peace each night, no matter what happened during the day. You could never sleep in peace during Saddam times. You never knew if someone would be coming for you in the middle of the night. If someone from your area was picked up by the intelligence, you could not sleep for weeks. You knew he was somewhere being tortured, saying names to make the pain stop, maybe your name. And they would come for you next. During Saddam times the city was quiet in the day, sure. But living through those nights was terror. That's the difference. That's why it's better now than it was before.

Sure, that's a good thing. But is having that worth all the tragedies that have come at the same time?

I think so, yes. You have to make sacrifices for freedom. And sacrifices have been made. In the end, after the Americans go, history will come to see their presence here as a curse on this country. But this is a curse we can bear. Gradually we will heal the wounds. Already as an Iraqi you can have a sense of self-respect, looking at other countries in the Middle East. None of them have endured what we have. The problem now is that we are still not free, despite all the sacrifices. The occupier is still here.

As of May 2009, Hassan Ali was continuing his work at the Bright Lights Foundation in Sadr City as well as working at a new job he had gotten as a member of a guard force at the Iraqi Ministry of Oil.

ACKNOWLEDGMENTS

FOREMOST THANKS MUST GO to all those Iraqis who shared their stories with me for the sake of this book. I cannot say enough how grateful I am to all the people who spoke with me. Not everyone who sat for an interview made it into the book, but each interview informed me and the book in some way. Each person who spoke took time out of their daily life to offer what were in many cases deeply painful memories. Tears flowed often, and I was moved again and again by the willingness of the people I met to give so much of themselves so that others might understand. Interviews posed more than emotional trials for the Iraqis who sat with me, however. To reach me at the *Time* bureau in central Baghdad, people had to journey through streets where bomb blasts still killed and maimed at random. Most of these interviews were conducted in the early months of 2009. Violence was rising noticeably then. The relative calm that had prevailed through the latter part of 2008 appeared to be slipping away, and people in Iraq in general seemed on edge, wondering what the country would be like as American troops moved to go. I ended most interviews by asking people whether they thought the war was over. I don't recall any saying yes. For most Iraqis, the war continued all around them even as America's role in the conflict began to draw to a close. To be so sharing with me during such a time was a gesture of openness on the part of those Iraqis who spoke that I will always cherish.

No one worked harder to find and arrange interviews for this book than Sami Hilali. Throughout my time in Iraq, Sami was there for me as a trusty driver, skilled chef, sharp reporter, avid chess partner, and close friend. But in helping with this book Sami took his companionship and dedication to a new level. I quickly lost track of how many people Sami brought for interviews. He spent countless afternoons combing Baghdad neighborhoods for good stories we might include and of course offered his own interesting tale. It's difficult to imagine this book being written without Sami's efforts, and I certainly cannot imagine working in Baghdad without him. Thank you, Sami, *habibi*. Moustafa Ahmed al-Ta'ee, a driver and bodyguard for *Time* in Baghdad, worked hard to find many interviews too, in addition to offering his own story. Moustafa would sometimes sense me growing concerned about getting one interview or another in the months we worked on the book together. The process of arranging interviews was often difficult and complicated for all involved. Moustafa would tell me in moments of frustration, Don't worry, Mr. Mark. Don't worry. I heard that phrase often in Iraq from Americans and Iraqis alike over the years. Don't worry. It was rarely comforting. But my worries did indeed ease a bit when I heard Moustafa say the words, because I knew then he would be using his considerable smarts and energy to solve whatever problem we faced. Ra'ad Obaeid Hussein, the bureau's head of security during my time there, deserves special mention too. He offered one of the most gripping tales I heard about the early days of the war, and he sought out many other such stories for the sake of the project. *Time* reporter Tariq Anmar Nazar was also invaluable in the search for interview subjects. Tariq often focused on getting the more difficult of our speakers, such as tribal sheiks hard to pin down for long conversations or former fighters of various stripes uneager to speak. It was an unenviable task, frankly. But Tariq set himself to it with professionalism and determination. All but a handful of these interviews were translated by either *Time* Baghdad bureau manager Ali al-Shaheen or the magazine's chief Iraqi reporter Mazin Ezzat. Ali and Mazin were much more than interpreters, however. They were fellow interviewers who showed much skill and sensitivity in drawing out the details of the stories we heard. Ali and Mazin deepened my understanding of both the interview subjects we met and the stories we heard through insights, observations, and questions during our recorded conversations. I was very fortunate indeed to have two such thoughtful men helping me and caring so much about the project.

None of my experiences in Iraq would have been possible without *Time* magazine and the editors there who entrusted me to cover the war. The first person I ever got to know at *Time* was Jay Carney, in 2000. Jay was then a correspondent for the magazine, covering the presidential race, and he was welcome company next to me during many flights aboard

George W. Bush's campaign plane as I reported for United Press International. Jay went on to become the Washington bureau chief for *Time*, and the two of us stayed in touch. In 2006, over coffee in Washington one afternoon, Jay offered to put my name forward for an open slot as a correspondent in the magazine's Baghdad bureau. I remember Jay at the time seeming concerned and troubled about the prospect of having a hand in sending someone to Iraq at that point given the dangers. But I was thrilled about the idea. I had wanted to cover Iraq for some time but could not figure out a way to do so as an independent journalist. Iraq had become too dangerous in my estimation simply to turn up as a freelancer. In order to operate as a journalist with a reasonable amount of safety and effectiveness, one needed costly resources such as professional security, translators, vehicles, and guarded living quarters fortified roughly to the standards of a military outpost. *Time* was one of the few news organizations truly committed to coverage of Iraq then and offered all of the above to its correspondents. I was more than eager to go to Iraq for *Time*, and I remain deeply grateful to Jay for being the first to send me on my way.

In my time with the magazine I wound up working alongside a host of other talented individuals. Richard Stengel led a team of editors in New York City when I joined that included Romesh Ratnesar, Adi Ignatius, Josh Tyrangiel, and Howard Chua-Eoan. Working for them as a correspondent was a privilege, and I consider myself lucky for the chance to do so. In Iraq I was very fortunate to be working alongside Aparisim "Bobby" Ghosh, who served as Baghdad bureau chief for *Time* when I first arrived. Bobby's support and guidance helped me as a newbie reporter on the Iraq scene to run when I might have stumbled, and for that I will always be deeply appreciative. I am especially grateful too for all the help and encouragement I got from Mark Thompson, the magazine's longtime lead military reporter. Mark was an invaluable voice of wisdom from Washington while I was in Iraq and has remained an exceptionally gracious friend since then.

Easily the person who came to mean the most to me at *Time*, however, was Sheila Charney. To this day I do not know what official title Sheila held during my time with the magazine. But to me she was something akin to a fairy godmother with a New York City attitude. She solved innumerable problems of mine, big and small, as I lived a strange life in which I called Baghdad home for nearly three years. Thank you, Sheila, for helping me so much and making me laugh so often along the way. And I will remain very grateful always to another quiet hero in the New York offices of *Time*, Ralph Spielman, who handled all my flight arrangements in and out of the Middle East. Ralph got me there and back again more times than I can count. Thank you, Ralph, for giving me wings.